KEYS TO
Business
Success

Martha S. Doran

Carol Carter   Joyce Bishop   Sarah Lyman Kravits

Prentice Hall
Upper Saddle River, New Jersey 07458

Library of Congress Cataloging-in-Publication Data

Keys to business success / Martha Doran . . . [et al.].
    p.   cm.
  Includes bibliographical references and index.
  ISBN 0-13-013304-3
  1. Business—Vocational guidance.   2. Success in business.   I.
Doran, Martha S. II. Title: Business success
  HF5381 .K49 2000
  650.1—dc21

                           99-15637
                            CIP

Publisher: *Carol Carter*
Acquisitions Editor: *Sue Bierman*
Managing Editor: *Mary Carnis*
Developmental Editor: *Kateri Drexler*
In-House Liaison: *Glenn Johnston*
Production: *Holcomb Hathaway, Inc.*
Director of Manufacturing and Production: *Bruce Johnson*
Manufacturing Buyer: *Marc Bove*
Cover Design: *Bruce Kenselaar*
Cover Illustrator: *Paul Gourhan*
Editorial Assistant: *Michelle M. Williams*
Marketing Manager: *Jeff McIlroy*
Marketing Assistant: *Barbara Rosenberg*

Copyright © 2000 by Prentice-Hall, Inc.
Upper Saddle River, New Jersey 07458

Printed in the United States of America

10 9 8 7 6 5 4 3 2 1

ISBN 0-13-013304-3

Prentice-Hall International (UK) Limited, *London*
Prentice-Hall of Australia Pty. Limited, *Sydney*
Prentice-Hall Canada Inc., *Toronto*
Prentice-Hall Hispanoamericana, S.A., *Mexico*
Prentice-Hall of India Private Limited, *New Delhi*
Prentice-Hall of Japan, Inc., *Tokyo*
Prentice-Hall Pte. Ltd., *Singapore*
Editora Prentice-Hall do Brasil, Ltda., *Rio de Janeiro*

Contents

4   CRITICAL AND CREATIVE THINKING   87
Tapping the Power of Your Mind

5   READING AND STUDYING   119
Maximizing Written Resources

6   NOTE TAKING AND WRITING   149
Harnessing the Power of Words and Ideas

7   LISTENING, MEMORY, AND TEST TAKING   183
Taking In, Retaining, and Demonstrating Knowledge

8   BUSINESS COMMUNICATION   211
Reporting Results

9 BUSINESS MATH   235
Finding Strength in Numbers

10 MOVING AHEAD   269
Building a Flexible Future

Preface

KEYS TO SUCCESS OWNER'S MANUAL: PLEASE READ BEFORE OPERATING

When you spend money on a coffeemaker, electric drill, television, car, tape deck, or anything else, getting your money's worth means knowing how to operate your purchase so that it delivers what you want (good coffee or clear channel reception or high-speed dubbing). When you bring the item home, you generally look over the manual or pamphlet that comes with it before you do anything else. The manual describes the parts, how they operate, and what should result if everything is functioning properly. With that in mind, think of this preface as your owner's manual for this book. Reading it might be one of the most helpful actions you take all semester.

We have spoken to people in a number of diverse fields. Through our talks with artists, entrepreneurs, managers, and engineers, we have discovered how important it is to have business skills in any field. As your authors, we have also talked to students across the country. We've learned that you are concerned about your future, you want your education to serve a purpose, you are adjusting to constant life changes, and you want honest and direct guidance on how to achieve your goals. We designed the features of *Keys to Business Success* based on what you have told us about your needs. Knowing how to use the features in this book—and making the most of your work in this class—will help you maximize the time, effort, and money you are putting into your education.

Following are descriptions of the different pieces of this book and how to use them to your advantage.

The Contents of the Package: What's Included

This addition to a great line of Prentice Hall texts has a very specific focus on business but takes a very broad definition of business, focusing on the business of living a productive life. We chose the topics in this book based on what you need to make the most of your educational experience. You need to *believe in yourself* just to believe that you are worth educating. You need a strong sense of *self*, *learning style*, and *goals* in order to discover and pursue the best course of study. You need good *study skills* to take in and retain what you learn both in and out of class. You need to *manage your time*, *money*, and *relationships* so you can handle the changes life hands you. *Keys to Business Success* can guide you in all of these areas and more.

THE PARTS: USEFUL FEATURES

The features (distinguishing characteristics and sections of this book) are designed to make your life easier by helping you take in and understand the material you read.

Lifelong Learning. If what you studied in this course only helped you to read textbooks and to pass tests, its usefulness would end at graduation, and you would have to start all over to learn how to deal with the real world. The ideas and strategies you learn that will help you succeed in school are the same ones that will bring you success in your career and in your personal life. Therefore, this book focuses on success strategies as they apply to *school*, *work*, and *life*, not just to the classroom.

Thinking Skills. Being able to remember facts and figures won't do you much good at school or beyond unless you can put that information to work through clear and competent thinking. Chapter 4 is a chapter on *critical and creative thinking* that will help you explore your mind's seven primary actions—the building blocks to competent thinking. You will also see how to combine those actions in order to perform thinking processes such as problem solving, decision making, and strategic planning.

Skill-Building Exercises. Today's graduates need to be effective thinkers, team players, writers, and strategic planners. The exercises at the end of the chapters will encourage you to develop these valuable career skills and to apply thinking processes to any topic or situation.

Applications and Team Building Exercises. These exercises are based on real-world dilemmas that give you a chance to interact and learn both individually and in a group setting, building your teamwork and leadership skills in the process.

Case Studies. These cases are based on real-world situations, followed by questions. You will be able to apply what you have learned in the chapter and analyze a real-life situation that a company has been confronted with.

Internet Exercises. The Internet is such an important tool in today's world, and these exercises give you a chance to see how the Internet can be used in business. These exercises will give you an opportunity to discover some important sites on the Internet. Then you will use the information you obtain to sharpen your critical-thinking skills.

Diversity of Voice. The world is becoming increasingly diverse in ethnicity, perspective, culture, lifestyle, race, choices, abilities, needs, and more. Each student, instructor, course, and school is unique. One point of view can't possibly apply to everyone. Therefore, many voices will speak to you from these pages. What you read will speak to your needs, offer ideas, and treat you with respect.

◆ *Real-World Perspective*, a question and answer feature, will appear once per chapter. In it, on person will present a question about an issue in his or her life, and another person who has had similar experiences will give advice in response.

◆ *Examples* throughout the text deal with different situations that different students face—working while in school, parenting, dealing with different financial needs, supporting various lifestyles and schedules, and so on.

◆ Most chapters will introduce you to a *foreign word or phrase* and will discuss how you might apply the meaning of that word or phrase to your own life.

◆ The *exercises* throughout the book recognize and reinforce your uniqueness; they are designed so that you apply what you learn to the particulars of your own life.

◆ *Success in the Real World* profiles different people in a variety of fields. People who have achieved certain successes in their lives offer advice and examples as to how their success was achieved.

ACKNOWLEDGMENTS

This book has come about through a heroic group effort. We would like to take this opportunity to acknowledge the people who have made it happen. Many thanks to:

◆ The Developmental Editor of this edition, Kateri Drexler, whose creativity, insight, effort, and energy made this edition possible.

◆ All the people who offered their stories for our Success in the Real World feature: Jamie Makuuchi, Mary Hey, Frank Borman, Andy Lauer, Carol Walton, Stuart Scott, Elizabeth Del Ferro, Monty Roberts, Scott Lehman, and Dick Rutan.

◆ Dr. Charles Beck for sharing his expertise in Managerial Communication.

◆ Will Drexler for taking many of the photographs used in the chapter openers.

◆ Michele Buetti and Kristin Groelig for their insightful comments.

◆ Editors Sue Bierman and Sande Johnson for their encouragement, insight, and constant support.

◆ Professor Barbara Soloman for granting us the use of her Learning Styles Inventory.

◆ Catherine Volland from the University of Colorado at Denver for use of her spreadsheet exercise.

◆ Dr. Frank T. Lyman for his generous permission to use and adapt his Thinktrix system.

About the Authors

Martha Doran, Ph.D., CPA, currently teaches accounting and student success at San Diego State University. She is also involved in teaching in the University's Freshman Success Program and is serving in the Faculty Fellow program designed to encourage informal interaction between faculty and resident hall members. She is the author of a textbook designed to teach accounting from a user's perspective as well as author of a series of accounting booklets based on real-world simulations and activities.

Carol Carter is Vice President and Director of Student Programs and Faculty Development at Prentice Hall. She has written *Majoring in the Rest of Your Life: College and Career Secrets for Students* and *Majoring in High School.* She has also co-authored *Graduating Into the Nineties, The Career Tool Kit, Keys to Career Success, Keys to Effective Learning,* and the first edition of *Keys to Success.* In 1992 Carol and other business people co-founded a nonprofit organization called LifeSkills, Inc., to help high school students explore their goals, their career options, and the real world through part-time employment and internships. LifeSkills is now part of the Tucson Unified School District and is featured in seventeen high schools in Tucson, Arizona.

Joyce Bishop holds a Ph.D. in psychology and has taught for more than twenty years, receiving a number of honors, including Teacher of the Year. For the past four years she has been voted "favorite teacher" by the student body and Honor Society at Golden West College, Huntington Beach, CA, where she has taught since 1986 and is a tenured professor. She is currently working with a federal grant to establish Learning Communities and Workplace Learning in her district, and has developed workshops and trained faculty in cooperative learning, active learning, multiple intelligences, workplace relevancy, learning styles, authentic assessment, team building, and the development of learning communities. She also co-authored *Keys to Effective Learning.*

Sarah Lyman Kravits comes from a family of educators and has long cultivated an interest in educational development. She co-authored *The Career Tool Kit, Keys to Study Skills,* and the first edition of *Keys to Success* and has served as Program Director for LifeSkills, Inc., a nonprofit organization that aims to further the career and personal development of high school students. In that capacity she helped to formulate both curricular and organizational elements of the program, working closely with instructors as well as members of the business community. She has also given faculty workshops in critical thinking, based on the Thinktrix critical thinking system. Sarah holds a B.A. in English and drama from the University of Virginia, where she was a Jefferson Scholar, and an M.F.A. from Catholic University.

1

The Business of Living

Getting the Big Picture

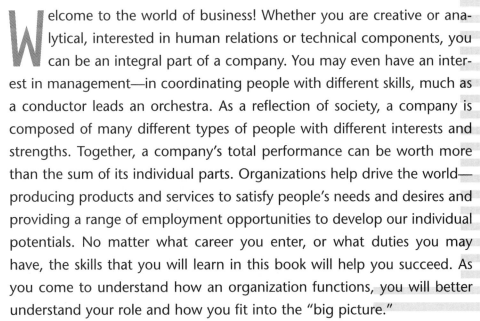

Welcome to the world of business! Whether you are creative or analytical, interested in human relations or technical components, you can be an integral part of a company. You may even have an interest in management—in coordinating people with different skills, much as a conductor leads an orchestra. As a reflection of society, a company is composed of many different types of people with different interests and strengths. Together, a company's total performance can be worth more than the sum of its individual parts. Organizations help drive the world—producing products and services to satisfy people's needs and desires and providing a range of employment opportunities to develop our individual potentials. No matter what career you enter, or what duties you may have, the skills that you will learn in this book will help you succeed. As you come to understand how an organization functions, you will better understand your role and how you fit into the "big picture."

In this chapter, you will discover the major fields of study in business that are offered by most colleges and universities. Following each description, you will find some career options for each field. The chapter ends with a list of good ideas about ways you can help yourself discover how to be successful in business *during* college.

In this chapter, you will explore the answers to the following questions:

◆ Who is working in business today?

◆ What is your role in a diverse world?

◆ What skills can you learn while pursuing a degree in business?

◆ What fields of study are in business administration?

◆ How can you increase your chances for success in the business world?

WHO IS WORKING IN BUSINESS TODAY?

We have seen organizations become much more diverse in recent years—in culture, education, age, and gender. Women represented 40 percent of the work force in 1976, but that number is estimated to grow to 47 percent by the year 2000. In addition, there are increasing opportunities for women. The percentage of women in managerial positions in the United States has increased from 15 percent to 40 percent during the years 1966 to 1990. Minorities are expected to account for over 30 percent of the new entrants in the U. S. work force by 2000. The average employee is also getting older. In the United States, the median age was twenty-seven in 1970 but is projected to reach thirty-nine by the year 2000. These changes present many opportunities for people, as well as challenges in managing the diversity.

Last year, almost one-half of the positions offered to graduating seniors were in the key areas of business: marketing, finance, economics, accounting, and management (see Figures 1-1 and 1-2). The average starting salary in these fields was approximately $30,000, second only to engineering.

Figure 1-1

Jobs offered—1998.

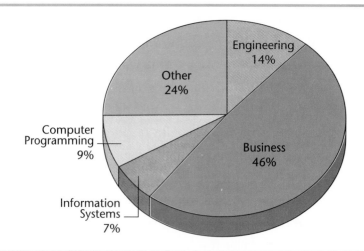

Source: Salary Survey, April 1998 (figures from September 1997–March 1998).

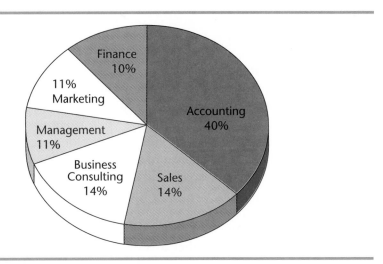

Figure 1-2

Job offers within business— 1998.

Source: Salary Survey, April 1998 (figures from September 1997–March 1998).

WHAT IS YOUR ROLE IN A DIVERSE WORLD?

Diversity isn't just what happens in an International Students' Club, in a business that tries to hire men and women from different backgrounds, or in an inner-city neighborhood that is home to various cultural groups. Diversity is the mosaic of differences that envelops your life, your communities, your nation, and the world. In addition to races and ethnic groups, diversity also occurs in desires, traditions, religions, family backgrounds, genders, abilities, economic levels, ages, habits, lifestyles, choices, careers, artistic expressions, modes of dress, foods, health conditions, perspectives, opinions, experiences, and more. Diversity touches each of you in a very personal way.

> "Let your soul stand cool and composed before a million universes."
>
> WALT WHITMAN

Diversity Is Real Life

You encounter diversity every day, even if you don't realize it. You are constantly bombarded with images and information in newspapers and magazines, on television, and on the radio that tell you about how different people think and live. People tend to focus on the kind of diversity they can see, such as skin color, hair type, or eye shape, but there are meaningful forms of diversity that aren't visible to the naked eye. People who look similar to you may actually be different in many important ways. Think about the qualities of the people you know. Your fellow student may have a different religion or a hidden disability; your cousin may oppose your political beliefs; your co-worker may have a different sexual orientation. Society is made up of millions of people who transcend labels and have limitless worth.

Diversity has become more important, partly because the world is becoming more interdependent. As people become more aware of other ways of living, they may tune in more to differences between "us" and "them." The knowledge of differences can be a benefit. Unfortunately, it can also be used to spread opinions that others are inferior. The problem is not in the differences but in the way in which people view and treat these differences.

Ethnocentrism

Ethnocentrism
The condition of thinking that one's particular ethnic group is superior to others.

When groups of people believe that their way of thinking is the only way, or a better way than anyone else's, they are being ethnocentric. Ethnocentrism creates an opinion that one's particular group is better than anyone else's. It's important to be proud of your identity, but it's one thing to think your group is terrific and another thing to think that your group is superior to all other groups.

A group can be organized around any sort of uniqueness—the same skin color, accent, country of origin, ideas, interests, religion, traditions, and much more. The problem arises when celebrating your own uniqueness leads to putting down someone else's. One example is thinking that when someone speaks with an accent, he or she doesn't know as much as you do. Another example is thinking that it is disrespectful for someone not to look you in the eye during a conversation. In certain other cultures, it is considered rude to look people in the eye, especially if that person happens to be an authority.

Ethnocentrism has many negative effects. It can get in the way of effective communication, as you will see in more detail when you read Chapter 8. It can prevent you from getting to know people from different backgrounds. It can result in people being shut out and denied opportunities that all people deserve. It limits you and your potential because it denies you exposure to new ideas that could help you grow and learn. Finally, it can hinder your ability to work with others, which can cause problems for you both at school and on the job.

Diversity and Teamwork

"Joy is not in things, it is in us."

JEAN FRANCOIS MILLET

Much of what people accomplish they owe to teamwork. Think of the path of your accomplishments, and you will find that other people had roles in your success. When you earn a degree, complete a project, or raise a family, you don't do it alone. You are part of many hard-working teams. As the African proverb goes, it takes an entire village to raise a child.

Your success at school and at work depends on your ability to cooperate in a team setting. At school you will work with study groups, complete group projects, interact with instructors and administrators, and perhaps live with a roommate. At work you will regularly team up with co-workers to achieve goals. At home you work with family or housemates to manage the tasks and responsibilities of daily life. Your achievements depend on how you communicate, share tasks, and develop a common vision.

Any team will gain strength from the diversity of its members. In fact, diversity is an asset in a team. Consider a five-person basketball team, composed of a center, a power forward, a small forward, a shooting guard, and a point guard. Each person has a different role and a different style of play, but only by combining their abilities can they achieve success. The more diverse the team members, the greater the chance that new ideas and solutions will find their way to the table, increasing the chances of solving any problem. As a member of any team, use these three strategies to maximize team success.

1. Open your mind and accept that different team members have valuable roles.
2. Consider the new information and ideas that others offer.
3. Evaluate contributions based on how they help solve the problem or achieve the goal instead of based on the identity of the person who had the idea. Successful teams use what works.

> "He has not yet learned the lesson of life who does not every day surmount a fear."
>
> RALPH WALDO EMERSON

Living Your Role

It's not always easy to open your mind to differences. However, doing so can benefit both you and others around you. You may consider actions like these as you define your role in the diverse world:

- **To accept diversity as a fact of life.** The world will only continue to diversify. The more you adapt to and appreciate this diversity, the more enriched your life will be. Diversity is an asset, not a deficiency.

- **To explore differences.** Open your mind and learn about what is unfamiliar around you.

- **To celebrate your own uniqueness as well as that of others.** It's natural to think that your own way is the best way. Expand your horizons by considering your way as one good way and seeking out different and useful ways to which other people can introduce you.

- **To consider new perspectives.** The wide variety of ideas and perspectives brought by people from all different groups and situations creates a wealth of thought from which the world can find solutions to tough and complex problems.

- **To continue to learn.** Education is one of the most productive ways to combat discrimination and become more open-minded about differences. Classes such as sociology and ethics can increase your awareness of the lives, choices, and values of people in other cultures. Even though your personal beliefs may be challenged in the process, facing how you feel about others is a positive step toward harmony among people.

Throughout this book you will find references to a diverse mixture of people in different life circumstances. Chapter 8 will go into more detail about communicating across lines of difference and addressing the problems that arise when people have trouble accepting each other's differences. Diversity is not a subject that you study at one point in the semester and then leave behind. It is a theme that touches every chapter in this book and every part of your life. Note especially the "Real World Perspective" feature in every chapter, which highlights people from different backgrounds who are striving to learn about themselves and their world.

HAT SKILLS CAN YOU LEARN WHILE PURSUING A DEGREE IN BUSINESS?

Leadership

TERMS

Educere
Latin root for
word *education*
meaning "to lead
forth."

A business education allows you to learn from examples of others. Through case studies of companies and managers, you can evaluate many leadership styles. You can see successes and failures and be able to evaluate techniques that can help you succeed. Through group projects, you'll be able to work with other people, developing your interpersonal and group communication skills—the tools of leadership.

Finance Management

In business courses, you will learn the basics of finance and budgeting, which can help in your personal life whether you're buying a car, financing your education, or planning for a vacation. Understanding business helps us to manage our own lives by developing strategies and goals—critical building blocks for success.

Communication

There are many ways to communicate with others. We now have email, faxes, letters, memos, and telephones, to name a few. We can communicate either one on one or to groups. We are able to use technology in many new ways to present our ideas and to gather information. How we can effectively use these methods requires strategic thinking. Studying business can give insight into the advantages and disadvantages of using the methods, as well as developing our skills to make whichever method we choose the most effective.

Ability to Analyze Complex Business and Economic Issues

Every day, it seems, we hear news stories on major policy changes taking place, the effects of which can be far-reaching. To understand, for example, how a standard European currency will affect Americans, we need a basic understanding of business and economics. We will be able to make better decisions for our own lives if we learn about the factors that comprise our economy.

HAT FIELDS OF STUDY ARE IN BUSINESS ADMINISTRATION?

There are as many different fields within business as there are specialists in medicine. However, a good understanding of the core business fields will help you in any field you choose to enter. The core fields are: accounting, marketing, management, finance, economics, and information systems.

Accounting

What Is It?

Accounting is the system that measures business activities, processes that information into reports, and communicates the results to decision makers. For this reason it is called "the language of business." What grammar is to English composition, accounting is to business. There is much more to accounting than bookkeeping. Bookkeeping is the procedural element (much as arithmetic is a procedural element of mathematics). Accounting is much more than procedures—it is a process that begins and ends with decision making. It is such an important function of a successful business because it provides vital information that enables managers in production, marketing, and personnel to make informed decisions.

Accounting has a long history. Some scholars claim that writing arose in order to record accounting information. Indeed, accounting records date back to the ancient civilizations of China, Babylonia, Greece, and Egypt. The rulers of these civilizations used accounting to keep track of the costs of labor and materials used in building structures such as the great pyramids. The need for accounting has existed as long as there has been business activity. The double-entry system, developed by Lucca Pacioli, gave rise to a new profession during the Renaissance.

In the nineteenth century, the growth of corporations spurred the development of accounting. Corporation owners (stockholders) were no longer the managers of their businesses but still needed to know how well their companies were doing. With records and an accounting system, managers could report this information to the owners. However, because managers naturally want their performance to look good, there needed to be a way to ensure that the reported business information was very accurate.

In the United States, the Financial Accounting Standards Board (FASB) determines how accounting is practiced. The FASB works with the Securities and Exchange Commission (SEC) and the American Institute of Certified Public Accountants (AICPA), the largest professional organization of accountants. Accounting practices must follow certain guidelines. The rules that govern how accountants measure, process, and communicate financial information fall under the heading GAAP, which stands for generally accepted accounting principles. FASB wrote the framework for GAAP. In the United States we also have certified public accountants (CPAs) who are licensed to serve the general public rather than one particular company.

Computers have revolutionized accounting in the late twentieth century. Tasks that are time-consuming when done by hand are handled quickly and easily by computers. Computer programs today also assist with the financial applications of accounting and make decision making easier.

Sometimes the accounting procedures used will depend on the type of business or organization: proprietorship, partnership, or corporation. A proprietorship has a single owner who is also generally the manager. These organizations tend to be small retail establishments or individual professional businesses. Partnerships join two or more people together as owners. Most partnerships are small or medium-sized, but some are huge, exceeding 2,000 partners. A corporation is a business owned by stockholders, people who

Accounting
The system of recording and summarizing business and financial transactions and analyzing, verifying, and reporting the results.

own shares in the business. A business becomes a corporation when the state approves its articles of incorporation. It becomes a legal entity, an "artificial person" that conducts its business in its own name. From a legal standpoint, corporations differ significantly from proprietorships and partnerships, both of which are legally obligated for the business's debts. If corporations go bankrupt, the lenders cannot take the personal assets of the stockholders.

The accounting equation shows the relationship among assets, liabilities, and owner's equity. Assets appear on the left-hand side of the equation; the legal and economic claims against the assets—liabilities and owner's equity—appear on the right-hand side:

$$\text{Assets} = \text{Liabilities} + \text{Owner's Equity}$$

What Are the Career Options?

Accountants are needed in almost every industry. Specifically, you could be a cost, managerial, or systems and procedures accountant. Tax, budget, and forecast accountants and auditors are also needed. You can use an accounting degree in a number of other careers. For example, in the insurance industry, with some additional training, you could be an actuary or an underwriter. You could work in the banking industry as an administrator. In financial services, people with accounting degrees are needed as financial analysts, planners, and stockbrokers. In many industries, cost estimators and compensation analysts have an accounting background.

A master's degree in business administration (MBA) helps in certain careers, such as business and public administration. By passing an inclusive exam, you could also be a certified public accountant (CPA).

Marketing

What Is It?

Marketing
The act of determining and satisfying consumer needs.

Basically, marketing is learning what customers want and need and providing products or services to meet those wants and needs. Boiled down to a few words: Marketing satisfies needs! It sounds simple, but in today's business environment there are actually many functions of marketing that companies must perform in order to succeed.

Behind the scenes, businesses must analyze the environment, looking at external factors such as the economy, competition, and trends, and evaluate consumers' needs and characteristics before they begin planning the products themselves. The product that eventually ends up being bought has gone through a number of modifications, and decisions have been made on everything from the images and brand name to packaging and optional features.

Communicating with customers and the public through advertising, public relations, personal selling, and sales promotions is another important part of the marketing process. The price and distribution process must also be determined. Marketing managers coordinate all of these functions in order to make a product or service successful.

As marketers determine the best way to present a good or service for consumers' consideration, they have a number of decisions to make. The marketer's strategic toolbox is called the marketing mix, which consists of the factors that can be manipulated and used together to create a desired response in the marketplace. These factors are the product itself, the price of the product, the promotion that makes it known to consumers, and the place where it is made available.

1. Product. The product is a good, service, idea, place, person—whatever is being offered for sale in the marketing exchange process. But more than a good or service, a product is the quality and character of the offering. This aspect of the marketing mix includes the design and packaging of a good, as well as its physical features. There are different aspects to a product besides the tangible item. In marketing, we also refer to an augmented product, which includes not only the tangible elements of a product but also the accompanying cluster of image and service features. For example, a Rolex watch is popular not only because of the physical watch product but also because of the luxury and status it conveys. The generic product centers on consumer benefits—what the customer is buying. Charles Revlon, founder of Revlon, once said, "In the factory we make cosmetics, and in the drugstore we sell hope." The generic product is a consumer view of what the product represents. For example, people don't buy drills at the hardware store. They buy the holes that the drill will make.

> "I have learned that success is to be measured not so much by the position one has reached in life as by the obstacles which he has overcome while trying to succeed."
>
> BOOKER T. WASHINGTON

2. Price. Price refers to the assignment of value, or the amount the consumer must exchange in order to receive the offering. The decision about how much to charge for something is not as simple as it sounds. In order to determine a product's price, one of the factors we look at is what is known as the price elasticity of demand. This indicates how sensitive buyers are to price changes. Elastic demand means that when the prices go down, total revenues rise, and when prices are raised, total revenues actually decrease. If people believe that there are many similar goods or services from which to choose, demand is elastic and greatly influenced by price changes. With inelastic demand, total revenues will go up when prices go up and down when prices go down. If consumers believe that a firm's offering is unique or there is an urgency to buy, demand is inelastic and little influenced by price changes.

3. Promotion. Promotion refers to a marketer's efforts to inform or persuade consumers or organizations about goods, services, or ideas. It includes all of the marketing activities that are designed to encourage potential customers to buy the product and can take many forms, including personal selling, television advertising, store coupons, billboards, and publicity releases.

4. Distribution. Distribution planning involves movement and ownership in a channel of distribution. The channel of distribution refers to the series of firms that work together to get a product from a producer to a consumer. For consumer goods like Levi's jeans, these intermediary firms include wholesale firms that work together with the manufacturer and with retail firms, like JCPenney and The Gap, to have the right amount of jeans in the right styles

REAL WORLD PERSPECTIVE

How will a business education help me in the long run?

Sara Beck, University of Colorado, Boulder, Colorado

As a freshman, it has been really difficult for me to determine my major. I really feel like I don't have enough information on any field and am interested in many things all across the board, including art, marine biology, and engineering! This term I participated in a program where many successful people from around the country came to speak. From listening to their stories, I have started to see how business might also be an exciting field. The speakers who came to our school have been making a lot of innovative changes in the world, and I feel myself being motivated by their enthusiasm.

However, I'm not sure what I want to do. There are so many choices! What can I get out of a business degree? Most of my friends who are majoring in business say that they want to make a lot of money! I really want a little more than that—I want to do something that I enjoy and feel like I'm making a difference in the world. What if I do want to end up working in the engineering or biology field—how would I do that with a business education? And, would a business degree help or hinder me in the long run?

Michele Buetti, Chemical Engineer, South Carolina

Deciding what field to go into is a very difficult thing to do, and when beginning your undergraduate studies it can be a very daunting prospect. I know you must feel overwhelmed trying to make a decision right now about what you want to do with the rest of your life. This decision will influence a lot that you do in the future, but it is not as final and unchangeable as it seems. It is great that you are thinking ahead, but don't panic. I would recommend getting a solid base of skills in a general area before worrying about specializing. The world is changing much more quickly today than ever before, and the more solid skill base you have, the more quickly you will be able to adapt to the changes in the business world.

Business courses are important. They give you a solid understanding of how our society is set up and how the world interacts. These courses provide a basic knowledge of finance, supply-and-demand principles, and marketing basics. No matter what you do—or what industry you go into—these principles are applicable. Industry is run by business, and understanding business at its basic level will give you an edge in any industry that you decide to pursue.

Although I decided to go into a research field, I find that I use business skills in my job and my life. I also feel that by understanding some basics of finance and marketing, I have a much broader base of experience from which to work. I believe this broad base will enable me to achieve greater personal success in my research pursuits. My advice is to learn as much as you can about different areas before specializing in one field.

at the right time—say, for back-to-school shopping. Products can go directly to the consumer or pass through other parties, such as retailers, first. They may also go through wholesalers and distributors before reaching the final consumer. Today we see many products being sold through the Internet, which is another form of distribution. The channel used depends on the type of consumer, company, product, competition, and legalities.

What Are the Career Options?

Because marketing is an essential part of business today, there are a great number of career opportunities in many industries that are open to graduating students with marketing degrees. Many types of sales representative entry-level positions exist in several industries, which include advertising sales, direct sales, business-to-business sales, retail sales, and sales management. Besides sales, marketing majors can seek careers as brand, marketing, promotion, and product managers. Other positions that can be obtained by marketing majors in advertising include advertising copywriter and media director. Public relations is another career path in which a marketing degree can be very beneficial. Research can also be conducted as a marketing research analyst or at the university level with a higher degree.

Management

What Is It?

Management is the process of accomplishing goals, or sets of goals, with and through other people. There are many different types of managers, depending on their level—first-line managers (supervisors); middle managers; and top managers—but they all perform four basic functions:

TERMS

Management
Accomplishing goals, or sets of goals, with and through other people.

1. Planning. Planning is setting goals and deciding on courses of action, developing rules and procedures, developing plans, and forecasting what the future will likely be for the firm.

2. Organizing. Organizing entails identifying jobs to be done, hiring people to do them, establishing departments, delegating or pushing authority to subordinates, establishing a chain of command, and coordinating the work of the manager's subordinates.

3. Leading. Leading means motivating other people to get the job done, maintaining morale, molding company culture, and managing conflicts and communication.

4. Controlling. Controlling is setting standards (such as sales quotas or quality standards), comparing actual performance with these standards, and then taking corrective actions as needed.

Managers don't spend an equal amount of time on each function. Usually, top managers will spend more of their time planning, while first-line managers use most of their time leading and controlling. Through an understanding of general management principles, individual and group behavior, organizational change and design, and human resources management, managers can make an impact on the success of an organization.

Early hunting civilizations used management when people banded into tribes for protection; the Egyptians used it to build pyramids, and the Romans to control their empire. Management theory as we know it today began with an effort to study the management process with scientific rigor.

This began in the mid-1700s with the birth of the Industrial Revolution. The division and specialization of work led to enormous increases in productivity and output. Frank Taylor developed a set of principles that became known as *scientific management*, a basic theme of which was that managers should study work scientifically to determine the one best way to get the job done.

Scientific management became very popular but eventually scrutinized every detail of the work process in so much depth that individuals' needs were ignored. In 1927, Chicago's Hawthorne Plant of the Western Electric Company conducted what became known as the Hawthorne Studies. The original study focused on working conditions of the employees. They looked at the effect that lighting had on productivity—they studied how low light, medium light, and bright light affected the amount of work that was done. What they found surprised everyone at the time—no matter what they did, productivity increased. They concluded that the researchers' interaction with the employees during the study made them feel special and resulted in the productivity increase, and so began the *human relations movement* and *behavioral approach to management*.

Behavioral scientists like Douglas McGregor and Rensis Likert translated their ideas into methodologies that became the basis for participative management and management by objectives (MBO), where subordinates set their goals with their supervisors and are measured on the accomplishment of those goals.

After World War II, a trend of applying quantitative techniques to a wide range of managerial problems developed. This movement, called management science, like scientific management, uses the scientific method to find the best solution to industrial problems. This approach is closely associated with the systems approach, which views an organization as a system made up of different interrelated parts. Since the 1960s, organizations have started using the contingency approach to management—changing the management principles and organizational structure based on the rate of change in an organization's environment and technology.

What Are the Career Options?

A degree in business administration prepares you for a wide range of jobs in accounting, sales, production, and management. Although recent graduates don't usually go into higher-level management positions immediately, there are a lot of paths that will lead to these positions. Many industries look for graduates with management degrees for supervisory positions (if you have a knowledge of the particular industry, it will help). If you choose to go into the banking or financial services industries, you can also begin your career as an administrator, bank loan officer, or investor relations manager. Financial analysts and planners, management consultants, purchasing agents, salespeople, and information specialists are needed in many industries. With additional training, you can also go into hotel, airport, city, or hospital management. A master's degree in business administration (MBA) in conjunction with work experience can sometimes help to further your career into upper-level management.

Finance

What Is It?

Finance is the study of how to create and maintain wealth. It is the art of administering and managing money that is crucial to the success of every business. Although you learn and use many calculations, financial management is really concerned with the logic behind the techniques. For instance, you come to understand what factors determine interest rates and the effects of those rates on future earnings. You learn the valuation and characteristics of stocks and bonds and how to evaluate a firm's financial performance. You also examine the functions and purposes of monetary systems, credit, prices, money markets, and financial institutions.

Before money existed, people produced much of what they needed to live and traded with others for items they could not produce themselves. When only real, tangible assets existed, people could only save those items. This is inconvenient at best, and, in this case, there is no mechanism to transfer the savings for value.

When paper money, or cash, came into being, we could then store our savings in the form of money. This is better, but not perfect, because there is still no mechanism to transfer money. Very few people will just hand over their cash! The concept of a receipt that represents the transfer of savings from one economic unit to another moved the system further along. Receipts enabled a person, or firm, who had surplus savings to lend those savings and earn a rate of return that the borrower paid.

Once loan brokers came into existence, they could help locate pools of excess savings and channel them to people needing funds. Sometimes people will purchase the financial claims of the borrowers and sell them at a higher price to other investors. This process is called *underwriting*. In addition, *secondary markets* developed, which represent trading in already existing financial claims. For example, if you buy your parents' General Motors common stock, you have made a secondary market transaction. In advanced financial market systems, financial intermediaries come into existence. These are the major financial institutions such as banks, savings and loan associations, credit unions, life insurance companies, and mutual funds. They all offer their own financial claims, called *indirect securities*, for entities with excess savings. The proceeds from selling these indirect securities are used to purchase the financial claims of others, the *direct securities*. For example, a mutual fund company sells its own shares (indirect securities) and buys common stock from other corporations (direct securities). A developed financial market system provides for a greater level of wealth in the economy.

The field of finance has undergone a change over the past decade because of the wave of acquisitions, mergers, and divestitures. The U. S. Department of Labor statistics estimates that financial services will grow at a faster rate than services as a whole. With all of this growth has also come a lot of controversy and debates about the system's alterations. Since late 1986, there has been a renewal of public interest in the regulation of the country's financial markets. The key event was a massive insider trading scandal. Much debate also followed the collapse of the equity markets on October 19, 1987, when the Dow-Jones industrial average fell by an unprecedented 508 points. More

Finance
The study of how to create and maintain wealth.

recently, in early 1990, the investing community became increasingly concerned over a weakening in the junk bond market. With all of this new awareness has come an appreciation of the crucial role that regulation plays in the financial system.

What Are the Career Options?

There are four basic areas for careers in finance:

> Banking
> Consumer credit
> Corporate finance
> Securities

In the banking sector, positions for finance majors include commercial loan officer, consumer bank officer, trust administrator, and bank manager. There are also opportunities with the Federal Reserve as bank examiners and operations analysts.

In the consumer credit area, jobs related to installment cash, sales, and mortgage credit are available, as well as consumer credit counselors or credit officers and managers.

In corporate finance, the chief financial officer is at the top of the ladder. Other positions may include treasurer, controller, pension fund manager, and financial analyst; positions could also be in financial public relations.

Securities sales and trading, as well as financial planning and underwriting, need finance majors. The Securities and Exchange Commission (SEC) also hires people with finance degrees as investigators.

Becoming a certified public accountant (CPA) or earning a master's degree in business administration (MBA) could help when you're looking for a job in some of these fields. There is also a growing availability of positions in international finance.

Economics

What Is It?

Economics
A social science concerned chiefly with the description and analysis of the production, distribution, and consumption of goods and services.

The field of economics studies how people make choices when faced with scarcity. Because we don't have an unlimited amount of money (or time, land, etc. . . .), we must make difficult choices about how we will spend it. If we buy a less expensive car, we might be able to afford a needed computer, for example. Economics is the study of choices on an individual, national, and global level. Economists apply the principles of economics to weigh the alternatives for many decisions that will affect the well-being of people around the world. With the help of economics, we can understand the world and make better decisions for our lives.

Early economic theories were based on the principle that government should regulate economic activities because only government could ensure that trade was conducted fairly. In the 1700s, the idea emerged that government should participate less in economic life. The writings of Adam Smith

(1723–1790) advocated free competition and free trade as a way to promote economic growth. His book, *An Inquiry into the Nature and Causes of the Wealth of Nations* (published in 1776), provided the foundation for the free enterprise system and contained insights that guide modern economic analysis.

Smith argued that human progress is possible in a society where individuals follow their own self-interests, and this individualism leads to social order and progress. In order to make money, people produce things that other people are willing to buy. Buyers spend money for things they need or want most. When buyers and sellers meet in the market, a natural pattern of production develops that produces social harmony. Smith also believed that national income grows when profits are used to expand production, which creates more and more jobs and national prosperity. He advocated that governments stay out of business and provide only social needs not met by the market.

In the early 1900s, economists began to apply the scientific method to the study of economic problems. They discovered relationships between different aspects of the economy and studied the booms and depressions associated with free enterprise.

Today, the field of economics is studied from two perspectives: microeconomics and macroeconomics. Microeconomics is the study of the choices that are made by individuals, firms, and government, and how these choices affect the markets for all sorts of goods and services. Macroeconomics, on the other hand, is the study of the nation's economy as a whole. It is a policy-oriented subject that was developed during the 1930s, when the entire world suffered from massive unemployment.

What Are the Career Options?

Economists are needed in many industries and can apply their knowledge in a number of careers. In the insurance industry, economic majors are hired to be actuaries and underwriters. Because they understand the interactions of many economic variables and policies, economists are needed in the financial industry as bank administrators, financial analysts, and investor relations managers.

Economists working for other businesses and public utilities spend much of their time applying economic theory to analyze issues that are important to their firms. They may analyze the effects of economic activity in the United States and the world on the demand for the company's product, conduct a cost-benefit analysis of the projects that the company is considering, or determine the effects of government regulations on the company. Careers in these areas include compensation analyst, business administrator, market researcher, and cost estimator.

Economists in government agencies may forecast the effects of various policy proposals on the economy and study the impacts of government regulations and taxes on industries. Today, economists in international development and trade are especially needed. They may also be hired as regional planners, demographers, and statisticians.

Research and university teaching are open to individuals with master's and doctoral degrees. Economics also provides a very good basis for continuing on to law school.

Information Systems

What Is It?

There is a difference between data and information, even though these words are sometimes used interchangeably. Data is facts and figures alone. When you see that 46 percent of job offers went for business positions in 1996, this is a raw fact. Perhaps you may have other data as well that tells you, for example, the average salary of graduates in accounting, marketing, and management. When you interpret this data and put it together in a meaningful way, perhaps to decide on a major or emphasis, the data becomes information.

An information system is a way that you can collect data, process it, and turn it into useful information. These information systems are used extensively in marketing and management and are made up of hardware (computers), software (computer programs), data sources, and people. For example, consider what happens when you buy a stereo at Best Buy. You may talk to the salesperson, tell him or her what you want in a stereo, and purchase the product. The information system will collect information on what type of stereo you purchased, where the stereo was shipped from, and the amount of inventory of that stereo left in the stockroom. It may also have a record of your zip code, which can tell them a lot about your demographic information (approximate age, race, approximate income, etc.). Management will use the information to determine what types of stereos they should stock in the future, when they should reorder, and how to best market the stereos.

There is a tremendous amount of data available, and the amount will continue to grow. An information system can convert the data into usable information, though it will still be up to individuals to make use of the information. Through math skills and information management, people in all types of businesses can increase their opportunities and contribute to their success.

What Are the Career Options?

With the changing technology, jobs in all areas in business are also changing. The field of information systems, however, has been more visibly dynamic than many other fields. New jobs that could never have been imagined even a couple of years ago continue to emerge. Cybrarians, virtual reality evangelists, and network administrators are just a few examples of newly created positions. Jobs such as Webmasters, which had not previously existed, now are quite common. As business continues to become more "borderless," and we see the Internet used even more extensively for product purchases, we will see jobs in information systems integrate into the organization, spreading throughout other departments. Marketing, for example, will need someone skilled in information systems in order to facilitate the sale of products via the Internet. Although it will still be its own field, information systems will also permeate other jobs. Most large corporations will probably have a chief knowledge officer, whose job it may be to extract the best ideas from people, maintain these in electronic file cabinets, and facilitate knowledge sharing among employees. Network administrators and architects are additional examples. As technology continues to change, we will continue to see new jobs develop in this field.

HOW CAN YOU INCREASE YOUR CHANCES FOR SUCCESS IN THE BUSINESS WORLD?

There are many things you can do while in school that can help you tremendously in preparing for your career. College is the best time that you have to analyze your skills, learn about different careers, and determine the best possible match. Make the most of this time—set a good, solid foundation for the rest of your life. Internships, contact development, skill analysis, and research can help give you an edge and enable you to make a smooth transition from school to work.

Internships

Any kind of work experience related to your field that you can get while in school will greatly increase your chance of employment in that field after graduation. This work experience can come in several forms:

Part-time job

Paid internship

Unpaid internship

Co-op program

Volunteer work

To make the most of your work experience, you should concentrate on learning new skills, taking initiative, and meeting as many people as possible. It is very important to ensure that the work experience you acquire during your college years is directly related to the field you think you may be interested in. Even if you have to take an unpaid internship, the experience you gain will be worth more in the long run than the wages you can earn in the short term.

Networking

Throughout your education, try to meet as many people as you can who are in careers you find interesting. You can start with alumni from your university who are working in your area of interest. The career office can help locate alumni. Take the initiative yourself also, and call people in the human resources departments of companies for which you might like to work. They can arrange informational interviews—many managers are very willing to spend time helping students because they were students themselves not so long ago! Always ask the people you meet for names of other people you should speak with. Keep a log of all the contacts you make and develop your network.

TERMS

Networking
To make connections among people or groups.

Business Skills Assessment

In the classes you take and the work experience you get, keep a journal of skills that you learn. Note what you do that you really like—and what you don't like. This will help to formulate a base of skills that you like using. Then you will be able to better determine what kind of position and career you might like. Everybody is different. Some people really like people—talking to them, understanding them, leading them; others might really like analyzing numbers and putting them together to tell a story. You are unique. The key is to find what you—alone—like to do. One way to do that is to constantly analyze what you are doing and what skills you are using and developing.

Researching Industries and Companies

If you think you might want to work for a company or in a particular industry or field, you'll want to do a lot of research. Talk to as many people as possible who are currently working there—again, use informational interviews. Research the Internet—use a general search by name. Also use LEXIS-NEXIS or the *Wall Street Journal Index*, for example, to get more detailed information on particular companies. Look in the library or call the company and order its annual report, if it publishes one, and find trade journals for the industry.

MBA or Other Advanced Degrees

Advanced degrees can sometimes increase your chances of getting a position. Sometimes they can also increase your starting salary. However, they are the most valuable to you—in the long term—if you have some work experience in between degrees. Many recruiters and managers recommend working for a couple of years after obtaining a bachelor's degree before going back for a graduate degree. You can get more out of an advanced graduate program if you have some real-world experience and specific goals that you want to achieve in the program. With experience and goals, a graduate degree can ultimately help your career and long-term salary.

In Chinese writing, this character has two meanings: One is "chaos"; the other is "opportunity." The character communicates the belief that every challenging, chaotic, demanding situation in life also presents an opportunity. By responding to challenges in a positive and active way, you can discover the opportunity that lies within the chaos.

Let this concept reassure you as you begin college. You may feel that you are going through a time of chaos and change. Remember that no matter how difficult the obstacles, you have the ability to persevere. You can create opportunities for yourself to learn, grow, and improve.

Success in the Real World

Jamie Makuuchi

Jamie Makuuchi, the International Marketing Director for Johns Manville Corporation, has  what some people may consider a glamorous job. In his fast-paced job, he jet-sets between countries—fifty-two so far—"wines and dines" clients, and is in touch via his cell phone and laptop computer. But, the travel and stress are wearing, and he considers his job less than glamorous.

"Traveling for work is much different than traveling for pleasure. All I really see in the different countries I go to are hotel rooms and offices—I'm craning my neck in the taxi trips between meetings to get a peek at the country I'm in."

With so much time and money invested in his international travel, Jamie's schedule has to be tight. His time management skills are crucial to the success of a trip. Because of this, Jamie values all of his time and relies heavily on a schedule, even scheduling in his downtime.

Jamie also relies heavily on goal setting. He writes down his yearly goals, both personal and professional, and then breaks these into objectives to accomplish throughout the year. He tries to periodically remind himself of his overall goals, focusing on them but not dwelling on them.

Jamie deals with diversity on a daily basis—not only while traveling but also at his office. The work force today is composed of many different types of people in all stages of life, and Jamie finds that tolerance, understanding, and knowledge are the keys to his success.

There are all sorts of differences among various cultures, and Jamie reads a lot in order to know the idiosyncrasies of each. But it can be somewhat humorous at times because as he's learning the culture of the people with whom he's doing business, they are also studying American culture. When they communicate, he says, it can get a little mixed up! But Jamie believes that taking the time to learn about others and their culture can make all the difference between a successful and an unsuccessful business relationship.

Taking the time to learn is a valuable investment for Jamie, but it is hard to fit this into his schedule. However, continual learning has been one of the major keys to success for him, so he makes the time. While he is on the airplane, waiting in an airport, and before going to sleep, he reads journals and skims relevant books for important information. Information is useless unless it is used, and Jamie uses the information to generate creative solutions to problems and to respond quickly to market forces. To be successful in today's marketplace, Jamie believes that you have to develop the necessary skills and, above all else, invest in yourself by working very hard.

Chapter 1 Applications

Name _____ Date _____

KEY INTO YOUR LIFE
Opportunities to Apply What You Learn

1.1 *Skill Analysis*

1. Think about a class that you really enjoyed. Take a few minutes to write down what you enjoyed about the class and what you were required to do in the class. Be as specific as possible. What skills did you use? Did you analyze information? Work with people? Use mechanical ability? Make a list of five skills you used. Now rank them according to how much you like to use them (1 being the most favorite).

   a. _____

   b. _____

   c. _____

   d. _____

   e. _____

2. Think about something you accomplished in your life that made you really proud. Write a story about it. Now go over the story and analyze what you had to do to make that happen. What skills did you use? Make a list of five skills you used and rank them as you did in question 1.

   a. _____

   b. _____

   c. _____

   d. _____

   e. _____

1.2 *Leadership*

1. Describe a person whom you really admire. What makes that person unique? How can you develop the qualities that you admire?

_____

_____

_____

_____

_____

_____

2. Compare and contrast two world leaders. Research their lives and leadership styles. Do you consider them good leaders? Why or why not? What do you think has contributed to their success?

_____

_____

_____

_____

_____

_____

3. What are the differences between a leader and a manager?

_____

_____

_____

_____

1.3 *Researching Careers*

Choose three careers you think are interesting:

1. _____

2. _____

3. _____

Now, identify one person in each career with whom you could speak. Interview the people and have them answer the questions in the table below.

Question	Career 1: Name:	Career 2: Name:	Career 3: Name:
What is the most interesting part of your job?			
What do you like least about your job?			
What advice would you give to students who are interested in pursuing this career?			
What skills should one have in order to do a good job in your field?			
How could I find out more information about this field?			

Team-Building Exercise

After everyone has completed Exercise 3, gather in small groups. Discuss the skills that are needed in each career. Are there any similarities in the skills needed among the careers? Choose three skills and write down specific ways that students can begin to develop those skills.

Activity To Help Develop Skill	Skill #1	Skill #2	Skill #3
1.			
2.			
3.			
4.			

Understanding The U. S. Business System

Disney

Case Studies

There's no getting around it: The baby boom generation is aging. The oldest of 76 million baby boomers turned fifty in 1996; the next decade, the number of Americans over age fifty will increase by 50 percent, to nearly 38 million. Many of the people are couples whose children have left home. They thrive on personal and even physical challenge, but most have no interest in taking a Disney World vacation.

Creative minds at the Walt Disney Company saw these demographic and mood shifts as a commercial challenge requiring a tailor-made solution: They had to find a way to attract forty- and fifty-year-olds who were no longer as active or child-oriented as they once were and who wanted to return from their vacations with something more than a suntan. In other words, asks Orlando-based marketing researcher Peter Yesawich, "What do you do if you're forty-eight and your kids are grown up?"

Disney's answer is the Disney Institute, a seventy-five-acre resort within a resort. Located at Orlando's Disney World, the resort allows guests to try their hand at bird watching, cartoon animation, rock climbing, gourmet cooking, spiritual inquiry, and more. This $35 million solution—billed by Disney as "smart fun"—is pretty much like a summer camp for adults.

The vision for the Disney Institute began to take shape when Disney CEO Michael Eisner visited the Chautauqua Institution, an adult-learning community located in upstate New York that holds classes on politics, philosophy, and the performing arts. Eisner's 1985 visit convinced him that Disney could create a similar environment "Disney-style."

The greatest challenge for Disney was to convince the public to try a venture that was so far afield from Disney's traditional mass-market resorts. It had to build a new market by slowly creating demand. Disney responded to this need in several ways:

◆ By catering to the trend toward shorter vacations (3, 4, and 7 nights)

◆ By striking a balance between education and entertainment

◆ By offering special introductory rates as part of its "First 100 Days of Discovery"

◆ By relying on word of mouth as well as traditional advertising to build a base of support

◆ By deciding that the Institute would be a long-term investment

Underlying all of these efforts was an appeal to the needs and wants of each individual customer. The challenge of sustaining a business despite changing market forces is very common to all types of business. Responding to a changing marketplace requires vision, careful attention to quality and customer service, substantial financial commitment, and a well-defined marketing strategy that helps a business grow over time. These and other forces are the main themes in stories of success and failure that are told over and over again in the annals of enterprise in the United States. [Adapted from *Business Essentials* (Ebert and Griffin).]

1. Give as many details as you can about the type of person who might go to the Disney Institute.

2. Find two examples of companies that did NOT respond to a changing market. What happened?

3. Where can you find information about population changes in the United States?

4. What skills did Michael Eisner have to have in order for the Disney Institute to become a reality?

5. How can you find out what careers are available at the Disney Institute?

6. Do you think you would like to work for the Disney Institute? Why or why not?

Internet Exercise

If you are trying to decide what major you should pursue, or which emphasis you should have in your business studies, and you would like more information, you can access the Prentice Hall supersite at:

www.prenhall.com/success

1. Click on **College Student** and find the **Majors Exploration** category. Look at several of the majors listed, including accounting, finance, marketing, and management.
2. Click on each of the majors shown below, and list one new thing you discovered about the major.

MAJOR	NEW DISCOVERY ABOUT THE MAJOR
Accounting	
Finance	
Marketing	
Management	

3. Access the Weblinks page and pick one of the links to explore further. Print out one of the pages you found interesting.

Journal

Name _____   Date _____

2

Self-
Awareness

Knowing Who You Are
and How You Learn

Learning is not something you do just in college. Throughout your life, learning can help you keep up with the rapid pace at which the world is changing.

Technology, for example, is changing so fast that you cannot learn today about all of the computer operations that will be commonplace five years from now. However, you can learn how to be an effective learner in school and in the workplace so that you can keep pace with changes as they occur. In this chapter you will become aware of your learning style by completing three different learning-style assessments. Each assessment will add a different dimension to the picture you are forming of yourself. You will then explore other important elements of self: your self-perception, your preferences, your habits, your abilities, and your attitudes.

In this chapter, you will explore answers to the following questions:

◆ Is there one best way to learn?

◆ How can you discover your learning styles?

◆ What are the benefits of knowing your learning styles?

◆ How do you explore who you are?

◆ How does your learning style affect your choice of business major?

IS THERE ONE BEST WAY TO LEARN?

Your mind is the most powerful tool you will ever possess. You are accomplished at many skills and can process all kinds of information. However, when you have trouble accomplishing a particular task, you may become convinced that you can't learn how to do anything new. You may feel that those who can do what you can't have the "right" kind of ability. Not only is this perception incorrect, it can also damage your belief in yourself.

Every individual is highly developed in some abilities and underdeveloped in others. Many famously successful people were brilliant in one area but functioned poorly in other areas. Winston Churchill failed the sixth grade. Abraham Lincoln was demoted to a private in the Black Hawk War. Louis Pasteur was a poor student in chemistry. Walt Disney was fired from a job and told he had no good ideas. What some might interpret as a deficiency or disability may be simply a different method of learning.

There is no one "best" way to learn. Instead, there are many different learning styles, and different styles are suited to different situations. Your individual learning profile is made up of a combination of learning styles. Each person's profile is unique. Just like personality traits, learning styles are part of your personal characteristics. Knowing how you learn is one of the first steps in discovering who you are.

TERMS

Learning style
A particular way
in which the
mind receives
and processes
information.

HOW CAN YOU DISCOVER YOUR LEARNING STYLES?

"To be what we are, and to become what we are capable of becoming, is the only end of life."
ROBERT LOUIS STEVENSON

Your brain is so complex that one inventory cannot give you all the information you need to maximize your learning skills. You will learn about and complete three assessments: the *Learning Styles Inventory*, the *Pathways to Learning* inventory based on the Multiple Intelligences Theory, and the *Personality Spectrum*. Each of these assessments evaluates your mind's abilities in a different way, although they often have related ideas. Your results will combine to form your learning-styles profile, consisting of the styles and types that best fit the ways that you learn and interact with others. After you complete the various learning-styles inventories, you will read about strategies that can help you make the most of particular styles and types, both in school and beyond. Your learning-styles profile will help you to improve your understanding of yourself, how you learn, and how you may function as a learner in the workplace.

Learning Styles Inventory

One of the first instruments to measure psychological types, the Myers-Briggs Type Inventory (MBTI), was designed by Katharine Briggs and her daughter, Isabel Briggs Myers. Later David Keirsey and Marilyn Bates combined the sixteen Myers-Briggs types into four temperaments. Barbara Soloman, Associate Director of the University Undesignated Student Program at North Carolina State University, has developed the following Learning Styles Inventory based on these theories and on her work with thousands of students.[1]

"Students learn in many ways," says Professor Soloman. "Mismatches often exist between common learning styles and standard teaching styles. Therefore, students often do poorly and get discouraged. Some students doubt themselves and doubt their ability to succeed in the curriculum of their choice. Some settle for low grades and even leave school. If students understand how they learn most effectively, they can tailor their studying to their own needs."

"Learning effectively" and "tailoring studying to your own needs" means choosing study techniques that help you learn. For example, if a student responds more to visual images than to words, he or she may want to construct notes in a more visual way. Or, if a student learns better when talking to people than when studying alone, he or she may want to study primarily in pairs or groups.

This inventory has four "dimensions," within each of which are two opposing styles. At the end of the inventory, you will have two scores in each of the four dimensions. The difference between your two scores in any dimension tells you which of the two styles in that dimension is dominant for you. A few people will score right in between the two styles, indicating that they have fairly equal parts of both styles. Following are brief descriptions of the four dimensions. You will learn more about them after you complete all three assessments, in the section on study strategies.

Active/Reflective. *Active* learners learn best by experiencing knowledge through their own actions. *Reflective* learners understand information best when they have had time to reflect on it on their own.

Factual/Theoretical. *Factual* learners learn best through specific facts, data, and detailed experimentation. *Theoretical* learners are more comfortable with big-picture ideas, symbols, and new concepts.

Visual/Verbal. *Visual* learners remember best what they see: diagrams, flow-charts, time lines, films, and demonstrations. *Verbal* learners gain the most learning from reading, hearing spoken words, participating in discussion, and explaining things to others.

Linear/Holistic. *Linear* learners find it easiest to learn material presented step-by-step in a logical, ordered progression. *Holistic* learners progress in fits and starts, perhaps feeling lost for a while, but eventually seeing the big picture in a clear and creative way.

TERMS

Holistic
Relating to the wholes of complete systems rather than the analysis of parts.

Please complete this inventory by circling **a** or **b** to indicate your answer to each question. Answer every question and choose only one answer for each question. If both answers seem to apply to you, choose the answer that applies more often.

1. I study best
   a. in a study group.
   b. alone or with a partner.

2. I would rather be considered
   a. realistic.
   b. imaginative.

3. When I recall what I did yesterday, I am most likely to think in terms of
   a. pictures/images.
   b. words/verbal descriptions.

4. I usually think new material is
   a. easier at the beginning and then harder as it becomes more complicated.
   b. often confusing at the beginning but easier as I start to understand what the whole subject is about.

5. When given a new activity to learn, I would rather first
   a. try it out.
   b. think about how I'm going to do it.

6. If I were an instructor, I would rather teach a course
   a. that deals with real-life situations and what to do about them.
   b. that deals with ideas and encourages students to think about them.

7. I prefer to receive new information in the form of
   a. pictures, diagrams, graphs, or maps.
   b. written directions or verbal information.

8. I learn
   a. at a fairly regular pace. If I study hard, I'll "get it" and then move on.
   b. in fits and starts. I might be totally confused and then suddenly it all "clicks."

9. I understand something better after
   a. I attempt to do it myself.
   b. I give myself time to think about how it works.

10. I find it easier
    a. to learn facts.
    b. to learn ideas/concepts.

11. In a book with lots of pictures and charts, I am likely to
    a. look over the pictures and charts carefully.
    b. focus on the written text.

12. It's easier for me to memorize facts from
    a. a list.
    b. a whole story/essay with the facts embedded in it.

13. I will more easily remember
    a. something I have done myself.
    b. something I have thought or read about.

14. I am usually
    a. aware of my surroundings. I remember people and places and usually recall where I put things.
    b. unaware of my surroundings. I forget people and places. I frequently misplace things.

15. I like instructors
    a. who put a lot of diagrams on the board.
    b. who spend a lot of time explaining.

16. Once I understand
    a. all the parts, I understand the whole thing.
    b. the whole thing, I see how the parts fit.

17. When I am learning something new, I would rather
    a. talk about it.
    b. think about it.

18. I am good at
    a. being careful about the details of my work.
    b. having creative ideas about how to do my work.

19. I remember best
    a. what I see.
    b. what I hear.

20. When I solve problems that involve some math, I usually
    a. work my way to the solutions one step at a time.
    b. see the solutions but then have to struggle to figure out the steps to get to them.

21. In a lecture class, I would prefer occasional in-class
    a. discussions or group problem-solving sessions.
    b. pauses that give opportunities to think or write about ideas presented in the lecture.

22. On a multiple-choice test, I am more likely to
    a. run out of time.
    b. lose points because of not reading carefully or making careless errors.

23. When I get directions to a new place, I prefer
    a. a map.
    b. written instructions.

24. When I'm thinking about something I've read,
    a. I remember the incidents and try to put them together to figure out the themes.
    b. I just know what the themes are when I finish reading and then I have to back up and find the incidents that demonstrate them.

25. When I get a new computer or VCR, I tend to
    a. plug it in and start punching buttons.
    b. read the manual and follow instructions.

26. In reading for pleasure, I prefer
    a. something that teaches me new facts or tells me how to do something.
    b. something that gives me new ideas to think about.

27. When I see a diagram or sketch in class, I am most likely to remember
    a. the picture.
    b. what the instructor said about it.

28. It is more important to me that an instructor
    a. lay out the material in clear, sequential steps.
    b. give me an overall picture and relate the material to other subjects.

Scoring Sheet: Use Table 2-1 to enter your scores.

1. Put 1's in the appropriate boxes in the table (e.g., if you answered **a** to Question 3, put a **1** in the column headed **a** next to the number **3**).
2. Total the 1's in the columns and write the totals in the indicated spaces at the base of the columns.

| Table 2-1 | Learning styles inventory scores. |

Active/Reflective			Factual/Theoretical			Visual/Verbal			Linear/Holistic		
Q#	a	b	Q#	a	b	Q#	a	b	Q#	a	b
1			2			3			4		
5			6			7			8		
9			10			11			12		
13			14			15			16		
17			18			19			20		
21			22			23			24		
25			26			27			28		
Total			Total			Total			Total		

3. For each of the four dimensions, circle your two scores on the bar scale and then fill in the bar between the scores. For example, if under "ACTV/REFL" you had 2 **a** and 5 **b** responses, you would fill in the bar between those two scores, as this sample shows:

ACTV [▮▮▮▮▮▮▮▮▮] REFL
   7a 6a 5a 4a 3a 2a 1a 0 1b 2b 3b 4b 5b 6b 7b

LEARNING STYLES SCALES

ACTV [ ] REFL
   7a 6a 5a 4a 3a 2a 1a 0 1b 2b 3b 4b 5b 6b 7b

FACT [ ] THEO
   7a 6a 5a 4a 3a 2a 1a 0 1b 2b 3b 4b 5b 6b 7b

VISL [ ] VRBL
   7a 6a 5a 4a 3a 2a 1a 0 1b 2b 3b 4b 5b 6b 7b

LINR [ ] HOLS
   7a 6a 5a 4a 3a 2a 1a 0 1b 2b 3b 4b 5b 6b 7b

If your filled-in bar has the 0 close to its center, you are well balanced on the two dimensions of that scale. If your bar is drawn mainly to one side, you have a strong preference for that one dimension and may have difficulty learning in the other dimension.

Continue on to the next assessment. After you complete all three, the next section of the chapter will help you understand and make use of your results from each assessment.

Multiple Intelligences Theory

Howard Gardner, a Harvard University professor, has developed a theory called Multiple Intelligences. He believes there are at least eight distinct intelligences possessed by all people, and that every person has developed some intelligences more fully than others. Most people have experienced a time when they learned something very quickly and comfortably. Most have also had the opposite experience when, no matter how hard they tried, something they wanted to learn just would not sink in. According to the Multiple Intelligences Theory, when you find a task or subject easy, you are probably using a more fully developed intelligence; when you have more trouble, you may be using a less developed intelligence.[2]

Following are brief descriptions of the focus of each of the intelligences. Study skills that reinforce each intelligence will be described later in the chapter.

- Verbal/Linguistic Intelligence—ability to communicate through language (listening, reading, writing, speaking)

- Logical/Mathematical Intelligence—ability to understand logical reasoning and problem solving (math, science, patterns, sequences)

- Bodily/Kinesthetic Intelligence—ability to use the physical body skillfully and to take in knowledge through bodily sensation (coordination, working with hands)

- Visual/Spatial Intelligence—ability to understand spatial relationships and to perceive and create images (visual art, graphic design, charts and maps)

- Interpersonal Intelligence—ability to relate to others, noticing their moods, motivations, and feelings (social activity, cooperative learning, teamwork)

- Intrapersonal Intelligence—ability to understand one's own behavior and feelings (independence, time spent alone)

- Musical Intelligence—ability to comprehend and create meaningful sound (music, sensitivity to sound)

- Naturalistic Intelligence—ability to understand features of the environment (interest in nature, environmental balance, ecosystem, stress relief brought by natural environments)

Please complete the following assessment of your multiple intelligences, called Pathways to Learning, developed by Joyce Bishop. It will help you determine which of your intelligences are most fully developed. Don't be concerned if some of your scores are low. That is true of most people, even your instructors and your authors!

Intelligence
As defined by H. Gardner, an ability to solve problems or fashion products that are useful in a particular cultural setting or community.

Kinesthetic
Coming from physical sensation caused by body movements and tensions.

PATHWAYS TO LEARNING[3]

Directions: Rate each statement as follows: rarely 1; sometimes 2; usually 3; always 4.

Write the number of your response (1–4) in the box next to the statement and total each set of the six questions.

Developed by Joyce Bishop, Ph.D., and based upon Howard Gardner, *Frames of Mind: The Theory of Multiple Intelligences.*

□ 1. I enjoy physical activities.

□ 2. I am uncomfortable sitting still.

□ 3. I prefer to learn through doing.

□ 4. When sitting I move my legs or hands.

□ 5. I enjoy working with my hands.

□ 6. I like to pace when I'm thinking or studying.

□ **TOTAL for Bodily/Kinesthetic**

□ 7. I use maps easily.

□ 8. I draw pictures/diagrams when explaining ideas.

□ 9. I can assemble items easily from diagrams.

□ 10. I enjoy drawing or photography.

□ 11. I do not like to read long paragraphs.

□ 12. I prefer a drawn map over written directions.

□ **TOTAL for Visual/Spatial**

□ 13. I enjoy telling stories.

□ 14. I like to write.

□ 15. I like to read.

□ 16. I express myself clearly.

□ 17. I am good at negotiating.

□ 18. I like to discuss topics that interest me.

□ **TOTAL for Verbal/Linguistic**

□ 19. I liked math in high school.

□ 20. I like science.

□ 21. I problem-solve well.

□ 22. I question how things work.

□ 23. I enjoy planning or designing something new.

□ 24. I am able to fix things.

□ **TOTAL for Logical/Mathematical**

□ 25. I listen to music.

□ 26. I move my fingers or feet when I hear music.

□ 27. I have good rhythm.

□ 28. I like to sing along with music.

□ 29. People have said I have musical talent.

□ 30. I like to express my ideas through music.

□ **TOTAL for Musical**

□ 31. I like doing a project with other people.

□ 32. People come to me to help settle conflicts.

□ 33. I like to spend time with friends.

□ 34. I am good at understanding people.

□ 35. I am good at making people feel comfortable.

□ 36. I enjoy helping others.

□ **TOTAL for Interpersonal**

□ 37. I need quiet time to think.

□ 38. I think about issues before I want to talk.

□ 39. I am interested in self-improvement.

□ 40. I understand my thoughts and feelings.

□ 41. I know what I want out of life.

□ 42. I prefer to work on projects alone.

□ **TOTAL for Intrapersonal**

□ 43. I enjoy nature whenever possible.

□ 44. I think about having a career involving nature.

□ 45. I enjoy studying plants, animals, or oceans.

□ 46. I avoid being indoors except when I sleep.

□ 47. As a child I played with bugs and leaves.

□ 48. When I feel stressed, I want to be out in nature.

□ **TOTAL for Naturalistic**

Write each of your eight intelligences in the column where it fits below. For each, choose the column that corresponds with your total in that intelligence.

Scores of 20–24 Highly Developed		Scores of 14–19 Moderately Developed		Scores below 14 Underdeveloped	
Scores	Intelligences	Scores	Intelligences	Scores	Intelligences

Keys to Success, 2/e by Carter et al., 1998. Reprinted by permission of Prentice-Hall, Inc., Upper Saddle River, NJ.

Learning styles and multiple intelligences are gauges to help you understand yourself. Instead of labeling yourself narrowly using one category or another, learn as much as you can about your preferences and how you can maximize your learning. Most people are a blend of styles and preferences, with one or two being dominant. In addition, you may change preferences depending on the situation. For example, a student might find it easy to take notes in outline style when the instructor lectures in an organized way. However, if another instructor jumps from topic to topic, the student might choose to use the Cornell system or a think link (Chapter 6 goes into detail about note-taking styles).

The final assessment, through its evaluation of personality types, focuses on how you relate to others.

Personality Spectrum

A system that simplifies learning styles into four personality types has been developed by Joyce Bishop (1997). Her work is based on the Myers-Briggs and Keirsey theories discussed earlier in the chapter. The Personality Spectrum will give you a personality perspective on your learning styles. Please complete the following assessment.

PERSONALITY SPECTRUM

Step 1: Rank all four responses to each question from *most like you (4)* to **least** *like you (1)*. Place a 1, 2, 3, or 4 in each box next to the responses, and use each number only once per question.

1. I like instructors who
   - ☐ a. tell me exactly what is expected of me.
   - ☐ b. make learning active and exciting.
   - ☐ c. maintain a safe and supportive classroom.
   - ☐ d. challenge me to think at higher levels.

2. I learn best when material is
   - ☐ a. well organized.
   - ☐ b. something I can do hands-on.
   - ☐ c. about understanding and improving the human condition.
   - ☐ d. intellectually challenging.

3. A high priority in my life is to
   - ☐ a. keep my commitments.
   - ☐ b. experience as much of life as possible.
   - ☐ c. make a difference in other's lives.
   - ☐ d. understand how things work.

4. Other people think of me as
   - ☐ a. dependable and loyal.
   - ☐ b. dynamic and creative.
   - ☐ c. caring and honest.
   - ☐ d. intelligent and inventive.

5. When I experience stress, I would most likely
   - ☐ a. do something to help me feel more in control of my life.
   - ☐ b. do something physical and daring.
   - ☐ c. talk with a friend.
   - ☐ d. go off by myself and think about my situation.

6. The greatest flaw someone can have is to be
   - ☐ a. irresponsible.
   - ☐ b. unwilling to try new things.
   - ☐ c. selfish and unkind to others.
   - ☐ d. an illogical thinker.

7. My vacations could best be described as
   - ☐ a. traditional.
   - ☐ b. adventuresome.
   - ☐ c. pleasing to others.
   - ☐ d. a new learning experience.

8. One word that best describes me is
   - ☐ a. sensible.
   - ☐ b. spontaneous.
   - ☐ c. giving.
   - ☐ d. analytical.

Step 2: Add up the total points for each letter.

Total for (A)	Total for (B)	Total for (C)	Total for (D)
☐	☐	☐	☐
Organizer	Adventurer	Giver	Thinker

Step 3: Plot these numbers on the brain diagram on page 38.

When you have tallied your scores, plot them on Figure 2-1 to create a visual representation of your spectrum.

Your Personality Spectrum assessment can help you maximize your functioning at school and at work. Each personality type has its own abilities that improve work and school performance, suitable learning techniques, and ways of relating in interpersonal relationships. Table 2-2 explains what suits each type.

WHAT ARE THE BENEFITS OF KNOWING YOUR LEARNING STYLES?

Determining your learning-styles profile takes work and self-exploration. For it to be worth your while, you need to understand what knowing your profile can do for you. The following sections will discuss benefits specific to study skills, as well as more general benefits.

Study Benefits

Most students aim to maximize learning while minimizing frustration and time spent studying. If you know your particular learning style, you can use techniques that complement it. Such techniques take advantage of your highly developed areas while helping you through your less developed ones. For example, say you perform better in smaller, discussion-based classes. When you have the opportunity, you might choose a course section that is smaller or that is taught by an instructor who prefers group discussion. You might also apply specific strategies to improve your retention in a lecture situation.

PERSONALITY	STRENGTHS AT WORK AND SCHOOL	INTERPERSONAL RELATIONSHIPS
Organizer	◆ Can efficiently manage heavy work loads ◆ Good organizational skills ◆ Natural leadership qualities	◆ Loyal ◆ Dependable ◆ Traditional
Adventurer	◆ Adaptable to most changes ◆ Creative and skillful ◆ Dynamic and fast-paced	◆ Free ◆ Exciting ◆ Intense
Giver	◆ Always willing to help others ◆ Honest and sincere ◆ Good people skills	◆ Giving ◆ Romantic ◆ Warm
Thinker	◆ Good analytical skills ◆ Can develop complex designs ◆ Is thorough and exact	◆ Quiet ◆ Good problem-solver ◆ Inventive

Table 2-2

Personality spectrum at school and work.

| Figure 2-1 | Personality spectrum—Thinking preferences & learning styles. |

Place a dot on the appropriate number line for each of your 4 scores and connect the dots. A new shape will be formed inside each square. Color each shape in a different color.

THINKER

Technical
Scientific
Mathematical
Dispassionate
Rational
Analytical
Logical
Problem Solving
Theoretical
Intellectual
Objective
Quantitative
Explicit
Realistic
Literal
Precise
Formal

Left Brain   Right Brain

GIVER

Interpersonal
Emotional
Caring
Sociable
Giving
Spiritual
Musical
Romantic
Feeling
Peacemaker
Trusting
Adaptable
Passionate
Harmonious
Idealistic
Talkative
Honest

ORGANIZER

Systematic
Administrative
Procedural
Organized
Conservative
Confident
Structured
Safekeeping
Disciplined

Practical
Sequential
Predictable
Detailed
Tactical
Controlled
Dependable
Planning

ADVENTURER

Imaginative
Adventuresome
Open-minded
Fast-paced
Metaphoric
Original
Simultaneous
Visual

Impulsive
Experimental
Risking
Divergent
Artistic
Spatial
Skillful
Competitive
Active

Source: *Understanding Psychology*, 3/e, by Morris, © 1996. Adapted by permission of Prentice-Hall, Inc., Upper Saddle River, NJ.

This section describes the techniques that tend to complement the strengths and shortcomings of each style. Students in Professor Soloman's program made many of these suggestions according to what worked for their own learning styles. Concepts from different assessments that benefit from similar strategies are grouped together. In Figure 2-2 you can see which styles tend to be dominant among students.

Remember that you may have characteristics from many different styles, even though some are dominant. Therefore, you may see suggestions for styles other than your dominant ones that may apply to you. What's important is that you use what works. Note the boxes next to the names of each style or type. In order to spot your best suggestions quickly, mark your most dominant styles or types by making check marks in the appropriate boxes.

Are You Active or Reflective?

Active learners ☐ include **Bodily-Kinesthetic** ☐ and **Interpersonal** ☐ learners as well as **Adventurers.** ☐ They like to apply the information to the real world, experience it in their own actions, or discuss or explain to others what they have learned.

Student-suggested strategies for active learners:

◆ Study in a group in which members take turns explaining topics to each other and then discussing them.

◆ Think of practical uses for the course material.

◆ Pace and recite while you learn.

◆ Act out material or design games.

◆ Use flash cards with other people.

◆ Teach the material to someone else.

Reflective learners ☐ include **Intrapersonal** ☐ and **Logical/ Mathematical** ☐ learners as well as **Thinkers.** ☐ They retain and understand information better after they have taken time to think about it.

Student-suggested strategies for reflective learners:

◆ Study in a quiet setting.

◆ When you are reading, stop periodically to think about what you have read.

◆ Don't just memorize material; think about why it is important and what it relates to, considering the causes and effects involved.

◆ Write short summaries of what the material means to you.

VISUAL	VERBAL
80%	20%

ACTIVE	REFLECTIVE
80%	20%

FACTUAL	THEORETICAL
70%	30%

LINEAR	HOLISTIC
85%	15%

Figure 2-2

Percentages of students with particular learning styles.

Source: Barbara Soloman, North Carolina State University.

Are You Factual or Theoretical?

Factual learners ☐ and **Organizers** ☐ prefer concrete and specific facts, data, and detailed experimentation. They like to solve problems with standard methods and are patient with details. They don't respond well to surprises and unique complications that upset normal procedure. They are good at memorizing facts.

Student-suggested strategies for factual learners:

◆ Ask the instructor how ideas and concepts apply in practice.

◆ Ask for specific examples of the ideas and concepts.

◆ Brainstorm specific examples with classmates or by yourself.

◆ Think about how theories make specific connections with the real world.

Theoretical learners ☐ are often also **Logical/Mathematical** ☐ and prefer innovation and theories. They are good at grasping new concepts and big-picture ideas. They dislike repetition and fact-based learning. They are comfortable with symbols and abstractions, often connecting them with prior knowledge and experience. Most classes are aimed at theoretical learners.

Student-suggested strategies for theoretical learners:

◆ If a class deals primarily with factual information, try to think of concepts, interpretations, or theories that link the facts together.

◆ Because you become impatient with details, you may be prone to careless mistakes on tests. Read directions and entire questions before answering, and be sure to check your work.

◆ Look for systems and patterns that arrange facts in a way that makes sense to you.

◆ Spend time analyzing the material.

Are You Visual/Spatial or Verbal/Linguistic?

Visual/Spatial learners ☐ remember best what they see: diagrams, flowcharts, time lines, films, and demonstrations. They tend to forget spoken words and ideas. Classes generally don't include that much visual information. Note that although words written on paper or shown with an overhead projector are something you see, visual learners learn most easily from visual cues that don't involve words.

Student-suggested strategies for visual/spatial learners:

◆ Add diagrams to your notes whenever possible: Dates can be drawn on a time line; math functions can be graphed; percentages can be drawn in a pie chart.

◆ Organize your notes so that you can clearly see main points and supporting facts and how things are connected. You will learn more about different styles of note-taking in Chapter 6.

◆ Connect related facts in your notes by drawing arrows.

◆ Color-code your notes using different colored highlighters so that everything relating to a particular topic is the same color.

Verbal/Linguistic learners □ (often also **Interpersonal** □) remember much of what they hear and more of what they hear and then say. They benefit from discussion, prefer verbal explanation to visual demonstration, and learn effectively by explaining things to others. Because written words are processed as verbal information, verbal learners learn well through reading. The majority of classes, since they present material through the written word, lecture, or discussion, are geared to verbal learners.

Student-suggested strategies for verbal learners:

◆ Talk about what you learn. Work in study groups so that you have an opportunity to explain and discuss what you are learning.

◆ Read the textbook and highlight no more than 10 percent.

◆ Rewrite your notes.

◆ Outline chapters.

◆ Recite information or write scripts and debates.

Are You Linear or Holistic?

Linear learners □ find it easiest to learn material presented in a logical, ordered progression. They solve problems in a step-by-step manner. They can work with sections of material without yet fully understanding the whole picture. They tend to be stronger when looking at the parts of a whole rather than understanding the whole and then dividing it up into parts. They learn best when taking in material in a progression from easiest to more complex to most difficult. Many courses are taught in a linear fashion.

Student-suggested strategies for linear learners:

◆ If you have an instructor who jumps around from topic to topic, spend time outside of class with the instructor or a classmate who can help you fill the gaps in your notes.

◆ If class notes are random, rewrite the material according to whatever logic helps you understand it best.

◆ Outline the material.

Holistic learners □ learn in fits and starts. They may feel lost for days or weeks, unable to solve even the simplest problems or show the most basic understanding, until they suddenly "get it." They may feel discouraged when struggling with material that many other students seem to learn easily. Once they understand, though, they tend to see the big picture to an extent that others may not often achieve. They are often highly creative.

Student-suggested strategies for the holistic learner:

◆ Recognize that you are not slow or stupid. Don't lose faith in yourself. You will get it!

◆ Before reading a chapter, preview it by reading all the subheadings, summaries, and any margin glossary terms. The chapter may also start with an outline and overview of the entire chapter.

- Instead of spending a short time on every subject every night, try setting aside evenings for specific subjects and immerse yourself in just one subject at a time.
- Try taking difficult subjects in summer school when you are handling fewer courses.
- Try to relate subjects to other things you already know. Keep asking yourself how you could apply the material.

Study Techniques for Additional Multiple Intelligences

People who score high in the **Musical/Rhythmic** ☐ intelligence have strong memories for rhymes and can be energized by music. They often have a song running through their minds and find themselves tapping a foot or their fingers when they hear music.

Student-suggested strategies for musical/rhythmic people:

- Create rhymes out of vocabulary words.
- Beat out rhythms when studying.
- Play instrumental music while studying if it does not distract you, but first determine what type of music improves your concentration the most.
- Take study breaks and listen to music.
- Write a rap about your topic.

Naturalistic learners ☐ feel energized when they are connected to nature. Their career choices and hobbies reflect their love of nature.

Student-suggested strategies for naturalistic people:

- Study outside whenever practical but only if it is not distracting.
- Explore subject areas that reflect your love for nature. Learning is much easier when you have a passion for it.
- Relate abstract information to something concrete in nature.
- Take breaks with something you love from nature—a walk, watching your fish, or a nature video. Use nature as a reward for getting other work done.

Study Techniques for Different Personality Types

The different personality types of the Personality Spectrum combine the learning styles and multiple intelligences you have explored. Table 2-3 shows learning techniques that benefit each type.

General Benefits

Although schools have traditionally favored verbal/linguistic students, there is no general advantage to one style over another. The only advantage is in discovering your profile through accurate and honest analysis. Following are three general benefits of knowing your learning styles.

Table 2-3	Types and learning techniques.	
PERSONALITY TYPES	RELATED LEARNING STYLES	LEARNING TECHNIQUES TO USE
Organizer	Factual, Linear	◆ Organize material before studying. ◆ Whenever possible, select instructors who have well-planned courses. ◆ Keep a daily planner and to-do list.
Adventurer	Active, Bodily/Kinesthetic	◆ Keep study sessions moving quickly. ◆ Make learning fun and exciting. ◆ Study with other Adventurers but also with Organizers.
Giver	Interpersonal	◆ Form study groups. ◆ Help someone else learn. ◆ Pick classes that relate to your interest in people.
Thinker	Reflective, Intrapersonal, Logical/Mathematical, Theoretical	◆ Study alone. ◆ Allow time to think about material. ◆ Pick classes and instructors who are intellectually challenging.

1. You will have a better chance of avoiding problematic situations. If you don't explore what works best for you, you risk forcing yourself into career or personal situations that stifle your creativity, development, and happiness. Knowing how you learn and how you relate to the world can help you make smarter choices.

2. You will be more successful on the job. Your learning style is essentially your working style. If you know how you learn, you will be able to look for an environment that suits you best and you'll be able to work effectively on work teams. This will prepare you for successful employment in the twenty-first century.

3. You will be more able to target areas that need improvement. The more you know about your learning styles, the more you will be able to pinpoint the areas that are more difficult for you. That has two advantages. One, you can begin to work on difficult areas, step by step. Two, when a task comes up requiring a skill that is tough for you, you can either take special care with it or suggest someone else whose style may be better suited to it.

Your learning-style profile is one important part of self-knowledge. Next you will explore other important factors that help to define you.

REAL WORLD PERSPECTIVE

How can I adjust my learning style to my instructors' teaching styles?

Patti Reed-Zweiger, South Puget Sound Community College, Tacoma, Washington

This last year I took a class in math that left me extremely stressed and exhausted. The way the teacher presented the material just didn't work for me. He threw out way too much information in a short period of time with little or no tools for completing the tasks. I really think he was unprepared. When he'd get to class, he'd fumble through his book for a while until he latched onto something to share. Sometimes, he'd spend the whole class answering a question or two about the previous homework and then, at the very last minute, give us a new assignment for the next class. We'd leave without any understanding of what we were to accomplish. It seems to me this teacher did very little teaching.

I'm a state trooper, so I'm used to handling enormous pressure, but in this case, nothing seemed to work. I'd leave in tears, class after class. This is frustrating for me. I'm forty years old and very confident, and yet in this class I felt like I was back in grade school again. I felt inadequate, foolish, and out of control. So much so that I would become sick to my stomach—nauseous. I wouldn't wish this experience on my worst enemy. What can I do to succeed in math and still maintain my self-esteem? At this point, I'm ready to drop it altogether.

Jacque Hall, University of Georgia, Terry College of Business

You're not alone. Math is frightening to most people. When I began taking math classes, I felt like a total failure. In fact, I dropped out of my Math 102 class. I just couldn't handle it. That's the first thing I'd recommend to you. Get out of the class if the teacher is not what you need. But make sure you talk with the teacher first and see if there's something the two of you can do to make the class successful for you. If you feel that it just won't work, let it go and try to find a better situation for yourself. Math is hard enough without subjecting yourself to inadequate teaching. I found that networking with other students on what classes and instructors to take really helped. The younger students always seem to know who the best teachers are.

If you can afford the additional time, I recommend you audit a class. If that isn't an option, hire a math tutor or take advantage of the math lab on a regular basis. Most importantly, remember that you are not a failure. And you're also not alone. I have felt a great deal of despair over math myself. I have seen people cry in class and others leave in total frustration. At some time or other, every student is going to run into a teacher or a classroom situation that leaves them feeling dissatisfied. Do your part by communicating with the teacher. If that doesn't work, move on. I'm glad I did.

HOW DO YOU EXPLORE WHO YOU ARE?

You are an absolutely unique individual. Although you may share individual characteristics with others, your combination of traits is one-of-a-kind. It could take a lifetime to learn everything there is to know about yourself because you are constantly changing. However, you can start by exploring these facets of yourself: self-perception, interests, habits, and abilities (both strengths and limitations).

Self-Perception

Having an accurate image of yourself is difficult. Unfortunately, many people err on the side of negativity. Feeling inadequate from time to time is normal, but a constantly negative self-perception can have destructive effects. Look at people you know who think that they are less intelligent, capable, or attractive than they really are. Observe how that shuts down their confidence and motivation. You do the same to yourself when you perceive yourself negatively.

Negative self-perception has a series of effects that leads to a self-fulfilling prophecy, meaning something that comes true because you have convinced yourself it will: First you believe that you are incapable of being or doing something; then you neglect to try; finally, you most likely don't do or become what you had already decided was impossible.

For example, say you think you can't pass a certain course. Since you feel you don't have a chance, you don't put as much effort into the work for that course. Sure enough, at the end of the semester, you don't pass. The worst part is that you may see your failure as proof of your incapability, instead of realizing that you didn't allow yourself to try. This chain of events can occur in many situations. When it happens in the workplace, people lose jobs. When it happens in personal life, people lose relationships.

Refine your self-image so that it reflects more of your true self. These strategies might help.

- Believe in yourself. If you don't believe in yourself, others may have a harder time believing in you. Work to eliminate negative self-talk. Have faith in your abilities. When you set your goals, stick to them. Know that your mind and will are very powerful.

- Talk to other people whom you trust. People who know you well often have a more realistic perception of you than you do of yourself.

- Take personal time. Stress makes having perspective on your life more difficult. Take time out to clear your mind and think realistically about who you are and who you want to be.

- Look at all of the evidence. Mistakes can loom large in your mind. Consider what you do well and what you have accomplished as carefully as you consider your stumbles.

Building a positive self-perception is a lifelong challenge. If you maintain a bright but realistic vision of yourself, it will take you far along the road toward achieving your goals.

Interests

Taking some time now to explore your interests will help you later when you select a major and a career. You may be aware of many of your general interests already. For example, you can ask yourself:

TERMS

Self-perception
How one views
oneself, one's
opinion of
oneself.

◆ What areas of study do I like?

◆ What activities make me happy?

◆ What careers seem interesting to me?

◆ What kind of daily schedule do I like to keep (early riser, night owl)?

◆ What type of home and work environment do I prefer?

"The greatest discovery of any generation is that human beings can alter their lives by altering their attitudes of mind."

ALBERT SCHWEITZER

Interests play an important role in the workplace. Many people, however, do not take their interests seriously when choosing a career. Some make salary or stability their first priority. Some feel they have to take the first job that comes along. Some may not realize they can do better. Not considering what you are interested in may lead to an area of study or a job that leaves you unhappy, uninterested, or unfulfilled.

Choosing to consider your interests and happiness takes courage but brings benefits. Think about your life. You spend hours of time both attending classes and studying outside of class. You will spend at least eight hours a day, five or more days a week, up to fifty or more weeks a year as a working contributor to the world. Although your studies and work won't always make you deliriously happy, it is possible to spend your school and work time in a manner that suits you.

Here are three positive effects of focusing on your interests.

1. You will have more energy. Think about how you feel when you are looking forward to seeing a special person, participating in a favorite sports activity, or enjoying some entertainment. When you're doing something you like, time seems to pass very quickly. You will be able to get much more done in a subject or career area that you enjoy.

2. You will perform better. When you were in high school, you probably got your best grades in your favorite classes and excelled in your favorite activities. That doesn't change as you get older. The more you like something, the harder you work at it—and the harder you work, the more you will improve.

3. You will have a positive attitude. A positive attitude creates a positive environment and might even make up for areas in which you lack ability or experience. Because businesses currently emphasize teamwork to such a great extent, your ability to maintain a positive attitude might mean the difference between success and failure.

TERMS

Attitude
A state of mind or feeling toward something.

Habits

A preference for a particular action that you do a certain way, and often on a regular basis or at certain times, is a habit. You might have a habit of showering in the morning, eating raisins, channel surfing with the TV remote control, hitting the snooze button on your clock, talking for hours on the phone, or studying late at night. Your habits reveal a lot about you. Some may be bad habits and some habits you consider to be good habits.

Bad habits earn that title because they can prevent you from reaching important goals. Some bad habits, such as chronic lateness, cause obvious problems. Other habits, such as renting movies three times a week, may not seem bad until you realize that you needed to spend those hours studying. People maintain bad habits because they offer immediate, enjoyable rewards, even if later effects are negative. For example, going out to eat frequently may drain your budget, but at first it seems easier than shopping for food, cooking, and washing dishes.

Good habits are those that have positive effects on your life. You often have to wait longer and work harder to see a reward for good habits, which makes them harder to maintain. If you cut out fattening foods, you wouldn't lose weight in two days. If you reduced your nights out to gain study time, your grades wouldn't improve in a week. When you strive to maintain good habits, trust that the rewards are somewhere down the road. Changing a habit can be a long process.

Take time to evaluate your habits. Look at the positive and negative effects of each, and decide which are helpful and which harmful to you. Here are steps you can take to change a habit that has more negative effects than positive ones.

1. Be honest about your habits. Admitting negative or destructive habits can be hard to do. You can't change a habit until you admit that it is a habit.

2. Recognize the habit as troublesome. Sometimes the trouble may not seem to come directly from the habit. For example, spending every weekend working on the house may seem important, but you may be overdoing it and ignoring friends and family members.

3. Decide to change. You might realize what your bad habits are but do not yet care about their effects on your life. Until you are convinced that you will receive something positive and useful from changing, your efforts will not get you far.

4. Start today. Don't put it off until after this week, after the family reunion, or after the semester. Each day lost is a day you haven't had the chance to benefit from a new lifestyle.

5. Change one habit at a time. Changing and breaking habits is difficult. Trying to spend more time with your family, reduce TV time, increase studying, and save more money all at once can bring on a fit of deprivation, sending you scurrying back to all your old habits. Easy does it.

6. Reward yourself appropriately for positive steps taken. If you earn a good grade, avoid slacking off on your studies the following week. Choose a reward that will not encourage you to stray from your target.

7. Keep it up. To have the best chance at changing a habit, be consistent for at least three weeks. Your brain needs time to become accustomed to the new habit. If you go back to the old habit during that time, you may feel like you're starting all over again.

8. Don't get too discouraged. Rarely does someone make the decision to change and do so without a setback or two. Being too hard on yourself might cause frustration that tempts you to give up and go back to the habit.

> "To fall into a habit is to begin to cease to be."
> MIGUEL DE UNAMUMO

Abilities

Everyone's abilities include both strengths and limitations. Both are part of you. Examining both strengths and limitations is part of establishing the kind of clear vision of yourself that will help you maximize your potential.

Strengths

As you think about your preferences, your particular strengths will come to mind because you often like best the things you can do well. Some strengths seem to be natural—things you learned to do without ever having to work too hard. Others you struggled to develop and continue to work hard to maintain. Asking yourself these questions may help you define more clearly what your abilities are:

- What have I always been able to do well?
- What have others often praised me for?
- What do I like most about myself, and why?
- What is my learning-style profile?
- What are my accomplishments—at home, at school, at work?

As with your preferences, knowing your abilities will help you find a job that makes the most of them. When your job requires you to do work you like, you are more likely to perform to the best of your ability. Keep that in mind as you explore career areas. Assessments and inventories that will help you further assess your abilities may be available at your school's career center or library. Once you know yourself, you will be more able to set appropriate goals.

Limitations

Nobody is perfect, and no one is good at everything. Everyone has limitations. However, that doesn't mean they are any easier to take. Limitations can make you feel frustrated, stressed, or angry. You may feel as though no one else has the limitations you have, or that no one else has as many.

There are three ways to deal with your limitations. The first two—ignoring them or dwelling on them—are the most common. Both are natural, but neither is wise. The third way is to face them and to work to improve them while keeping the strongest focus on your abilities.

Ignoring your limitations can cause you to be unable to accomplish your goals. For example, say you are an active, global learner with a well-developed interpersonal intelligence. You have limitations in logical/mathematical intelligence and in linear thought. Ignoring that fact, you decide that you can make good money in computer programming, and you sign up for math and programming courses. You certainly won't automatically fail. However, if you ignore your limited ability in those courses and don't seek extra help, you may have more than a few stumbles.

Dwelling on your limitations can make you forget you have any strengths at all. This results in negative self-talk and a poor self-perception. Continuing the example, if you were to dwell on your limitations in math, you might very likely stop trying altogether.

Facing limitations and working to improve them is the best response. A healthy understanding of your limitations can help you avoid troublesome situations. In the example, you could face your limitations in math and explore other career areas that use your more well-developed abilities and intelligences. If you decided to stick with computer technology, you could study an area of the field that focuses on management and interpersonal relationships. Or you could continue to aim for a career as a programmer, taking care to seek special help in areas that give you trouble.

HOW DOES YOUR LEARNING STYLE AFFECT YOUR CHOICE OF BUSINESS MAJOR AND CAREER?

Knowing now what you do about your learning style and personality, you are probably more aware of what business field might better suit you. Be honest with yourself about your likes and dislikes. Your long-term success depends on this honesty. If there is a great job market for accounting, but you really don't like numbers and would prefer to deal with people, a career in marketing may better suit you. Likewise, if you don't like marketing but like to combine analytical and people skills, management may be your choice. Job markets will change over time, so try not to put your future in a force that lies outside of yourself. Realistically assess your skills, interests, personality, and abilities as you take a variety of courses.

Exploring Potential Majors

While many students come to college knowing what they want to study, many do not. That's completely normal. College is a perfect time to begin exploring your different interests. In the process, you may discover talents and strengths you never realized you had.

Here are some steps to help you explore majors that may interest you.

Take a variety of classes. Although you will generally have core requirements to fulfill, use your electives to branch out. Try to take at least one class in each area that sparks your interest.

Don't rule out subject areas that aren't classified as "safe." Friends or parents may have warned you against pursuing certain careers, encouraging you to stay with "safe" careers that pay well. Even though financial stability is important, following your heart's dreams and desires is equally important. Choosing between the "safe" path and the path of the heart can be challenging. Only you can decide which is the best for you.

Spend time getting to know yourself, your interests, and your abilities. The more you know about yourself, the more ability you will have to focus on areas that make the most of who you are and what you can do. Pay close attention to which areas inspire you to greater heights and which areas seem to deaden your initiative.

> **TERMS**
>
> **Major**
> A subject of academic knowledge chosen as a field of specialization, requiring a specific course of study.

Work closely with your advisor. Begin discussing your plans early on with your advisor. You may also discuss with your advisor the possibility of a double major (completing the requirements for two different majors) or designing your own major, if your school offers an opportunity to do so.

Take advantage of other resources. Seek opinions from instructors, friends, and family members. Talk to students who have declared majors that interest you. Explore the course materials your college gives you in order to see what majors your college offers.

Develop your critical-thinking skills. Working toward any major will help you develop your most important skill—knowing how to use your mind. Critical thinking is the most crucial ingredient in any recipe for school and career success. More than anything, your future career and employer will depend on your ability to think clearly, effectively, creatively, and wisely, and to contribute to the workplace by truly making a difference.

Changing Majors

Some people may change their minds several times before honing in on a major that fits. Although this may add to the time you spend in college, being happy with your decision is important.

If changing majors happens to you, don't be discouraged. You're certainly not alone. Changing a major is much like changing a job. Skills and experiences from one job will assist you in your next position, and some of the courses from your first major may apply—or even transfer as credits—to your next major. Talk with your academic advisor about any desire to change majors. Sometimes an advisor can speak to department heads in order to get the maximum number of credits transferred to your new major.

Whatever you decide, realize that you do have the right to change your mind. Continual self-discovery is part of the journey. No matter how many detours you make, each interesting class you take along the way helps to point you toward a major that feels like home.

Sabiduría

In Spanish, the term *sabiduría* represents the two sides of learning—both knowledge and wisdom. Knowledge—building what you know about how the world works—is the first part. Wisdom—deriving meaning and significance from knowledge, and deciding how to use that knowledge—is the second. As you continually learn and experience new things, the *sabiduría* you build will help you make knowledgeable and wise choices about how to lead your life.

Think of this concept as you discover more about how you learn and receive knowledge in all aspects of your life—in school, work, and personal situations. As you learn how your unique mind works and how to use it, you can more confidently assert yourself. As you expand your ability to use your mind in different ways, you can create lifelong advantages for yourself.

Success in the Real World

Mary Hey

Mary Hey is living proof that you can change your career or life path more than once. It took Mary almost thirty years to discover art as her true calling, but she believes that all of her past experiences played a role in getting her where she is today. Mary will be the first to admit that she has led a very "colorful" life. Though she's now a successful artist, Mary has traveled a variety of other career paths, including lawyer,

 editor, congressional aide, political organizer, and bus driver. She finally found her true passion and meaning in art, and then believed in herself enough to mold that calling into a career.

"I became completely passionate about art and recognized that I loved it. Art is a joy and pleasure that I find sustaining. I have a sense of what is coming next, of the kind of paintings I want to do. I don't know exactly what they are, but I know that they're there—I just have to keep going to make them happen. This vision of what is ahead has allowed me to overcome all types of obstacles. I want what's coming."

Mary believes that you have to discover your talent and then take advantage of it. Every person has a talent for something. Your true interest can be found, as long as you allow yourself the opportunity to find it.

"Talent is simply what comes easily to you—that's all. And that can be any number of things, from stand-up comedy to fixing cars to helping people get through hard times to solving equations. It's important to recognize what comes easily and not try to do things that are inherently too difficult. Go where your talent is, and then get some training and work hard to develop that talent. When I was young, I didn't take my talents seriously because I thought if something was fun, it couldn't be considered real work. Every voice was saying 'You've got to get serious about a career.' I sure wish I had given myself the chance to begin painting earlier. My advice is to let yourself do what you want . . . go where your talent takes you. It may be a place you never dreamed you could go."

Mary has learned firsthand how frustrating an ill-fitted career can be. She found her law career so difficult that she had to set her jaw every morning and force herself to work. It was like pushing water uphill. Now she works with purpose and joy, and is finding a way to make a living at it. She is happy she studied law, though, because the same problem-solving skills she used as an attorney now apply to her art making. In fact, she needs many of the skills she has picked up throughout her life—time management, writing, accounting, marketing, networking—in order to run a successful art business.

Mary's keys to success include:

- Have integrity—make sure your actions match your words and feelings.
- Have a vision of what you want to achieve and stay focused on your goal. Don't let the daily ups and downs discourage you.
- Attack obstacles individually—one by one, they're not so overwhelming as a big knot of problems.
- Be flexible about how you reach your goal. Many roads can get you there, so focus on what you want and don't get hung up on which is the perfect path.
- Be extremely reliable. Showing up is 90 percent of success.
- Do every job well. You'll earn respect, and that will lead to greater credibility and more responsibility.
- Pay close attention to detail. Returning phone calls and ensuring things are correct show that you respect your work and are proud of what you do.

Chapter 2 Applications

Name _____ Date _____

KEY INTO YOUR LIFE
Opportunities to Apply What You Learn

 How Do You Learn Best?

Start by writing your scores next to each term.

LEARNING STYLES INVENTORY	PATHWAYS TO LEARNING	PERSONALITY SPECTRUM
_____ Active	_____ Bodily/Kinesthetic	_____ Organizer
_____ Reflective	_____ Visual/Spatial	_____ Adventurer
_____ Factual	_____ Verbal/Linguistic	_____ Giver
_____ Theoretical	_____ Logical/Mathematical	_____ Thinker
_____ Visual	_____ Musical	
_____ Verbal	_____ Interpersonal	
_____ Linear	_____ Intrapersonal	
_____ Holistic	_____ Naturalist	

Circle your highest preferences (largest numbers) for each assessment.

What positive experiences have you had at work and school that you can link to the strengths you circled?

_____

_____

_____

_____

_____

_____

What negative experiences have you had that may be related to your least developed learning styles or intelligences?

_____

_____

_____

_____

_____

 2.2 *Making School More Enjoyable*

List two required classes that you are not necessarily looking forward to taking. Discuss what parts of your learning-style profile may relate to your lack of enthusiasm. Name learning-styles–related study techniques that may help you get the most out of the class and enjoy it more.

CLASS	REASON FOR LACK OF ENTHUSIASM	LEARNING OR STUDY TECHNIQUES
1.		
2.		

 2.3 *Your Habits*

You have the power to change your habits. List three habits that you want to change. Discuss the effects of each and how those effects keep you from reaching your goals.

HABIT	EFFECTS THAT PREVENT YOU FROM REACHING GOALS
1.	
2.	
3.	

Out of these three, put a star by the habit you want to change first. Write down a step you can take today toward overcoming that habit.

_____

_____

_____

What helpful habit do you want to develop in its place? For example, if your problem habit were a failure to express yourself when you are angry, a replacement habit might be to talk calmly about situations that upset you as soon as they arise. If you have a habit of cramming for tests at the last minute, you could replace it with a regular study schedule that allows you to cover your material bit by bit over a longer period of time.

_____

_____

_____

One way to help yourself abandon your old habit is to think about how your new habit will improve your life. List two benefits of your new habit.

1. _____

2. _____

Give yourself one month to complete your habit shift. Set a specific deadline. Keep track of your progress by indicating on a chart or calendar how well you did each day. If you avoided the old habit, write an X below the day. If you used the new one, write an N. Therefore, a day when you only avoided the old habit will have an X, a day when you did both will have both letters, and a day when you did neither will be left blank. You can use the chart below or mark your own calendar. Try pairing up with another student and arranging to check up on each other's progress.

1	2	3	4	5	6	7	8	9	10	11	12	13	14	15	16
17	18	19	20	21	22	23	24	25	26	27	28	29	30	31	

Don't forget to reward yourself for your hard work. Write here what your reward will be when you feel you are on the road to a new and beneficial habit.

_____

_____

_____

Interests, Majors, and Careers

Start by listing activities and subjects you like.

1. _____

2. _____

3. _____

4. _____

5. _____

6. _____

Name three majors that might relate to your interests and help you achieve your career goals.

1. _____

2. _____

3. _____

For each major, name a corresponding career area you may want to explore.

1. _____

2. _____

3. _____

Keep these majors and career areas in mind as you gradually narrow your course choices in the time before you declare a major.

Team-Building Exercise

After everyone has completed the Personality Spectrum exercise in the chapter, divide into groups according to your best fit in one of the following groups:

Adventurer

Thinker

Organizer

Giver

Each group should discuss and make a list of the following traits:

◆ Strengths—What do you really like about your type of personality?
◆ Areas for Improvement—What traits do you have that might annoy others?
◆ Stresses—What causes stress in your life? How might you clash with other personality styles?
◆ Careers—What types of careers do you think might best suit your personality?

Fill in the chart below and be prepared to share your results with the class.

Strengths

1. _____
2. _____
3. _____
4. _____
5. _____

Areas for Improvement

1. _____
2. _____
3. _____
4. _____
5. _____

Stresses

1. _____
2. _____

3. _____

4. _____

5. _____

Careers

1. _____

2. _____

3. _____

4. _____

5. _____

Looking for a Needle in a Haystack

YAHOO!

Suppose you want to find some quick information for a report that you're doing on the history and animals of the Galápagos Islands, which lie off the country of Ecuador in South America. One of the easiest ways to begin your research is to search for information on the Internet. You can find a lot of information, some of which can be useful. At the very least, searching is a quick way to get you started. How do you search through the massive amounts of information on the Internet, though? There are several search engines that will do the searching for you. Yahoo is one of those search engines, though the company is also trying to be even more than a search engine. You type in what information you want, and you will get a list of sites with information on the topic.

The interesting thing about Yahoo! is that although it is not the most technologically advanced search engine that can be found on the Internet, it is extremely popular. Competitors, such as Lycos and Infoseek, employ faster systems and more advanced computer technology to relay search. It is calculated, however, that more people visit Yahoo! than use AOL or Netscape. Between 25 million and 40 million people will visit Yahoo! in one month.

Yahoo! has two keys things: a catchy name and a commitment to developing a better service than can be done using automation alone. This seems to appeal to the common Internet browser. It has taken the small revenues that it does make and invested in people to run and support the search engine system. They are not investing in large computers or fancy buildings. The people of Yahoo! keep the service running, and the number of people who visit the site indicate that it's working. On top of this, the vision of Yahoo! is to produce a search engine that is useful, though not necessarily the best or most advanced.

It seems to be the setup of Yahoo! that attracts its customers. The human perspective is what makes Yahoo! special—it is developed and maintained by people who also use the Internet to find information, so they understand the needs of a browser (a person looking for information). Instead of giving into automated service, the Stanford University engineers who created Yahoo!

continue to develop the directories themselves, even as Yahoo! becomes immensely popular. It is this personal feel from Yahoo! that seems to be appealing to Net surfers.

Yahoo! does not give all the possible sites on the Internet for a given topic. It will list the popular sites or those that most closely match the intended search topic—what it defines as the "best of the Web" for a given subject. It has taken the overwhelming size of the Internet and made it feel more personable. Yahoo! also has a directory system that seems to be more amenable to an average Internet user. The directories found in Yahoo!'s search engine are created with the "human touch"—set up in such a way that the most popular categories are displayed and each category is linked to sub-categories.

The promotion that Yahoo! has used has paid off in terms of number of users. Yahoo! developed a focused promotional strategy that included free services and products for browsers, free online services like email, and access to stock quotes, maps, chat rooms, and classifieds. Yahoo! became a site that users went looking for deliberately, just to discover what new offer would appear on the site next. It has the feel of an online service such as AOL. This was an advertiser's dream—millions of people were visiting the site. The visibility that Yahoo! could provide to its advertisers was enticing. Suddenly, there were investors everywhere, and the stock soared to over 500 percent of what it had been in 1996. Yahoo! has 1,700 advertisers and the search engine is becoming an integral part of the Internet. It is now competing with companies like Microsoft, AOL, and Netscape in the Internet market. Yahoo! is no longer just another search engine for the Internet—it is an online service for Internet users.

However, while Yahoo! enjoys immense popularity, its revenues are not close to those of a company rendering service to millions of people. It is the market capitalization that seems to show the real story behind Yahoo! Revenues (money coming into the company) for 1997 were a mere $67 million, with an actual loss of $23 million (after expenses), but the market cap by comparison was $2.8 billion. It is in the same league with other companies such as Office Depot, Wendy's, and Ryder.

1. How is Yahoo! changing to meet the needs and wants of its customers?
2. In what ways does the company show that it is looking at its business with a long-term perspective in mind?
3. What is the difference between revenues and profit/loss?
4. What are some of the opportunities that Yahoo! might have?
5. If Yahoo! were a person, what would its self-awareness process be like?
6. Does exploring who you are (as a business or a person) ever end?

Internet Exercise

There are a number of search engines that you can use to search the Internet for information. To get a feel for what kind of information you can get from each one, access the Internet and search for "Galápagos Islands" on each of the following search engines:

Yahoo!: **www.yahoo.com**
Infoseek: **www.infoseek.com**
Lycos: **www.lycos.com**
AltaVista: **www.altavista.com**

◆ What differences did you notice among the search engines?
◆ What type of information could you find?
◆ Did you see several of the same sites listed?
◆ How could you narrow your search to types of animals found on the Galápagos Islands?

Record your findings to these questions in the table below:

SEARCH ENGINE	DIFFERENCES?	TYPES OF INFORMATION?	LIST SOME OF THE SITES FOUND	HOW CAN YOU NARROW THE SEARCH?
Yahoo!				
Infoseek				
Lycos				
AltaVista				

Journal

Name _____ Date _____

3

Business

Goal Setting and Time Management

Mapping Your Course

P eople dream of what they want out of life, but not everyone knows how to turn dreams into reality. Often dreams seem far off in time, too difficult, or even completely unreachable. You can build paths to your dreams, however, by identifying the goals you need to achieve, one by one, to arrive at your destination. When you set goals, prioritize, and manage your time effectively, you increase your ability to take those steps to achieve your long-term goals.

This chapter explains how taking specific steps toward goals can help you turn your dreams into reality. You will explore how your values relate to your goals, how to create a framework for your life's goals, how to set long-term and short-term goals, and how to set priorities. The section on time management will discuss how to translate those goals into daily, weekly, monthly, and yearly steps. Finally, you will explore the effects of procrastination.

In this chapter, you will explore answers to the following questions:

◆ What defines your values?

◆ How do you set and achieve goals?

◆ What are your priorities?

◆ How can you manage your time?

◆ Why is procrastination a problem?

WHAT DEFINES YOUR VALUES?

Your personal values are the beliefs that guide your choices. Examples of values include family togetherness, a good education, caring for others, and worthwhile employment. The sum total of all your values is your *value system.* You demonstrate your particular value system in the priorities you set, how you communicate with others, your family life, your educational and career choices, and even the material things with which you surround yourself.

Choosing and Evaluating Values

Examining the sources of your values can help you define those values, trace their origin, and question the reasons why you have adopted them. Value sources, however, aren't as important as the process of considering each value carefully to see if it makes sense to you. Some of your current values may have come from television or other media but still ring true. Some may come from what others have taught you. Some you may have constructed from your own personal experience and opinion. You make the final decision about what to value, regardless of the source.

"Obstacles are
what people see
when they take
their eyes off
the goal."

NEW YORK CITY
SUBWAY BULLETIN
BOARD

Each individual value system is unique, even if many values come from other sources. Your value system is yours alone. Your responsibility is to make sure that your values are your own choice, and not the choice of others. Make value choices for yourself based on what feels right for you, for your life, and for those who are touched by your life.

You can be more sure of making choices that are right for you if you try to always question and evaluate your values. Before you adopt a value, ask yourself: Does it feel right? What effects might it have on my life? Am I choosing it to please someone else, or is it truly my choice? Values are a design for life, and you are the one who has to live the life you design.

Because life change and new experiences may bring a change in values, try to continue to evaluate values as time goes by. Periodically evaluate the effects that having each value has on your life, and see if a shift in values might suit your changing circumstances. For example, losing your sight may cause you to value your hearing intensely. The difficulty of a divorce may have a positive result: a new value of independence and individuality. After growing up in a homogeneous community, a student who meets other students from unfamiliar backgrounds may learn a new value of living in a diverse community. Your values will grow and develop as you do if you continue to think them through.

How Values Relate to Goals

Understanding your values will help you set career and personal goals because the most ideal goals help you achieve what you value. If you value spending time with your family, related goals may include living near your parents or writing to your grandmother every week. A value of financial independence may generate goals, such as working while going to school and keeping credit-card debt low, that reflect that value. If you value helping others, try to make time for volunteer work.

Goals enable you to put values into practice. When you set and pursue goals that are based on values, you demonstrate and reinforce values through taking action. The strength of those values, in turn, reinforces your goals. You will experience a much stronger drive to achieve if you build goals around what is most important to you.

How DO YOU SET AND ACHIEVE GOALS?

A goal can be something as concrete as buying a health insurance plan or as abstract as working to control your temper. When you set goals and work to achieve them, you engage your intelligence, abilities, time, and energy in order to move ahead. From major life decisions to the tiniest day-to-day activities, setting goals will help you define how you want to live and what you want to achieve.

Paul Timm, a best-selling author and teacher who is an expert in self-management, feels that focus is a key ingredient in setting and achieving goals. "Focus adds power to our actions. If somebody threw a bucket of water on you, you'd get wet, and probably get mad. But if water was shot at you through a high-pressure nozzle, you might get injured. The only difference is focus."[1] Each part of this section will explain ways to focus your energy through goal setting. You can set and achieve goals by identifying a personal mission statement, placing your goals in long-term and short-term time frames, and linking your goals to your values.

Identifying Your Personal Mission Statement

Some people go through their lives without ever really thinking about what they can do or what they want to achieve. If you choose not to set goals or explore what you want out of life, you may look back on your past with a sense of emptiness. You may not know what you've done or why you did it. However, you can avoid that emptiness by periodically taking a few steps back and thinking about where you've been and where you want to be.

One helpful way to determine your general direction is to write a *personal mission statement*. Dr. Stephen Covey, author of the best-seller *The Seven Habits of Highly Effective People*, defines a mission statement as a philosophy

TERMS

Goal
An end toward which effort is directed; an aim or intention.

that outlines what you want to be (character), what you want to do (contributions and achievements), and the principles by which you live. Dr. Covey compares the personal mission statement to the Constitution of the United States, a statement of principles that gives this country guidance and standards in the face of constant change.[2]

Your personal mission isn't written in stone. It should change as you move from one phase of life to the next—from single person to spouse, from parent to single parent to caregiver of an older parent. Stay flexible and reevaluate your personal mission from time to time.

Here is an example of author Carol Carter's personal mission statement:

My mission is to use my talents and abilities to help people of all ages, stages, backgrounds, and economic levels achieve their human potential through fully developing their minds and their talents.

A company, like a person, needs to establish standards and principles that guide its many activities. Companies often have mission statements so that each member of the organization, from the custodian to the president, clearly understands what to strive for. If a company fails to identify its mission, a million well-intentioned employees might focus their energies in just as many different directions, creating chaos and low productivity.

Here is a mission statement from Northwest Airlines. It is displayed inside its company buildings and on the back of every employee's business card. Notice how it reinforces the company's goals of teamwork, leadership, and excellence:

To build together the world's most preferred airline with the best people; each committed to exceeding our customer's expectations every day.

Another example is from Prentice Hall, the company that publishes this text:

To provide the most innovative resources—books, technology, programs—to help students of all ages and stages achieve their academic and professional goals inside the classroom and out.

You will have an opportunity to write your own personal mission statement at the end of this chapter. Writing a mission statement is much more than an in-school exercise. It is truly for you. Thinking through your personal mission can help you begin to take charge of your life. It helps to put you in control instead of allowing circumstances and events to control you. If you frame your mission statement carefully so that it truly reflects your goals, it can be your guide in everything you do.

Placing Goals in Time

Everyone has the same twenty-four hours in a day, but it often doesn't feel like enough. Have you ever had a busy day flash by so quickly that it seems you accomplished nothing? Have you ever felt that way about a longer period of time, like a month or even a year? Your commitments can overwhelm you unless you decide how to use time to plan your steps toward goal achievement.

If developing a personal mission statement establishes the big picture, placing your goals within particular time frames allows you to bring individual areas of that picture into the foreground. Planning your progress step-by-step will help you maintain your efforts over the extended time period often needed to accomplish a goal. Goals fall into two categories: long-term goals and short-term goals.

Setting Long-Term Goals

Establish first the goals that have the largest scope, the *long-term goals* that you aim to attain over a lengthy period of time, up to a few years or more. As a student, you know what long-term goals are all about. You have set yourself a goal to attend school and earn a degree or certificate. Becoming educated is an admirable goal that takes a good number of years to reach.

Some long-term goals are lifelong, such as a goal to continually learn more about yourself and the world around you. Others have a more definite end, such as a goal to successfully complete a course. To determine your long-term goals, think about what you want out of your professional, educational, and personal life. Here is Carol Carter's long-term goal statement.

Carol's Goals: To accomplish my mission through writing books, giving seminars, and developing programs that create opportunities for students to learn and develop. To create a personal, professional, and family environment that allows me to manifest my abilities and duly tend to each of my responsibilities.

For example, you may establish long-term goals such as these:

◆ I will graduate from school and know that I have learned all that I could, whether my grade point average shows it or not.

◆ I will build my leadership and teamwork skills by forming positive, productive relationships with classmates, instructors, and co-workers.

Long-term goals don't have to be lifelong goals. Think about your long-term goals for the coming year. Considering what you want to accomplish in a year's time will give you clarity, focus, and a sense of what needs to take place right away. When Carol thought about her long-term goals for the coming year, she came up with the following:

1. Develop programs to provide internships, scholarships, and other quality initiatives for students.
2. Allow time in my personal life to eat well, run five days a week, and spend quality time with family and friends. Allow time daily for quiet reflection and spiritual devotion.

In the same way that Carol's goals are tailored to her personality and interests, your goals should reflect who you are. Personal missions and goals are as unique as each individual. Continuing the example above, you might adopt these goals for the coming year:

- I will earn passing grades in all my classes.
- I will join two clubs and make an effort to take leadership roles in each.

Setting Short-Term Goals

When you divide your long-term goals into smaller, manageable goals that you hope to accomplish within a relatively short time, you are setting *short-term goals*. Short-term goals narrow your focus, helping you to maintain your progress toward your long-term goals. They are the steps that take you where you want to go. Say you have set the two long-term goals you just read in the previous section. To stay on track toward those goals, you may want to accomplish these short-term goals in the next six months:

- I will pass Business Writing I so that I can move on to Business Writing II.
- I will attend four of the monthly meetings of the Journalism Club.

These same goals can be broken down into even smaller parts, such as one month:

- I will complete five of the ten essays for Business Writing.
- I will write an article for next month's Journalism Club newsletter.

In addition to monthly goals, you may have short-term goals that extend for a week, a day, or even a couple of hours in a given day. Take as an example the article you have planned to write for the next month's Journalism Club newsletter. Such short-term goals may include the following:

- Three weeks from now: Have a final draft ready. Submit it to the editor of the newsletter.
- Two weeks from now: Have a second draft ready, and give it to one more person to review.
- One week from now: Have a first draft ready. Ask my writing instructor if he will review it.
- Today by the end of the day: Freewrite about the subject of the article, and narrow it down to a specific topic.
- By 3 p.m. today: Brainstorm ideas and subjects for the article (more on brainstorming and freewriting in Chapter 6).

"Even if you're on the right track, you'll get run over if you just sit there."

WILL ROGERS

As you consider your long-term and short-term goals, notice how all of your goals are linked to one another. As Figure 3-1 shows, your long-term goals establish a context for the short-term goals. In turn, your short-term goals make the long-term goals seem clearer and more reachable. The whole system works to keep you on track.

Linking Goals With Values

If you are not sure how to start formulating your mission, look to your values to guide you. Define your mission and goals based on what is important to you.

| Figure 3-1 | Linking goals together. |

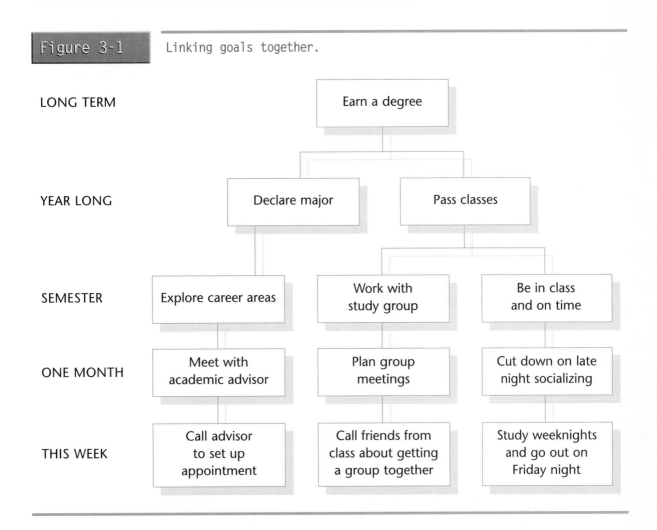

If you value physical fitness, your mission statement might emphasize your commitment to staying in shape throughout your life. Your long-term goal might be to run a marathon, while your short-term goals might involve your weekly exercise and eating plan. Similarly, if you value a close family, your personal mission might emphasize how you want to maintain family ties and stability. In this case, your long-term goals might involve finding a job that allows for family time or living in a town close to your parents. Your short-term goals may focus on helping your son learn a musical instrument or having dinner with your family at least twice a week.

Current and Personal Values Mean Appropriate Goals

When you use your values as a compass for your goals, make sure the compass is pointed in the direction of your real feelings. Watch out for the following two pitfalls that can occur.

Setting goals according to other people's values. Friends or family may encourage you to strive for what they think you should value, rather than what is right for you. If you follow their advice without believing in it, you may have a harder time sticking to your path. For example, someone who attends school primarily because a parent or spouse thought it was right may have less motivation and initiative than someone who made an independent decision to become a student. Look hard at what you really want, and why. Staying in tune with your own values will help you make decisions that are right for you.

Setting goals that reflect values you held in the past. What you felt yesterday may no longer apply because life changes can alter your values. The best goals reflect what you believe today. For example, a person who has been through a near-fatal car accident may experience a dramatic increase in how he or she values time with friends and family, and a drop in how he or she values material possessions. Someone who survives a serious illness may value healthy living above all else. Keep in touch with your life's changes so your goals can reflect who you are.

Values Can Help You Identify Educational Goals

Education is a major part of your life right now. In order to define a context for your school goals, explore what you value about pursuing an education. People have many reasons for attending college. You may identify with one or more of the following possible reasons:

- I want to earn a higher salary.
- I want to build marketable skills.
- My supervisor at work says that a degree will help me move ahead in my career.
- Most of my friends were going.
- I want to be a student and learn all that I can.
- It seems like the only option for me right now.
- I am recently divorced and need to find a way to earn money.
- Everybody in my family goes to college; it's expected.
- I don't feel ready to jump into the working world yet.
- I got a scholarship.
- My friend loves her job and encouraged me to take courses in the field.
- My parent (or a spouse or partner) pushed me to go to college.
- I am pregnant and need to increase my skills so I can provide for my baby.
- I am studying for a specific career.
- I don't really know.

All of these answers are legitimate, even the last one. Being honest with yourself is crucial if you want to discover who you are and what life paths make sense for you. Whatever your reasons are for being in school, you are at the gateway to a journey of discovery.

It isn't easy to enroll in college, pay tuition, decide what to study, sign up for classes, gather the necessary materials, and actually get yourself to the school and into the classroom. Many people drop out at different places along the way, but somehow your reasons have been compelling enough for you to have arrived at this point. Thinking about why you value your education will help you stick with it.

Achieving goals becomes easier when you are realistic about what is possible. Setting priorities will help you make that distinction.

WHAT ARE YOUR PRIORITIES?

When you set a priority, you identify what's important at any given moment. *Prioritizing* helps you focus on your most important goals, even when they are difficult to achieve. If you were to pursue your goals in no particular order, you might tackle the easy ones first and leave the tough ones for later. The risk is that you might never reach for goals that are important to your success. Setting priorities helps you focus your plans on accomplishing your most important goals.

To explore your priorities, think about your personal mission and look at your goals in the five life areas: personal, family, school/career, finances, and lifestyle. These five areas may not all be equally important to you right now. At this stage in your life, which two or three are most critical? Is one particular category more important than others? How would you prioritize your goals from most important to least important?

You are a unique individual, and your priorities are yours alone. What may be top priority to someone else may not mean that much to you, and vice versa. You can see this in Figure 3-2, which compares the priorities of two very different students. Each student's priorities are listed in order, with the first priority at the top and the lowest priority at the bottom.

> **TERMS**
>
> **Priority**
> An action or intention that takes precedence in time, attention, or position.

Figure 3-2   Two students compare priorities.

K. Cole, Returning Adult Student		M. Connell, Traditional-Aged Freshman
1 Caring for my daughter	Education/classes	1 Close friends
2 Working at my part-time job	Work	2 Classes and studying
3 Studying, classes, projects	Family	3 School and community group responsibilities
4 Relationships and entertainment	Friends/relationships	4 Extracurricular events and entertainment
5 Household tasks and chores	Personal time	5 Personal time for exercise and relaxation
6 Personal time and wellness	Chores/household tasks	6 Chores, errands, groceries
7 Church and meditation	Extracurricular activities	7 Time spent with parents and sisters
	School and community involvement	
	Spiritual life	

First and foremost, your priorities should reflect your personal goals. In addition, they should reflect your relationships with others. For example, if you are a parent, your children's needs will probably be high on the priority list. You may decide to go back to school so you can get a better job, earn more money, and give them a better life. If you are in a committed relationship, you may consider the needs of your partner. You may schedule your classes so that you and your partner are home together as often as possible. Even as you consider the needs of others, though, never lose sight of your personal goals. Be true to your goals and priorities so that you can make the most of who you are.

Setting priorities moves you closer to accomplishing specific goals. It also helps you begin planning to achieve your goals within specific time frames. Being able to achieve your goals is directly linked to effective time management.

How CAN YOU MANAGE YOUR TIME?

Time is one of your most valuable and precious resources. Unlike money or opportunity or connections, time doesn't discriminate—everyone has the same twenty-four hours in a day, every day. Your responsibility and your potential for success lie in how you use yours. You cannot manipulate or change how time passes, but you can spend it taking steps to achieve your goals. Efficient time management helps you achieve your goals in a steady, step-by-step process.

People have a variety of different approaches to time management. Your learning style (explained in more detail in Chapter 2) can help you identify the particular way you currently use your time. For example, factual and linear learners tend to organize activities within a framework of time. Because they stay aware of how long it takes them to do something or travel somewhere, they are usually prompt. Theoretical and holistic learners tend to miss the passing of time while they are busy thinking of something else. Because they focus on the big picture, they may neglect details such as structuring their activities within available time. They frequently lose track of time and can often be late without meaning to be.

Time management, like physical fitness, is a lifelong pursuit. No one can plan a perfect schedule or build a terrific physique and then be "done." You'll work at time management throughout your life, and it can be tiring. Your ability to manage your time will vary with your mood, your stress level, your activity level, and other factors. You're human; don't expect perfection. Just do your best. Time management involves building a schedule and making your schedule work through lists and other strategies.

Building a Schedule

Being in control of how you manage your time is a key factor in taking responsibility for yourself and your choices. When you plan your activities with an eye toward achieving your most important goals, you are taking personal responsibility for how you live. Building a schedule helps you be responsible.

Just as a road map helps you travel from place to place, a *schedule* is a time-and-activity map that helps you get from the beginning of the day (or week or month) to the end as smoothly as possible. A written schedule helps you gain control of your life. Schedules have two major advantages: They allocate segments of time for the fulfillment of your daily, weekly, monthly, and longer-term goals; they serve as a concrete reminder of tasks, events, due dates, responsibilities, and deadlines. Few moments are more stressful than suddenly realizing you have forgotten to pick up a prescription, take a test, or be on duty at work. Scheduling can help you avoid events like these.

Keep a Date Book

Gather the tools of the trade: a pen or pencil and a *date book* (sometimes called a planner). Some of you already have date books and may have used them for years. Others may have had no luck with them or have never tried. Even if you don't feel you are the type of person who would use one, give it a try. A date book is indispensable for keeping track of your time. Paul Timm says, "Most time management experts agree that rule number one in a thoughtful planning process is: Use some form of a planner where you can write things down."

There are two major types of date books. The *day-at-a-glance* version devotes a page to each day. While it gives you ample space to write the day's activities, this version makes it difficult to see what's ahead. The *week-at-a-glance* book gives you a view of the week's plans but has less room to write per day. If you write out your daily plans in detail, you might like the day-at-a-glance version. If you prefer to remind yourself of plans ahead of time, try the book that shows a week's schedule all at once. Some date books contain additional sections that allow you to note plans and goals for the year as a whole and for each month. You can also create your own sheets for yearly and monthly notations in a notepad section, if your book has one, or on plain paper that you can then insert into the book.

Another option to consider is an *electronic planner*. These are compact mini-computers that can hold a large amount of information. You can use them to schedule your days and weeks, make to-do lists, and create and store an address book. Electronic planners are powerful, convenient, and often fun. On the other hand, they certainly cost more than the paper version, and you can lose a lot of important data if something goes wrong with the computer inside. Evaluate your options and decide what you like best.

Set Daily and Weekly Goals

The most ideal time management starts with the smallest tasks and builds to bigger ones. Setting short-term goals that tie in to your long-term goals lends the following benefits:

♦ Increased meaning for your daily activities
♦ Shaping your path toward the achievement of your long-term goals
♦ A sense of order and progress

For college students as well as working people, the week is often the easiest unit of time to consider at one shot. Weekly goal setting and planning allow you to keep track of day-to-day activities while giving you the larger perspective of what is coming up during the week. Take some time before each week starts to remind yourself of your long-term goals. Keeping long-term goals in mind will help you determine related short-term goals you can accomplish during the week to come.

Figure 3-3 shows parts of a daily schedule and a weekly schedule.

Link Daily and Weekly Goals With Long-Term Goals

After you evaluate what you need to accomplish in the coming year, semester, month, week, and day in order to reach your long-term goals, use your schedule to record those steps. Write down the short-term goals that will enable

Figure 3-3

Daily and weekly schedules.

Monday, March 22		1999
Time	Tasks	Priority
7:00 AM		
8:00	Up at 8am — finish homework	*
9:00		
10:00	Business Administration	
11:00	Renew driver's license @ DMV	*
12:00 PM		
1:00	Lunch	
2:00	Writing Seminar (peer editing today)	*
3:00	↓	
4:00	check on Ms. Scwartz's office hrs.	
5:00	5:30 work out	
6:00	↳6:30	
7:00	Dinner	
8:00	Read two chapter for Business Admin.	
9:00	↓	
10:00		
11:00		

Monday, March 22

8		Call: Maggie Blair	1
9	BIO 212	Finanical Aid Office	2
10		EMS 262 *Paramedic*	3
11	CHEM 203	role-play	4
12			5
Evening	6pm yoga class		

Tuesday, March 23

8	Finish reading assignment!	Work @ library	1
9			2
10	ENG 112	(study for quiz)	3
11	↓		4
12			5
Evening		↓ until 7pm	

Wednesday, March 24

8		Meet w/advisor	1
9	BIO 212		2
10		EMS 262	3
11	CHEM 203 *Quiz		4
12		Pick up photos	5
Evening	6pm Aerobics		

you to stay on track. Here is how a student might map out two different goals over a year's time:

This year: Complete enough courses to graduate.

Improve my physical fitness.

This semester: Complete my accounting class with a B average or higher.

Lose 10 pounds and exercise regularly.

This month: Set up study-group schedule to coincide with quizzes.

Begin walking and weight lifting.

This week: Meet with study group; go over material for Friday's quiz.

Go for a fitness walk three times; go to weight room twice.

Today: Go over Chapter 3 in accounting text.

Walk for 40 minutes.

Prioritize Goals

Prioritizing enables you to use your date book with maximum efficiency. On any given day, your goals will have varying degrees of importance. Record your goals first, and then label them according to level of importance, using these categories: Priority 1, Priority 2, and Priority 3. Identify these categories using any code that makes sense to you. Some people use numbers, as above. Some use letters (A, B, C). Some write activities in different colors according to priority level. Some use symbols (*, +, -).

Priority 1 activities are the most important things in your life. They may include attending class, picking up a child from day care, putting gas in the car, and paying bills.

Priority 2 activities are part of your routine. Examples include grocery shopping, working out, participating in a school organization, or cleaning. Priority 2 tasks are important but more flexible than priority 1 items.

Priority 3 activities are those you would like to do but can reschedule without much sacrifice. Examples might be a trip to the mall, a visit to a friend, a social phone call, a sports event, a movie, or a hair appointment. As much as you would like to accomplish them, you don't consider them urgent. Many people don't enter priority 3 tasks in their date books until they are sure they have time to get them done. You may want to list priority 3 tasks separately and refer to the list when you have some extra time.

Prioritizing your activities is essential for two reasons. First, some activities are more important than others, and effective time management requires that you focus most of your energy on priority 1 items. Second, looking at all your priorities helps you plan when you can get things done. Often, it's not possible to get all your priority 1 activities done early in the day, especially if these activities involve scheduled classes or meetings. Prioritizing helps you set priority 1 items and then schedule priority 2 and 3 items around them as they fit.

Keep Track of Events

Your date book also enables you to schedule *events*. Rather than thinking of events as separate from goals, tie them to your long-term goals just as you would your other tasks. For example, attending a wedding in a few months

"The right time is anytime that one is still so lucky as to have . . . Live!"

HENRY JAMES

REAL WORLD PERSPECTIVE

How can I stay focused on my goals?

Karin Lounsbury, Gonzaga University, Spokane, Washington

I decided to return to school when I had just turned 40. I didn't like feeling dependent on my husband for my financial security so I thought that I'd do something about it. I also did it for my two children. My marriage had been shaky for quite a few years, and I was scared to death that I wouldn't be able to provide for them on my own. Even though I'd worked in the business world for a long time, the salary was never very good. I was overexperienced and underpaid. I thought that by completing my education, I could find a great job that allowed me to support my family. Although I knew that college would be challenging, I wasn't concerned with the work load—I'm used to carrying a lot of responsibilities. In fact, probably more than most people. Besides my two young children, I'm married to a man who lost both his legs in the Vietnam war. He's in a wheelchair, which means a lot of extra work falls on my shoulders.

These last few months everything seems to be falling apart: My husband and I decided to get a divorce; my son has been struggling at school; my mother was just diagnosed with cancer; and I feel like I can hardly keep my head above water. All of this is taking a toll on my grades. I'm usually so emotionally and physically exhausted by the end of the day, I just don't have the energy to put into my work. When I'm at school, I'm distracted thinking about the future. I don't want to drop out of school, but I also don't want my kids to suffer when they need me so badly. How can I get through this difficult time and still accomplish my educational goals?

Shirley Williamson, University of Georgia

To begin with, I want to encourage you to hold on to your dream of finishing your education. Even though there are probably going to be some very cloudy days ahead, don't give up. The long-term rewards are worth all the extra effort it's going to take for a while. If you could lighten your academic load in any way, I think it would be wise to do so. It might take you a little longer to graduate, but you and your children will appreciate the extra time you get with one another. Right now, maintaining your family life is extremely important. It's healthy for children to learn that you have goals and that they may have to make compromises sometimes, but they should never suffer at the expense of those goals. If that means putting off your studies until after they're in bed, then that's what you should do. You might even try studying at the same time they are doing their homework. Make it a family activity. But whatever you do, try and keep your family structure consistent.

My heart goes out to you. You really have a lot on your plate right now. I would also suggest you find some time to care for yourself. I think the greatest stress reducer is exercise. It gets your adrenaline going and keeps your body and mind healthy. You may have to get up a little earlier or work out on your lunch hour like I do, but it's worth the extra effort.

contributes to your commitment to spending time with your family. Being aware of quiz dates, due dates for assignments, and meeting dates will aid your goals to achieve in school and become involved.

Note events in your date book so that you can stay aware of them ahead of time. Write them in daily, weekly, monthly, or even yearly sections, where a quick look will remind you that they are approaching. Writing them down will also help you see where they fit in the context of all your other activities. For example, if you have three big tests and a presentation all in one week, you'll want to take time in the weeks before to prepare for them all.

Following are some kinds of events worth noting in your date book:

- Due dates for papers, projects, presentations, and tests
- Important meetings, medical appointments, or due dates for bill payments
- Birthdays, anniversaries, social events, holidays, and other special occasions
- Benchmarks for steps toward a goal, such as due dates for sections of a project or a deadline for losing five pounds on your way to twenty

Time Management Strategies

Managing time takes thought and energy. Here are some additional strategies to try:

1. **Plan your schedule each week.** Before each week starts, note events, goals, and priorities. Look at the map of your week to decide where to fit activities like studying and priority 3 items. For example, if you have a test on Thursday, you can plan study sessions on the days up until then. If you have more free time on Tuesday and Friday than on other days, you can plan workouts or priority 3 activities at those times. Looking at the whole week will help you avoid being surprised by something you had forgotten was coming up.

2. **Make and use to-do lists.** Use a *to-do list* to record the things you want to accomplish. If you generate a daily or weekly to-do list on a separate piece of paper, you can look at all tasks and goals at once. This will help you consider time frames and priorities. You might want to prioritize your tasks and transfer them to appropriate places in your date book. Some people create daily to-do lists right on their date book pages. You can tailor a to-do list to an important event, such as exam week, or to an especially busy day, such as when you have a family gathering or a presentation to make. This kind of specific to-do list can help you prioritize and accomplish an unusually large task load.

3. **Post monthly and yearly calendars at home.** Keeping a calendar on the wall will help you stay aware of important events. You can purchase one or draw it yourself, month by month, on plain paper. Use a yearly or a monthly version (Figure 3-4 shows part of a monthly calendar), and keep it where you can refer to it often. If you live with family or friends, make the calendar a group project so that you stay aware of each other's plans. Knowing each other's schedules can also help you avoid schedul-

Figure 3-4	Monthly calendar.

AUGUST 1999

SUNDAY	MONDAY	TUESDAY	WEDNESDAY	THURSDAY	FRIDAY	SATURDAY
1	2 WORK	3 Turn in English paper	4 Dentist 2pm	5 Chem. test	6	7
8 Frank's B-day	9 Psych test	10 6:30 pm Meeting at Student Center	11 Statistics quiz WORK	12 History study group	13 WORK	14 WORK
15	16 WORK	17	18 WORK	19	20	21
22	23	24	25	26	27	28
29	30	31				

ing problems, such as two people needing the car at the same time or one partner scheduling a get-together when the other has to work.

4. Schedule downtime. When you're wiped out from too much activity, you don't have the energy to accomplish much with your time. A little downtime will refresh you and improve your attitude. Even half an hour a day will help. Fill the time with whatever relaxes you—having a snack, reading, watching TV, playing a game or sport, walking, writing, or just doing nothing. Make downtime a priority.

5. Be flexible. Since priorities determine the map of your day, week, month, or year, any priority shift can jumble your schedule. Be ready to reschedule your tasks as your priorities change. On Monday, a homework assignment due in a week might be priority 2. By Saturday, it has become priority 1. On some days a surprise priority, such as a medical emergency or a family situation, may pop up and force you to cancel everything else on your schedule. Other days a class may be canceled and you will have extra time on your hands. Adjust to whatever each day brings.

No matter how well you schedule your time, you will have moments when it's hard to stay in control. Knowing how to identify and avoid procrastination and other time traps will help you get back on track.

WHY IS PROCRASTINATION A PROBLEM?

Procrastination occurs when you postpone unpleasant or burdensome tasks. People procrastinate for different reasons. Having trouble with goal setting is one reason. People may project goals too far into the future, set unrealistic goals that are too frustrating to reach, or have no goals at all. People also procrastinate because they don't believe in their ability to complete a task or don't

TERMS

Downtime
Quiet time
set aside for
relaxation and
low-key activity.

TERMS

Procrastination
The act of
putting off some-
thing that needs
to be done.

believe in themselves in general. As natural as these tendencies are, they can also be extremely harmful. If continued over a period of time, procrastination can develop into a habit that will dominate a person's behavior. Following are some ways to face your tendencies to procrastinate and *just do it!*

Strategies to Fight Procrastination

Weigh the benefits (to you and others) of completing the task versus the effects of procrastinating. What rewards lie ahead if you get it done? What will the effects be if you continue to put it off? Which situation has better effects? Chances are you will benefit more in the long term from facing the task head-on.

Set reasonable goals. Plan your goals carefully, allowing enough time to complete them. Unreasonable goals can be so intimidating that you do nothing at all. "Pay off the credit-card bill next month" could throw you. However, "Pay off the credit-card bill in six months" might inspire you to take action.

Get started. Going from doing nothing to doing something is often the hardest part of avoiding procrastination. Once you start, you may find it easier to continue.

Break the task into smaller parts. If it seems overwhelming, look at the task in terms of its parts. How can you approach it step-by-step? If you can concentrate on achieving one small goal at a time, the task may become less of a burden.

Ask for help with tasks and projects at school, work, and home. You don't always have to go it alone. For example, if you have put off an intimidating assignment, ask your instructor for guidance. If you need accommodations due to a disability, don't assume that others know about it. Once you identify what's holding you up, see who can help you face the task.

Don't expect perfection. No one is perfect. Most people learn by starting at the beginning and wading through plenty of mistakes and confusion. It's better to try your best than to do nothing at all.

Procrastination is natural, but it can cause you problems if you let it get the best of you. When it does happen, take some time to think about the causes. What is it about this situation that frightens you or puts you off? Answering that question can help you address what causes lie underneath the procrastination. These causes might indicate a deeper problem that needs to be solved.

In Hebrew, the word *chai* means "life," representing all aspects of life—spiritual, emotional, family, educational, and career. Individual Hebrew characters have number values. Because the characters in the word *chai* add up to 18, the number 18 has come to be associated with good luck. The word *chai* is often worn as a good-luck charm. As you plan your goals, think about your view of luck. Many people feel that a person can create his or her own luck by persistently pursuing goals and staying open to possibilities and opportunities. Canadian novelist Robertson Davies once said, "What we call luck is the inner man externalized. We make things happen to us."

Consider that your vision of life may largely determine how you live. You can prepare the way for luck by establishing a personal mission and forging ahead toward your goals. If you believe that the life you want awaits you, you will be able to recognize and make the most of luck when it comes around. *L'Chaim*—to life, and good luck.

Success in the Real World

Colonel Frank Borman

Retired Colonel Frank Borman has experienced a great deal of success—in and *out* of this world. As an astronaut, CEO, and award-winning aircraft rebuilder, Frank's achievements seem endless. As commander of the *Apollo 8* mission, he made world history with crew members Jim Lovell and Bill Anders by being the first to orbit the moon.

After Frank's career as an astronaut was over, he eventually went on to be the CEO of Eastern Airlines in Miami, Florida. He believes that in order to be truly successful in today's workplace, you have to use your integrity. With integrity, a person will have good "situational ethics" and will know how to act appropriately in certain tough situations, which are almost certainly encountered throughout one's career. He believes that you need to concentrate on having a code of ethics for yourself in order to be truly successful.

Frank suggests that one sure way to achieve success is to pick one mission, focus on it, and give the best of your ability to accomplishing that mission. Frank puts the mission, or goal, above his own desires and is willing to make huge sacrifices for the good of the organization. If the organization succeeds, then so does he.

Frank demonstrated strong leadership as the *Apollo 8* commander and as CEO. He has been called a "leader's leader." According to Frank, good leadership skills can be taught. Good leaders:

◆ Have integrity

◆ Have a certain degree of intelligence

◆ Have knowledge about the industry in which they are working

◆ Genuinely care for people they are leading

◆ Are completely committed to their mission

◆ Subordinate personal desires for the good of the whole

◆ Are very clear about their goals

◆ Find people they can trust and then let them do their own thing

The successes that Frank has achieved in life have surely not come without sacrifice. When he was working at NASA, he was away from his family for 240 days a year for eight years. Working toward his mission was an incredible sacrifice. Frank credits a lot of his successes to the partnership with his wife. Both were committed to the overall mission.

Currently, Frank is winning awards for rebuilding antique wartime aircrafts. He's also won several other awards, including the Congressional Space Medal of Honor, and inductions into the International Space Hall of Fame and U.S. Astronaut Hall of Fame.

Frank has his share of critics, also. For a long time, he was hurt by the comments of his detractors until he decided that he couldn't please everyone. He deals with criticism by taking what he believes is useful information that can help him and disregarding the rest: "You just have to give the best of your ability to accomplishing your mission once you decide what that is. Focus on it and you will achieve success."

Chapter 3   Applications

Name _____   Date _____

KEY INTO YOUR LIFE
Opportunities to Apply What You Learn

 Your Values

Begin to explore your values by rating the following values on a scale from 1 to 4, 1 being least important to you and 4 being most important. If you have values that you don't see in the chart, list them in the blank spaces and rate them.

VALUE	RATING	VALUE	RATING
Knowing yourself		Mental health	
Physical health		Fitness and exercise	
Spending time with your family		Having an intimate relationship	
Helping others		Education	
Being well-paid		Being employed	
Being liked by others		Free time/vacations	
Enjoying entertainment		Time to yourself	
Spiritual/religious life		Reading	
Keeping up with the news		Staying organized	
Being financially stable		Close friendships	
Creative/artistic pursuits		Self-improvement	
Lifelong learning		Facing your fears	

Considering your priorities, write your top five values here:

1. _____

2. _____

3. _____

4. _____

5. _____

Why Are You Here?

Why did you decide to enroll in school? Do any of the reasons listed in the chapter fit you? Do you have other reasons all your own? Many people have more than one answer. Write up to five here.

_____

_____

_____

_____

_____

Take a moment to think about your reasons. Which reasons are most important to you? Why? Prioritize your reasons above by writing 1 next to the most important, 2 next to the second most important, etc.

How do you feel about your reasons? You may be proud of some. On the other hand, you may not feel comfortable with others. Which do you like or dislike and why?

_____

_____

_____

_____

_____

Short-Term Scheduling

Take a close look at your schedule for the coming month, including events, important dates, and steps toward goals. On the calendar layout on p. 82, fill in the name of the month and appropriate numbers for the days. Then record what you hope to accomplish, including the following:

- Due dates for papers, projects, and presentations
- Test dates
- Important meetings, medical appointments, and due dates for bill payments
- Birthdays, anniversaries, and other special occasions
- Steps toward long-term goals

This kind of chart will help you see the big picture of your month. To stay on target from day to day, check these dates against the entries in your date book and make sure that they are indicated there as well.

 ## 3.4 *To-Do Lists*

Make a to-do list for what you have to do tomorrow. Include all tasks— priority 1, 2, and 3—and events.

TOMORROW'S DATE: _____

1. _____
2. _____
3. _____
4. _____
5. _____
6. _____
7. _____
8. _____
9. _____
10. _____

Use a coding system of your choice to indicate priority level of both tasks and events. Place a check by the items that are important enough to note in your date book. Use this list to make your schedule for tomorrow in the date book, making a separate list for priority 3 items. At the end of the day, evaluate this system. Did the to-do list help you? How did it make a difference? If you liked it, use this exercise as a guide for using to-do lists regularly.

_____
_____
_____
_____

MONTH CHART

Team-Building Exercise: Individual Priorities

In a group of three or four people, brainstorm a list of long-term goals, and have one member of the group write them down. From that list, pick out ten goals that everyone can relate to most. Each group member should then take five minutes alone to evaluate the relative importance of the ten goals and rank them in the order that he or she prefers. Use a 1 to 10 scale, with 1 being the highest priority and 10 the lowest.

Display the rankings of each group member side by side. How many different orders are there? Discuss why each person has a different set of priorities, and be open to different views. What factors in different people's lives have caused them to select particular rankings? If you have time, discuss how priorities have changed for each group member over the course of a year, perhaps by having each person re-rank goals according to his or her needs a year ago.

Racing Against Themselves

Nike

Almost everyone, it seems, has owned a pair of Nike tennis shoes. If you have not, you probably at least recognize the Nike name and have heard the company's "Just do it" slogan. So you know what a giant Nike has become in the shoe industry. However, after seeing such a shining success in the past two decades, Nike is now on the decline. There is no one competitor in the market on which Nike can place the blame for its downturn. This is something Nike seems to have done to itself. We now see a flooded market of Nike athletic shoes, and people have become bored with Nike products. How did this happen?

There are several reasons that appear to have caused Nike's slowdown. The key reason may lie in the brand's appeal in the marketplace. After Nike was started in 1972, it became very popular largely because it marketed its athletic shoes on what it called the "Five Cool Guys" concept. Chief Executive Officer (CEO) Phil Knight believed that if he could show popular sports figures wearing Nike shoes, everyone would want to wear them. It is obvious how successful this was, especially with the Michael Jordan line that started in the 1980s. Nike had found a key marketing strategy and made millions on it. Now, Nike is all over the place. The appeal of the product as the "cool" thing to wear now, though, is gone because almost everyone has the products. They are worn by members of most sports teams and advertised frequently. The target market of teens and young adults (12–24 years) does not find Nike appealing because of its familiarity. They look at other brands that are less common such as Adidas, Timberland, and Reebok.

Nike has traditionally been a very resilient company. It had always come out on top because it had consistently produced new, exciting products and/or developed better marketing strategies than anyone else. Nike thought that

Case Studies

they would rebound again, as they had consistently done previously, and launched into the Asian market while also raising their prices in the U.S. to combat inflation. The retailers bought the shoes and apparel expecting a large demand in American and Asian markets, but they found that no one was buying. People thought that the Nike lines were the same, and the prices were higher. The Asian market collapsed and Nike found itself in trouble. The stock price fell from its high of $76 per share to $46 per share within one year. Nike did not respond quickly enough to the obvious fall in sales—the company simply did not admit that it was having problems until it was too late. Investors decided that the stock was not worth its previous value and lost some of their faith in Nike as an investment.

1. What mistakes did Nike make?

2. What would you do now to regain sales if you were Nike?

3. Why do you think that the "Five Cool Guys" marketing strategy worked? What other companies have employed a similar strategy to sell their products?

4. Why did the Nike brand become less popular?

5. Is a marketing slogan the same thing as a mission statement?

6. What were Nike's seeming goals? Can goals be conflicting?

7. Is avoiding the truth a form of procrastination?

Internet Exercise

The names of sites on the Internet are called domain names. Anything that ends with ".gov" is a government site. Access the Internet and go to NASA's page at:

www.nasa.gov

1. Briefly describe the main article on the page.

_____

_____

_____

_____

_____

Scroll down to the bottom of the page and double-click on the **Multimedia Gallery.**

Double-click on the **Photo Gallery.**

2. Can you find the Astronomy Picture of the Day? What is it?

_____

_____

Find the **Nasa Image Exchange** and double click on this.

You can browse or search for a particular topic. Search for photos of astronaut Frank Borman. Hint: Type the following as it appears here:

Frank "AND" Borman

Can you find a photo of Frank Borman and Jim Lovell? Can you find a photo of _Apollo 8?_

_____

_____

Journal

Name _____   Date _____

Critical and Creative Thinking

Tapping the Power of Your Mind

Your mind's powers show in everything you do, from the smallest chores (comparing prices on cereals at the grocery store) to the most complex situations (figuring out how to earn money after being laid off). Your mind is able to process, store, and create with the facts and ideas it encounters. Critical and creative thinking are what enable those skills to come alive.

Understanding how your mind works is the first step toward critical thinking. When you have that understanding, you can perform the essential critical-thinking task: asking important questions about ideas and information. This chapter will show you both the mind's basic actions and the thinking processes that use those actions. You will explore what it means to be an open-minded critical and creative thinker, able to ask and understand questions that promote your success in college, career, and life.

In this chapter, you will explore answers to the following questions:

◆ What is critical thinking?

◆ How does your mind work?

◆ How does critical thinking help you solve problems and make decisions?

◆ Why shift your perspective?

◆ Why plan strategically?

◆ How can you develop your creativity?

WHAT IS CRITICAL THINKING?

Critical thinking is thinking that goes beyond the basic recall of information. If the word *critical* sounds negative to you, consider that the dictionary defines its meaning as "indispensable" and "important." Critical thinking is important thinking that involves asking questions. Using critical thinking, you question established ideas, create new ideas, turn information into tools to solve problems and make decisions, and take the long-term view as well as the day-to-day view.

A critical thinker asks as many kinds of questions as possible. The following are examples of possible questions about a given piece of information: *Where did it come from? What could explain it? In what ways is it true or false, and what examples could prove or disprove it? How do I feel about it, and why? How is this information similar to or different from what I already know? Is it good or bad? What causes led to it, and what effects does it have?* Critical thinkers also try to transform information into something they can use. They ask themselves whether the information can help them solve a problem, make a decision, create something new, or anticipate the future. Such questions help the critical thinker learn, grow, and create.

Not thinking critically means not asking questions about information or ideas. A person who does not think critically tends to accept or reject information or ideas without examining them. Table 4-1 compares how a non-critical thinker and critical thinker might respond to particular situations.

Asking questions (the focus of the table), considering without judgment as many responses as you can, and choosing responses that are as complete and accurate as possible are some primary ingredients that make up the skill of critical thinking.

Critical Thinking Is a Skill

Anyone can develop the ability to think critically. Critical thinking is a skill that can be taught to students at all different levels of ability. One of the most crucial components of this skill is learning information. For instance, part of

| Table 4-1 | | Not thinking critically vs. thinking critically. | |

YOUR ROLE	SITUATION	NON-QUESTIONING RESPONSE	QUESTIONING RESPONSE
STUDENT	Instructor is lecturing on the causes of the Vietnam War.	You assume that everything your instructor tells you is true.	You consider what the instructor says; you write down questions about issues you want to clarify; you initiate discussion with the professor or other classmates.
PARENT	Instructor discovers your child lying about something at school.	You're mad at your child and believe the instructor, or you think the instructor is lying.	You ask both instructor and child about what happened, and you compare their answers, evaluating who you think is telling the truth; you discuss the concepts of lying/honesty with your child.
SPOUSE/ PARTNER	Your partner feels that he or she no longer has quality time with you.	You think he or she is wrong and defend yourself.	You ask how long he or she has felt this way; you ask your partner and yourself why this is happening; you explore how you can improve the situation.
EMPLOYEE	Your supervisor is angry at you.	You ignore or avoid your supervisor, or you deny responsibility for what the supervisor is angry about.	You are willing to discuss the situation; you ask what you could have done better; you ask what changes you can make in the future.
NEIGHBOR	People different from you move in next door.	You ignore or avoid them; you think their way of living is weird.	You introduce yourself; you offer to help if they need it; you respectfully explore what's different about them.
CITIZEN	You encounter a homeless person.	You avoid the person and the issue.	You examine whether the community has a responsibility to the homeless, and if you find that it does, you explore how to fulfill that responsibility.
CONSUMER	You want to buy a car.	You decide on a brand-new car and don't think through how you will handle the payments.	You consider the different effects of buying a new car vs. buying a used car; you examine your money situation to see what kind of payment you can handle each month.

the skill of critical thinking is comparing new information with what you already know. Your prior knowledge provides a framework within which to ask questions about and evaluate a new piece of information. Without a solid base of knowledge, critical thinking is harder to achieve. For example, thinking critically about the statement "Shakespeare's character King Richard III is like an early version of Adolf Hitler" is impossible without basic knowledge of Shakespeare's play *Richard III* and World War II.

The skill of critical thinking focuses on generating questions about statements and information. To examine potential critical-thinking responses in more depth, explore the different questions that a critical thinker may have about one particular statement.

A Critical-Thinking Response to a Statement

Consider the following statement of opinion: *"My obstacles are keeping me from succeeding in school. Other people make it through school because they don't have to deal with the obstacles that I have."*

Non-questioning thinkers may accept an opinion such as this as an absolute truth, believing that their obstacles will hinder their success. As a result, on the road to achieving their goals, they may lose motivation to overcome those obstacles. In contrast, critical thinkers would take the opportunity to examine the opinion through a series of questions. Here are some examples of questions one student might ask (the type of each question is indicated in parentheses):

> *"What exactly are my obstacles?* Examples of my obstacles are a heavy work schedule, single parenting, being in debt, and returning to school after ten years out." (**recall**)

> *"Are there other cases different from mine?* I do have one friend who is going through problems worse than mine, and she's getting by. I also know another guy who doesn't have too much to deal with that I can tell, and he's struggling just like I am." (**difference**)

> *"Who has problems similar to mine?* Well, if I consider my obstacles specifically, I might be saying that single parents and returning adult students will all have trouble in school. That is not necessarily true. People in all kinds of situations may still become successful." (**similarity**)

> *"Why do I think this?* Maybe I am scared of returning to school and adjusting to a new environment. Maybe I am afraid to challenge myself, which I haven't done in a long time. Whatever the cause, the effect is that I feel bad about myself and don't work to the best of my abilities, and that can hurt both me and my family, who depends on me." (**cause and effect**)

> *"What is an example of someone who has had success despite having to overcome obstacles?* What about Oseola McCarty, the cleaning woman who saved money all her life and raised $150,000 to create a scholarship at the University of Southern Mississippi? She didn't have what anyone would call advantages, such as a high-paying job or a college education." (**idea to example**)

"What conclusion can I draw from my questions? From thinking about my friend and about Oseola McCarty, I would say that people can successfully overcome their obstacles by working hard, focusing on their abilities, and concentrating on their goals." (**example to idea**)

"How do I evaluate the effects of this statement? I think it's harmful. When we say that obstacles equal difficulty, we can damage our desire to try to overcome those obstacles. When we say that successful people don't have obstacles, we might overlook that some very successful people have to deal with hidden disadvantages such as learning disabilities or abusive families." (**evaluation**)

Remember these types of questions. When you explore the seven mind actions later in the chapter, refer to these questions to see how they illustrate the different actions your mind performs.

The Value of Critical Thinking

Critical thinking has many important advantages. Following are some of the positive effects, or benefits, of putting energy into critical thinking.

You will increase your ability to perform thinking processes that help you reach your goals. Critical thinking is a learned skill, just like shooting a basketball or using a word-processing program on the computer. As with any other skill, the more you use it, the better you become. The more you ask questions, the better you think. The better you think, the more effective you will be when completing schoolwork, managing your personal life, and performing on the job.

You can produce knowledge rather than just reproduce it. The interaction of new information with what you already know creates new knowledge. The usefulness of such knowledge can be judged by how you apply it to new situations. For instance, it won't mean much for an early-childhood-education student to quote the stages of child development on an exam unless he or she can make judgments about children's needs when on the job.

You can be a valuable employee. You certainly won't be a failure in the workplace if you follow directions. However, you will be even more valuable if you think critically and ask strategic questions about how to make improvements, large or small. Questions could range from "Is there a better way to deliver phone messages?" to "How can we increase business to keep from going under?" An employee who shows the initiative to think critically will be more likely to earn responsibility and promotions.

You can increase your creativity. You cannot be a successful critical thinker without being able to come up with new and different questions to ask, possibilities to explore, and ideas to try. Creativity is essential in producing what is new. Being creative generally improves your outlook, your sense of humor, and your perspective as you cope with problems. Later in this chapter, you will look at ways to awaken and increase your natural creativity.

"We do not live to think but, on the contrary, we think in order that we may succeed in surviving."
JOSÉ ORTEGA Y GASSETT

In the next section, you will read about the seven basic actions your mind performs when asking important questions. These actions are the basic blocks you will use to build the critical-thinking processes you will explore later in the chapter.

 OW DOES YOUR MIND WORK?

Critical thinking depends on a thorough understanding of the workings of the mind. Your mind has some basic moves, or actions, that it uses to understand relationships among ideas and concepts. Sometimes it uses one action by itself, but most often it uses two or more in combination.

Mind Actions: The Thinktrix

You can identify your mind's actions using a system called the Thinktrix, originally conceived by educators Frank Lyman, Arlene Mindus, and Charlene Lopez[1] and developed by numerous other instructors. They studied how students think and named seven mind actions that are the basic building blocks of thought. These actions are not new to you, although some of their names may be. They represent the ways in which you think all the time.

Through exploring these actions, you can go beyond just thinking and learn *how* you think. This will help you take charge of your own thinking. The more you know about how your mind works, the more control you will have over thinking processes such as problem solving, decision making, creating, and strategic planning.

Following are explanations of each of the mind actions. Each explanation names the action, defines it, and explains it with examples. As you read, write your own examples in the blank spaces provided. Each action is also represented by a picture or *icon* that helps you visualize and remember it.

Recall: *Facts, sequence, and description.* This is the simplest action. When you **recall,** you describe facts, objects, or events, or you put them into sequence. *Examples:*

- Naming the steps of a geometry proof, in order.
- Remembering your best friends' phone numbers.

Your example: Recall some important events this month. _____

_____

_____

_____

    The icon: A string tied around a finger is a familiar image of recall or remembering.

Similarity: *Analogy, likeness, comparison.* This action examines what is **similar** about one or more things. You might compare situations, ideas, people, stories, events, or objects. *Examples:*

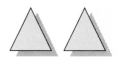

◆ Comparing notes with another student to see what facts and ideas you both have considered important.

◆ Analyzing the arguments you've had with your partner this month and seeing how they all seem to be about the same problem.

Your example: Tell what is similar about two of your best friends. _____

_____

_____

_____

   The icon: Two alike objects, in this case triangles, indicate similarity.

Difference: *Distinction, contrast.* This action examines what is **different** about one or more situations, ideas, people, stories, events, or objects, contrasting them with one another. *Examples:*

◆ Seeing how two instructors differ in style—one divides the class into small groups and encourages discussion; the other keeps desks in straight lines and lectures for most of the class.

◆ Contrasting a weekday where you work a half-day and go to school a half-day with a weekday when you attend class and then have the rest of the day to study.

Your example: Explain how your response to a course you like differs from how you respond to a course you don't like as much. _____

_____

_____

_____

   The icon: Two differing objects, in this case a triangle and a square, indicate difference.

Cause and Effect: *Reasons, consequences, prediction.* Using this action, you look at what has caused a fact, situation, or event, and/or what **effects,** or consequences, come from it. In other words, you examine both what led up to something and what will follow because of it. *Examples:*

◆ You see how staying up late at night causes you to oversleep, which has the effect of your being late to class. This causes you to miss some of the material, which has the further effect of your having problems on the test.

◆ When you pay your phone and utility bills on time, you create effects such as a better credit rating, uninterrupted service, and a better relationship with your service providers.

Your example: Name what causes you to like your favorite class, and the effects that liking the class has on you. _____

_____

_____

_____

The icon: The water droplets making ripples indicate causes and their resulting effects.

Example to Idea: *Generalization, classification, conceptualization.* From one or more **examples** (facts or events), you develop a general idea or ideas. Grouping facts or events into patterns may allow you to make a general statement about several of them at once. Classifying a fact or event helps you build knowledge. This mind action moves from the specific to the general. *Examples:*

♦ You have had trouble finding a baby-sitter who can match your schedule. A classmate even brought her child to class once. Your brother has had to drop off his daughter at your mom's and doesn't like being unable to see her all day. From these examples, you derive the idea that your school needs an on-campus day-care program.

♦ You see a movie and you decide it is mostly about pride.

Your example: Name examples of activities you enjoy, and from them, come up with an idea of your choice of vacation. _____

_____

_____

_____

The icon: The arrow and "Ex" pointing to a light bulb on the right indicate how an example or examples lead to the idea (the light bulb, lit up).

Idea to Example: *Categorization, substantiation, proof.* In a reverse of the previous action, you take an idea or ideas and think of examples (events or facts) that support or prove that idea. This mind action moves from the general to the specific. *Examples:*

♦ When you write a paper, you start with a thesis statement, which communicates the central idea: "Men are favored over women in the modern workplace." Then you gather examples to back up that idea: Men make more money on average than women in the same jobs; there are more men in upper management positions than there are women; women can be denied advancement when they make their families a priority.

♦ You talk to your instructor about changing your major, giving examples that support your idea: You have worked in the field you want to change to, you have fulfilled some of the requirements for that major already, and you are unhappy with your current course of study.

Your example: Name a person whom you consider to be admirable. Give three examples that show how that person is admirable. _____

_____

_____

_____

The icon: In a reverse of the previous icon, this one starts with the light-bulb and has an arrow pointing to "Ex." This indicates that you start with the idea, the lit bulb, and then branch into the example or examples that support the idea.

Evaluation: *Value, judgment, rating.* Here you judge whether something is useful or not useful, important or unimportant, good or bad, or right or wrong by identifying and weighing its positive and negative effects (pros and cons). Be sure to consider the specific situation at hand (a cold drink might be good on the beach in August, not so good in the snowdrifts in January). With the facts you have gathered, you determine the value of something in terms of both predicted effects and your own needs. Cause and effect analysis always accompanies evaluation. *Examples:*

◆ You decide to try taking later classes for a semester. You schedule classes in the afternoons and spend your nights on the job. You find that instead of getting up early to use the morning time, you tend to sleep in and then get up not too long before you have to be at school. From those harmful effects, you evaluate that it doesn't work for you. You decide to schedule earlier classes next time.

◆ Someone offers you a chance to cheat on a test. You evaluate the potential effects if you are caught. You also evaluate the long-term effects on you of not actually learning the material. You decide that it isn't worth your while to participate in the plan to cheat.

Your example: Evaluate your mode of transportation to school. _____

_____

_____

_____

The icon: A set of scales out of balance indicates how you weigh positive and negative effects to arrive at an evaluation.

You may want to use a *mnemonic device*—a memory tool, explained in more detail in Chapter 7—to remember the seven mind actions. Try recalling them using the word DECRIES—each letter is the first letter of a mind action. You can also make a sentence where each word starts with a mind action's first letter. Here's an example: "Really Smart Dogs Cook Eggs In Enchiladas" (the first letter of each word stands for one of the mind actions).

How Mind Actions Build Thinking Processes

The seven mind actions are the fundamental building blocks that your mind uses every day. Note that you will rarely use them one at a time in a step-by-step process, as they are presented here. You will usually combine them, overlap them, and repeat them more than once, using different actions for different situations. For example, when you want to say something nice at the end of a date, you might consider past comments that had an effect *similar* to what you want now. When a test question asks you to explain what prejudice is, you might name similar *examples* that show your *idea* of what prejudice means.

When you combine mind actions in working toward a specific goal, you are performing a thinking process. The next few sections will explore some of the most important critical-thinking processes: solving problems, making decisions, shifting your perspective, and planning strategically. Each thinking process helps you succeed by directing your critical thinking toward the achievement of your goals. Figure 4-3, appearing later in the chapter, shows all of the mind actions and thinking processes together and reminds you that the mind actions form the core of the thinking processes.

HOW DOES CRITICAL THINKING HELP YOU SOLVE PROBLEMS AND MAKE DECISIONS?

Problem solving and decision making are probably the two most crucial and common thinking processes. Each one requires various mind actions. They overlap somewhat because every problem that needs solving requires you to make a decision. However, not every decision requires that you solve a problem (for example, not many people would say that deciding what to order in a restaurant is a problem). Each process will be considered separately here. You will notice similarities in the steps involved in each.

Although both of these processes have multiple steps, you will not always have to work your way through each step. As you become more comfortable with solving problems and making decisions, your mind will automatically click through the steps you need whenever you encounter a problem or decision. Also, you will become more adept at evaluating which problems and decisions need serious consideration and which can be taken care of more quickly and simply.

Problem Solving

Life constantly presents problems to be solved, ranging from average daily problems (how to manage study time or learn not to misplace your keys) to life-altering situations (how to care for a sick elderly relative or design a custody plan during a divorce). Choosing a solution without thinking critically may have negative effects. For example, if you decide to move a sick elderly relative into your home without considering the effects of your work schedule, the relative may be alone in the evenings with no one to help should a medical emergency arise. However, if you use the steps of the following problem-solving process to think critically, you have the best chance of coming up with a favorable solution.

You can apply this problem-solving plan to any situation or issue that you want to resolve. Using the following steps will maximize the number of possible solutions you generate and will allow you to explore each one as fully as possible.

1. State the problem clearly. What are the facts? *Recall* the details of the situation. Be sure to name the problem specifically, without focusing on causes or effects. For example, a student might state this as a problem: "I'm not understanding the class material." However, that may be a *cause* of the actual problem at hand: "I'm failing my economics quizzes."

2. Analyze the problem. What is happening that, in your opinion, needs to change? In other words, what *effects* does the situation have that cause a problem for you? What *causes* these effects? Look at the *causes and effects* that surround the problem. Continuing the example of the economics student, if some effects of failing quizzes include poor grades in the course and disinterest, some causes may include poor study habits, poor test-taking skills, lack of sleep, or not understanding the material.

3. Brainstorm possible solutions. Brainstorming will help you think of examples of other similar problems and how you solved them. Consider what is different about this problem, and see if the thoughts you generate might lead you to new possible solutions. You will find more about brainstorming on p. 106 of this chapter. *It's very important to base your possible solutions upon causes rather than effects.* Getting to the heart of a problem requires addressing the cause rather than putting a bandage on the effect. If the economics student were to aim for better assignment grades to offset the low quiz grades, that might raise his GPA but wouldn't address the cause of not understanding the material. Looking at this cause, on the other hand, might lead him to work on study habits or seek help from his instructor, a study group, or a tutor.

4. Explore each solution. Why might your solution work? Why not? Might a solution work partially, or in a particular situation? *Evaluate* ahead of time the pros and cons, or the positive and negative effects, of each plan. Create a chain of causes and effects in your head, as far into the future as you can, to see where you think this solution would lead. The economics student might consider the effects of improved study habits, more sleep, tutoring, or dropping the class.

5. Choose and execute the solution you decide is best. Decide how you will put your solution to work. Then, execute your solution. The economics student could decide on a combination of improved study habits and tutoring.

6. Evaluate the solution that you acted upon, looking at its *effects*. What are the positive and negative effects of what you did? In terms of your needs, was it a useful solution or not? Could the solution use any adjustments or changes in order to be more useful? Would you do the same again or not? Evaluating his choice, the economics student may decide that the effects are good but that his fatigue still causes a problem.

7. Continue to refine the solution. Problem solving is always a process. You may have opportunities to apply the same solution over and over again.

TERMS

Brainstorming
The spontaneous, rapid generation of ideas or solutions, undertaken by a group or an individual, often as part of a problem-solving process.

Figure 4-1

Problem-solving plan.

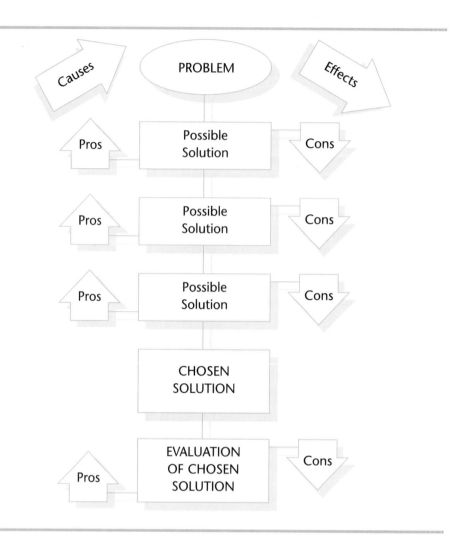

Evaluate repeatedly, making changes that you decide make the solution better. The economics student may decide to continue to study more regularly but, after a few weeks of tutoring, could opt to trade in the tutoring time for some extra sleep. He may decide to take what he has learned from the tutor so far and apply it to his increased study efforts.

Using this process will enable you to solve personal, educational, and workplace problems in a thoughtful, comprehensive way. Figure 4-1 is a think link that demonstrates a way to visualize the flow of problem solving. Figure 4-2 contains a sample of how one person used this plan to solve a problem. Figure 4-2 represents the same plan as 4-1 but gives room to write so that it can be used in the problem-solving process.

Decision Making

Although every problem-solving process involves making a decision (when you decide which solution to try), not all decisions involve solving problems. Decisions are choices. Making a choice, or decision, requires thinking criti-

Figure 4-2   How one student worked through a problem.

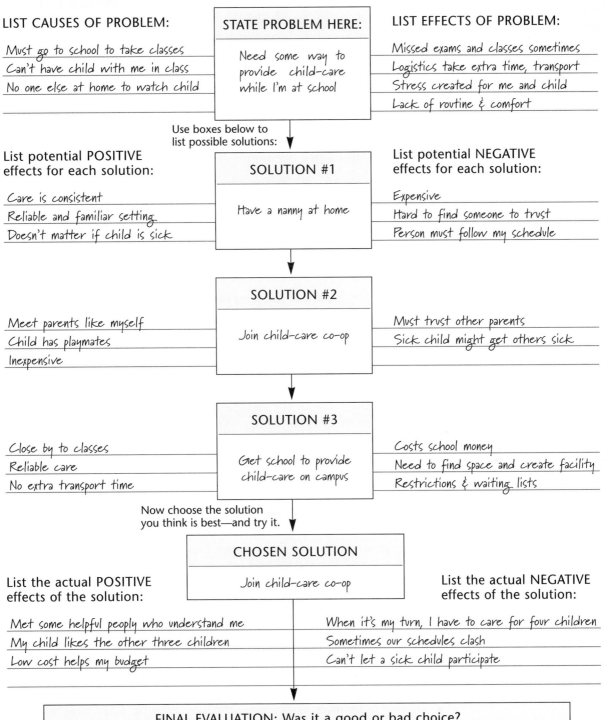

LIST CAUSES OF PROBLEM:

Must go to school to take classes

Can't have child with me in class

No one else at home to watch child

STATE PROBLEM HERE:

Need some way to provide child-care while I'm at school

LIST EFFECTS OF PROBLEM:

Missed exams and classes sometimes

Logistics take extra time, transport

Stress created for me and child

Lack of routine & comfort

Use boxes below to list possible solutions:

List potential POSITIVE effects for each solution:

Care is consistent

Reliable and familiar setting

Doesn't matter if child is sick

SOLUTION #1

Have a nanny at home

List potential NEGATIVE effects for each solution:

Expensive

Hard to find someone to trust

Person must follow my schedule

SOLUTION #2

Join child-care co-op

Meet parents like myself

Child has playmates

Inexpensive

Must trust other parents

Sick child might get others sick

SOLUTION #3

Get school to provide child-care on campus

Close by to classes

Reliable care

No extra transport time

Costs school money

Need to find space and create facility

Restrictions & waiting lists

Now choose the solution you think is best—and try it.

CHOSEN SOLUTION

Join child-care co-op

List the actual POSITIVE effects of the solution:

Met some helpful people who understand me

My child likes the other three children

Low cost helps my budget

List the actual NEGATIVE effects of the solution:

When it's my turn, I have to care for four children

Sometimes our schedules clash

Can't let a sick child participate

FINAL EVALUATION: Was it a good or bad choice?

All in all, I think this is the best I could do on my budget. There are times when I have to stay home with a sick child, buy I'm mostly able to stay committed to both parenting and school.

Source: Adapted from a heuristic developed by Frank T. Lyman Jr., Ph.D., University of Maryland, 1983.

cally through all of the possible choices and evaluating which will work best for you and for the situation. Decisions large and small come up daily, hourly, even every few minutes. Do you call your landlord when the heat isn't coming on? Do you drop a course? Should you stay in a relationship? Can you work part-time without interfering with school?

Before you begin the decision-making process, evaluate the level of the decision you are making. Do you have to decide what to have for lunch (usually a minor issue), or whether to quit a good job (often a major life change)? Some decisions are little, day-to-day considerations that you can take care of quickly on your own. Others require thoughtful evaluation, time, and perhaps the input of others you trust. The following is a list of steps to take in order to think critically through a decision:

1. **Decide on a goal.** Why is this decision necessary? In other words, what result do you want from this decision, and what is its value? Considering the *effects* you want can help you formulate your goal. For example, say a student currently attends a small private college. Her goal is to become a physical therapist. The school has a good program, but her financial situation has changed and has made this school too expensive for her.

2. **Establish needs.** *Recall* the needs of everyone (or everything) involved in the decision. The student needs a school with a full physical therapy program; she and her parents need to cut costs (her father changed jobs and her family cannot continue to afford the current school); she needs to be able to transfer credits.

3. **Name, investigate, and evaluate available options.** Brainstorm possible choices, and then look at the facts surrounding each. *Evaluate* the good and bad effects of each possibility. Weigh these effects and judge which is the best course of action. Here are some possibilities that the student in the college example might consider:

   ◆ *Continue at the current college.* **Positive effects:** I wouldn't have to adjust to a new place or to new people. I could continue my course work as planned. **Negative effects:** I would have to find a way to finance most of my tuition and costs on my own, whether through loans, grants, or work. I'm not sure I could find time to work as much as I would need to, and I don't think I would qualify for as much aid as I now need.

   ◆ *Transfer to the state college.* **Positive effects:** I could reconnect with people there whom I know from high school. Tuition and room costs would be cheaper than at my current school. I could transfer credits. **Negative effects:** I would still have to work some or find minimal financial aid. The physical therapy program is small and not very strong.

   ◆ *Transfer to the community college.* **Positive effects:** They have many of the courses I need to continue with the physical therapy curriculum. The school is twenty minutes from my parents' house, so I could live at home and avoid paying housing costs. Credits will transfer. The tuition is extremely reasonable. **Negative effects:** I don't know anyone there. I would be less independent. The school doesn't offer a bachelor's degree.

4. Decide on a plan of action and pursue it. **Make a choice based on your evaluation, and act on your choice. In this case the student might decide to go to the community college for two years and then transfer back to a four-year school to earn a bachelor's degree in physical therapy. Although she might lose some independence and contact with friends, the positive effects are money saved, opportunity to spend time on studies rather than working to earn tuition money, and the availability of classes that match the physical therapy program requirements.**

5. Evaluate the result. **Was it useful? Not useful? Some of both? Weigh the positive and negative effects. The student may find with her transfer decision that it can be hard living at home, although her parents are adjusting to her independence and she is trying to respect their concerns as parents. Fewer social distractions result in her getting more work done. The financial situation is much more favorable. All things considered, she evaluates that this decision was a good one.**

Making important decisions can take time. Think through your decision thoroughly, considering your own ideas as well as those of others you trust, but don't hesitate to act once you have your plan. You cannot benefit from your decision until you act upon it and follow through.

WHY SHIFT YOUR PERSPECTIVE?

Seeing the world only from your perspective, or point of view, is inflexible, limiting, and frustrating to both you and others. You probably know how hard it can be to relate to someone who cannot understand where you are coming from—a co-worker who's annoyed that you leave early on Thursdays for physical therapy, a parent who doesn't see why you can't take a study break to visit, a friend who can't understand why you would date someone of a different race. Seeing beyond one's own perspective can be difficult, especially when life problems and fatigue take their toll.

On the other hand, when you shift your own perspective to consider someone else's, you open the lines of communication. Trying to understand what other people feel, need, and want makes you more responsive to them. They then may feel respected by you and respond to you in turn. For example, if you want to add or drop a course and your advisor says it's impossible, not waiting to hear you out, the last thing you may feel like doing is pouring your heart out. On the other hand, if your advisor asks to hear your point of view, you may sense that your needs are respected. Because the advisor wants to hear from you, you feel valued; that may encourage you to respond, or even to change your mind.

Every time you shift your perspective, you can also learn something new. There are worlds of knowledge and possibilities outside your individual existence. You may learn that what you eat daily may be against someone else's religious beliefs. You may discover people who don't fit a stereotype. You may find different and equally valid ways of getting an education, living as a family, relating to one another, having a spiritual life, or spending free time. Above all else, you may see that each person is entitled to his or her own perspective, no matter how foreign it may be to you.

TERMS

Perspective
A mental point of view or outlook, based on a cluster of related assumptions, incorporating values, interests, and knowledge.

REAL WORLD PERSPECTIVE

How can I find a satisfactory solution to my problem?

Chelsea Phillips, Hampshire College, Amherst, Massachusetts

I attend Hampshire College in Massachusetts. This year I'm involved in a field study program called Earth Lands. The college gives me credits, but the program is not affiliated with Hampshire. I live and work in a sustainable community and study ecological issues. There are nine of us who live together. All of us are environmental activists and we agree to live by certain principles. The lodge we live in is run by solar power. We use kerosene and flashlights, too. Our food is entirely vegan, which means we not only don't eat meat, we also don't eat other foods that come from animals, like milk and butter.

Five of the participants in the program, including myself, are here as paying students. The other members are brought in to live with us and support us as we learn about the environment and community living. When we got involved, we believed the program was an entirely collaborative effort—at least that's what the brochure said. We're coming to find out there is a subtle power structure that exists between the five of us and the group called the "centering Team." We don't have as much input as we'd like into the schedule or decisions that need to be made. Because we're learning how to build community and resolve problems, I'd like to find a way to resolve this feeling of separation between the two groups. I'd like to see much more dialogue and collaboration so that we're all equal participants. What process could I initiate that would address this problem and allow for more equality within our community?

Raymond Reyes, Community and Organizational Consultant

There seems to be a "tale of two cities" where there are two distinct groups of people. I would recommend that you revisit and "reclaim" the core principles that you have said were agreed upon by everyone in the community. There is an obvious gap between what has been said and reality. As a community, you need to journey into the gap, or what Plato called "the fertile void." You may want to give serious consideration to identifying and inviting an individual who can guide you through a process to establish a greater level of trust and authenticity and to do some team building.

Communities and other "learning organizations" need to address what I often refer to as the "other three R's" of education: relationship, relevance, and respect. First, address the need for honest and healthy relationships by specifically identifying and working through the trust and power issues. Secondly, make the core principles upon which your community is based more relevant so that the members truly "own" them, whether they are paying students or part of the "centering Team." Lastly, your community needs to establish a social culture that has "wake-up" calls that remind everyone to practice respect. Just as you are practicing respect for our Earth Mother, your community needs to have the daily fellowship behaviors that are likewise respectful.

Asking questions like these will help you maintain flexibility and openness in your perspective:

◆ What is similar and different about this person/belief/method and me/my beliefs/my methods?

◆ What positive and negative effects come from this different way of being/acting/believing? Even if this perspective seems to have negative effects for me, how might it have positive effects for others and, therefore, have value?

◆ What can I learn from this different perspective? Is there anything I could adopt for my own life—something that would help me improve who I am or what I do? Is there anything I wouldn't do myself but that I can still respect and learn from?

Shifting your perspective is at the heart of all successful communication. Each person is unique. Even within a group of people similar to yourself, there will be a great variety of perspectives. Whether you see that each world community has different customs or you understand that a friend can't go out on weekends because he spends that time with his mother, you have increased your wealth of knowledge and shown respect to others. Being able to shift perspective and communicate more effectively may mean the difference between success and failure in today's diverse working world.

W HY PLAN STRATEGICALLY?

If you've ever played a game of chess or checkers, participated in a wrestling or martial arts match, or had a drawn-out argument, you have had experience with strategy. In those situations and many others, you continually have to think through and anticipate the moves the other person is about to make. Often you have to think about several possible options that person could put into play, and you consider what you would counter with should any of those options occur. In competitive situations, you try to outguess the other person with your choices. The extent of your strategic skills can determine whether you will win or lose.

Strategy is the plan of action, the method, the "how" behind any goal you want to achieve. Specifically, strategic planning means having a plan for the future, whether you are looking at the next week, month, year, ten years, or fifty years. It means exploring the future positive and negative effects of the choices you make and actions you take today. You are planning strategically right now just by being in school. You made a decision that the requirements of attending college are a legitimate price to pay for the skills, contacts, and opportunities that will help you in the future. As a student, you are challenging yourself to achieve. You are learning to set goals for the future, analyze what you want in the long term, and prepare for the job market to increase your career options. Being strategic with yourself means challenging yourself as you would challenge a competitor, urging yourself to work toward your goals with conviction and determination.

What are the benefits, or positive effects, of strategic planning?

TERMS

Strategy
A plan of action designed to accomplish a specific goal.

Strategy is an essential skill in the workplace. A food company that wants to develop a successful health-food product needs to examine the anticipated trends in health consciousness. A lawyer needs to think through every aspect of the client's case, anticipating how to respond to any allegation the opposing side will bring up in court. Strategic planning creates a vision into the future that allows the planner to anticipate all kinds of possibilities and, most importantly, to be prepared for them.

Strategic planning powers your short-term and long-term goal setting. Once you have set goals, you need to plan the steps that will help you achieve those goals over time. For example, a strategic thinker who wants to own a home in five years' time might drive a used car and cut out luxuries, put a small amount of money every month into a mutual fund, and keep an eye on current mortgage percentages. In class, a strategic planner will think critically about the material presented, knowing that information is most useful later on if it is clearly understood.

Strategic planning helps you keep up with technology. As technology develops more and more quickly, jobs become obsolete. It's possible to spend years in school training for a career area that will be drying up when you are ready to enter the work force. When you plan strategically, you can take a broader range of courses or choose a major and career that are expanding. This will make it more likely that your skills will be in demand when you graduate.

Effective critical thinking is essential to strategic planning. If you aim for a certain goal, what steps will move you toward that goal? What positive effects do you anticipate these steps will have? How do you evaluate your past experiences with planning and goal setting? What can you learn from similar or different previous experiences in order to take different steps today? Critical thinking runs like a thread through all of your strategic planning.

Here are some tips for becoming a strategic planner:

Develop an appropriate plan. What approach will best achieve your goal? What steps toward your goal will you need to take one year, five years, ten years, or twenty years from now?

Anticipate all possible outcomes of your actions. What are the positive and negative effects that may occur?

Ask the question "how?" How do you achieve your goals? How do you learn effectively and remember what you learn? How do you develop a productive idea on the job? How do you distinguish yourself at school and at work?

Use human resources. Talk to people who are where you want to be, whether professionally or personally. What caused them to get there? Ask them what they believe are the important steps to take, degrees to have, training to experience, knowledge to gain.

Figure 4-3 shows how the seven mind actions form the core of the thinking processes. In each thinking process, you use your creativity to come up with ideas, examples, causes, effects, and solutions. You have a capacity to be creative, whether you are aware of it or not. Open up your

| Figure 4-3 | The wheel of thinking. |

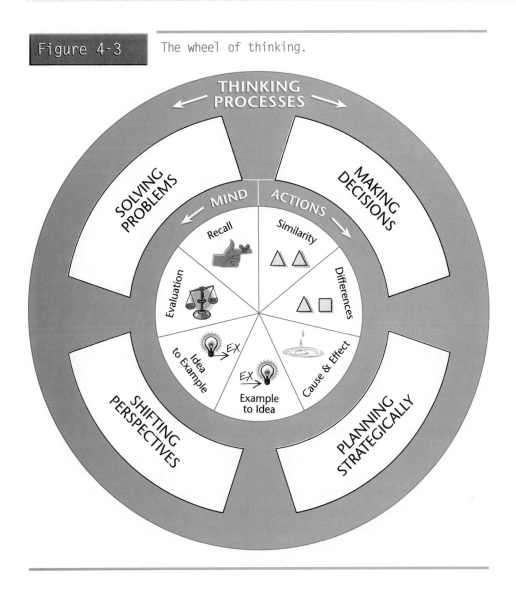

mind and awaken your creativity. It will enhance your critical thinking and make life more enjoyable.

How CAN YOU DEVELOP YOUR CREATIVITY?

Everyone is creative. Although the word "creative" may seem to refer primarily to artists, writers, musicians, and others who work in fields whose creative aspects are in the forefront, creativity comes in many other forms. It is the power to create anything, whether it is a solution, idea, approach, tangible product, work of art, system, program—anything at all. To help you expand your concept of creativity, here are some examples of day-to-day creative thinking:

♦ Figuring out an alternative plan when your baby-sitter unexpectedly cancels on you

♦ Planning how to coordinate your work and class schedules

TERMS

Creativity
The ability to produce something new through imaginative skill.

◆ Talking through a problem with an instructor, and finding a way to understand each other

Creative innovations introduced by all kinds of people continually expand and change the world. Here are some that have had an impact:

◆ Susan B. Anthony and other women fought for and won the right for women to vote.
◆ Art Fry and Spencer Silver invented the Post-it™ note in 1980, enabling people to save paper and protect documents by using removable notes.
◆ Henry Ford introduced the assembly-line method of automobile construction, making cars cheap enough to be available to the average citizen.
◆ Rosa Parks refused to give up her seat on the bus to a white person, thus setting off a chain of events that gave rise to the civil rights movement.
◆ Alicia Diaz, Director of the Center of Hispanic Policy, Research, and Development, developed corporate partnerships and internship programs that have become models for small, efficient government.

Even though these particular innovations had wide-ranging effects, the characteristics of these influential innovators can be found in all people who exercise their creative capabilities.

Characteristics of Creative People

Creative people think in fresh new ways that improve the world and increase productivity, consistently responding to change with new ideas. Roger van Oech, an expert on creativity, highlights this kind of flexibility.[2] "I've found that the hallmark of creative people is their mental flexibility," he says. "Like race-car drivers who shift in and out of different gears depending on where they are on the course, creative people are able to shift in and out of different types of thinking depending on the needs of the situation at hand. . . . they're doggedly persistent in striving to reach their goals."

Creative people combine ideas and information in ways that form completely new solutions, ideas, processes, uses, or products. Children often can tap into this creative freedom more easily than adults. Whether they make up a new game, wear a bowl as a hat, or create forts from chairs and blankets, they create naturally without worrying that their ideas might not be "right." See if you can retrieve some of that creative freedom from your childhood when you use the following creative technique.

Brainstorming Toward a Creative Answer

You are brainstorming when you approach a problem by letting your mind free-associate and come up with as many possible ideas, examples, or solutions as you can, without immediately evaluating them as good or bad. Brainstorming is also referred to as divergent thinking—you start with the issue or problem and then let your mind diverge, or go in as many different directions as it wants, in search of ideas or solutions. You can use brainstorming for problem solving, decision making, preparing to write an essay, or any time you want to open your mind to new possibilities. Here are some rules for successful brainstorming:[3]

Don't evaluate or criticize an idea right away. Write down your ideas so that you remember them. Evaluate later, after you have had a chance to think about them. Try to avoid criticizing other people's ideas as well. Students often become stifled when their ideas are evaluated during brainstorming.

Focus on quantity; don't worry about quality until later. Try to generate as many ideas or examples as you can. The more thoughts you generate, the better the chance that one may be useful. Brainstorming works well in groups. Group members can become inspired by, and make creative use of, one another's ideas.

Let yourself consider wild and wacky ideas. Trust yourself to fall off the edge of tradition when you explore your creativity. Sometimes the craziest ideas end up being the most productive, positive, workable solutions around.

Remember, creativity can be developed if you have the desire and patience. Be gentle with yourself in the process. Most people are harsher with themselves and their ideas than is necessary. Your creative expression will become more free with practice.

> "The world of reality has its limits. The world of imagination is boundless."
>
> JEAN-JACQUES ROUSSEAU

Creativity and Critical Thinking

Creativity and critical thinking work hand in hand. Critical thinking is inherently creative because it requires you to take the information you are given and come up with original ideas or solutions to problems. For example, you can brainstorm to generate possible causes of a certain effect. If the effect you were examining was fatigue in afternoon classes, you might come up with possible causes such as lack of sleep, too much morning caffeine, a diet heavy in carbohydrates, a natural tendency toward low energy at that time, or an instructor who doesn't inspire you. Through your consideration of causes and solutions, you have been thinking both creatively and critically.

Creative thinkers and critical thinkers have similar characteristics—both consider new perspectives, ask questions, don't hesitate to question accepted assumptions and traditions, and persist in the search for answers. Only through thinking creatively and critically can you freely question, brainstorm, and evaluate in order to come up with the most fitting ideas, solutions, decisions, arguments, and plans.

You use critical-thinking mind actions in everything you do both in school and in your daily life. In this chapter and in some of the other study skills chapters, you will notice mind action icons placed where they can help you to label your thinking.

Κρινειν

The word "critical" is derived from the Greek word *krinein*, which means to separate in order to choose or select. To be a mindful and aware critical thinker, you need to be able to separate, evaluate, and select ideas, facts, and thoughts.

Think of this concept as you apply critical thinking to your reading, writing, and interaction with others. Be aware of the information you take in and of your thoughts, and be selective as you process them. Critical thinking gives you the power to make sense of life by deliberately selecting how to respond to the information, people, and events that you encounter.

Success in the Real World

Andy Lauer

Andy Lauer is an actor or, as he terms it, an "artist in the visual media." This is a more fitting title for how Andy lives because he finds his success in how he performs his art. He has  been a key figure in numerous television sitcoms and movies and is currently directing a film. Although he has experienced a great deal of material wealth, this is not how he judges his success.

Andy received a bachelor's degree in journalism and advertising but had known that he wanted to be an actor since he was nine years old. Andy saw the value in education, though, and decided to complete his degree while also pursuing his acting career. His education has made him a more well-rounded person and helped him achieve success in his career. The business skills he learned in school he finds invaluable today. He manages his time and finances better. He sets his goals high and then begins the process of accomplishing them. And, he understands people better—their motivations and their challenges. In his field, Andy works with different types of people who have different ideologies. Understanding people, and accepting the differences, has helped him get to where he is now.

College life set the tone for the rest of Andy's life. He still cannot get away from the semester system. He finds that it is a healthy system to be in, though. He works hard, studies, crams for deadlines, takes summer breaks, goes to the library, and explores new environments. Andy believes that his success has come about largely because he knows the value of balances. Although he works incredibly hard and has several projects going on at the same time, he makes time for fun and exploration. This becomes more difficult to do the older people get, he thinks, perhaps because we have to give up more to do it, but it is so necessary. The time off rejuvenates him and is crucial for continued success.

Success to Andy is doing what you love. He has a passion for acting and believes that everyone should find something to do that they are passionate about. Even when projects don't work out well, he finds that everything he does is a great experience. By being passionate about his career and balanced in his life, he finds success even in "failures" because he has learned something new. Nothing lasts forever, and both successes and failures are fleeting.

Andy advises students to find their passion and to keep a balanced life. He believes that we all need to be kind and considerate to everyone we interact with. Doing so will help each of us live more successful lives. He believes that stability is a trap and every once in a while we need to walk away from our security blanket, no matter what our age. Andy practices what he preaches. He recently walked away from a very lucrative acting job on a sitcom because he felt he was going through the motions and not living up to his potential. He has since been concentrating on finding additional work that will challenge him and just received a movie offer, which he believes will do just that. By taking stock of yourself every so often, Andy thinks you will once again see talents and skills that may have been hidden.

Chapter 4   Applications

Name _____ Date _____

KEY INTO YOUR LIFE
Opportunities to Apply What You Learn

4.1   *Making a Decision*

In this series of exercises you will make a personal decision using the seven mind actions and the decision-making steps described in this chapter. Before you proceed through each of the steps, write here an important personal decision you have to make. Choose a decision that you want to act on and will be able to address soon.

_____

_____

_____

_____

_____

Step 1 Name Your Goal

Be specific: What goal, or desired effects, do you seek from this decision? For example, if your decision is a choice between two jobs, the effects you want might be financial security, convenience, experience, or anything else that is a priority to you. It could also be a combination of these effects. Write down the desired effects that together make up your goal. Note priorities by numbering the effects in order of importance.

_____

_____

_____

_____

_____

Step 2 Establish Needs

Who and what will be affected by your decision? If you are deciding how to finance your education and you have a family to support, you must take into consideration their financial needs as well as your own when exploring options.

List here the people/things/situations that may be affected by your decision and indicate how your decision will affect them.

_____

_____

_____

_____

_____

Step 3 Check Out Your Options

Look at all the options you can imagine. Consider options even if they seem impossible or unlikely—you can evaluate them later. Some decisions only have two options (to move to a new apartment or not, to get a new roommate or not); others have a wider selection of choices. For example, if you are a full-time student and the parent of a child, you must coordinate your class schedule with the child's needs. Options could be the following: (1) put the child in day care, (2) ask a relative to care for the child, (3) hire a full-time nanny, or (4) arrange your class schedule so that you can balance the duties with another parent.

First, list the possible options for your own personal decision. Then evaluate the good and bad effects of each.

Option 1 _____

Positive effects _____

Negative effects _____

Option 2 _____

Positive effects _____

Negative effects _____

Option 3 _____

Positive effects _____

Negative effects _____

Option 4 _____

Positive effects _____

Negative effects _____

Have you or someone else ever made a decision similar to the one you are about to make? What can you learn from that decision that may help you?

_____

_____

_____

_____

_____

Step 4 Make Your Decision and Pursue It to the Goal

Taking your entire analysis into account, decide what to do. Write your decision here.

EX →

_____

_____

_____

_____

Next is perhaps the most important step: Act on your decision.

Step 5 Evaluate the Result

After you have acted on your decision, evaluate how everything turned out. Did you achieve the effects you wanted to achieve? What were the effects on you? On others? On the situation? To what extent were they positive, negative, or some of both?

List four effects here. Name each effect, circle *Positive* or *Negative*, and explain that evaluation.

Effect _____

      Positive   *Negative*

Why? _____

Effect _____

      Positive   *Negative*

Why? _____

Effect _____

      Positive   *Negative*

Why? _____

Effect _____

      Positive   *Negative*

Why? _____

Final evaluation: Write one statement in reaction to the decision you made. Indicate whether you feel the decision was useful or not useful, and why. Indicate any adjustments that could have made the effects of your decision more positive.

_____

_____

_____

_____

Brainstorming on the Idea Wheel

Your creative mind can solve problems when you least expect it. Many people report having sudden ideas while exercising, driving, showering, upon waking, or even when dreaming. When the pressure is off, the mind is often more free to roam through uncharted territory and bring back treasures.

To make the most of this mind-float, grab ideas right when they surface. If you don't, they roll back into your subconscious as if on a wheel. Since you never know how big the wheel is, you can't be sure when that particular idea will roll to the top again. That's one of the reasons why writers carry notebooks—they need to grab thoughts when they come to the top of the wheel.

Name a problem, large or small, to which you haven't yet found a satisfactory solution. Brainstorm without the time limit. Be on the lookout for ideas, causes, effects, solutions, or similar problems coming to the top of your wheel. The minute it happens, grab this book and write your idea next to the problem. Take a look at your ideas later and see how your creative mind may have pointed you toward some original and workable solutions. You may want to keep a book by your bed to catch ideas that pop up before, during, or after sleep.

Problem:

Ideas:

_____

_____

_____

_____

_____

_____

_____

_____

Team-Building Exercise

As a class, brainstorm a list of problems in your lives. Write the problems on the board or on a large piece of paper attached to an easel. Include any problems you feel comfortable discussing with others. Such problems may be in the categories of schoolwork, relationships, job stress, discrimination, parenting, housing, procrastination, and others. Divide into groups of two to four, with each group choosing or being assigned one problem to work on. Use the empty problem-solving flowchart on the next page to fill in your work.

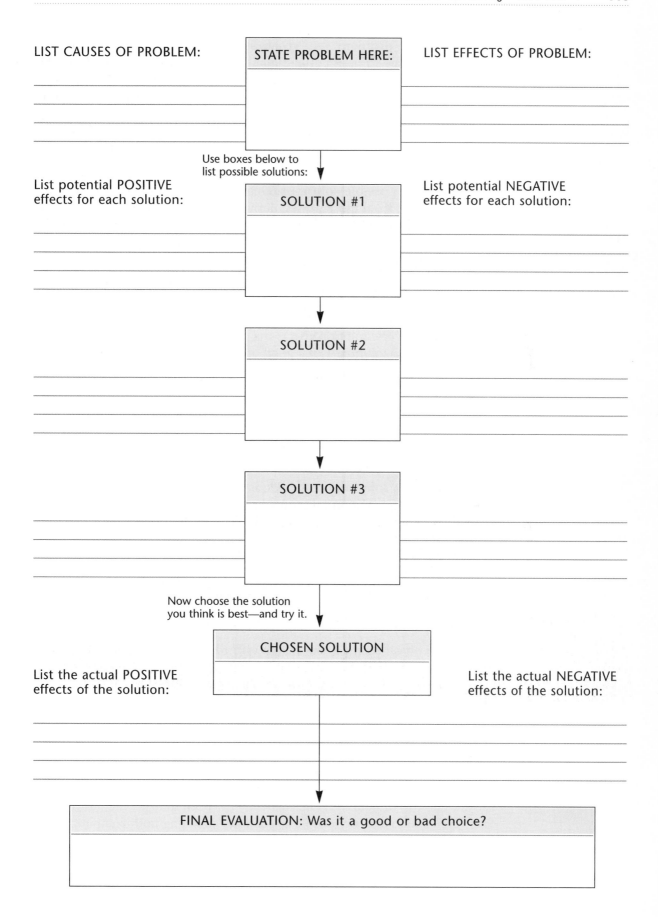

LIST CAUSES OF PROBLEM:

STATE PROBLEM HERE:

LIST EFFECTS OF PROBLEM:

Use boxes below to
list possible solutions:

List potential POSITIVE
effects for each solution:

SOLUTION #1

List potential NEGATIVE
effects for each solution:

SOLUTION #2

SOLUTION #3

Now choose the solution
you think is best—and try it.

CHOSEN SOLUTION

List the actual POSITIVE
effects of the solution:

List the actual NEGATIVE
effects of the solution:

FINAL EVALUATION: Was it a good or bad choice?

1. **Identify the problem.** As a group, state your problem specifically, without causes ("I'm not attending all of my classes" is better than "lack of motivation"). Then, look at the causes and effects that surround it. Record the effects that the problem has on your lives. List what causes the problem. Remember to look for "hidden" causes (you may perceive that traffic makes you late to school, but the hidden cause might be that you don't get up early enough to have adequate commuting time in the morning).

2. **Brainstorm possible solutions.** Determine the most likely causes of the problem; from those causes, derive possible solutions. Record all the ideas that group members offer. After ten minutes or so, each group member should choose one possible solution to explore independently.

3. **Explore each solution.** In thinking independently through the assigned solution, each group member should (a) weigh the positive and negative effects, (b) consider similar problems, (c) determine whether the problem requires a different strategy from other problems like it, and (d) describe how the solution affects the causes of the problem. Evaluate your assigned solution. Is it a good one? Will it work?

4. **Choose your top solution(s).** Come together again as a group. Take turns sharing your observations and recommendations; then take a vote: Which solution is the best? You may have a tie or may combine two different solutions. Either way is fine. Different solutions suit different people and situations. Although it's not always possible to reach agreement, try to find the solution that works for most of the group.

5. **Evaluate the solution you decide is best.** When you decide on your top solution or solutions, discuss what would happen if you went through with it. What do you predict would be the positive and negative effects of this solution? Would it turn out to be a truly good solution for everyone?

Case Studies

Navigating the Superhighway

America Online

The Internet has become a "superhighway" for millions of people who "surf the Web" looking for information on current events, entertainment news, and business updates. The Internet has also become a place to conduct business. Products and services are sold online, similar to ordering from a giant catalog. Accessing information has gotten easier in the past few years for the average person. Web sites are common places to find facts and figures about companies and special-interest topics. Email is becoming a global form of communication for business, as well as for pleasure, linking people around the world. With the tremendous amount of information available, the question becomes how to organize it. The challenge has been to make the information easily available to as many people as possible, including both computer savvy groups and new users.

Enter America Online, also known as AOL. AOL provides Internet access and email service but is also set up as its own type of "community." When you sign on to AOL, you get a number of menus, including News, Sports,

Entertainment, Personal Finance, Travel, Shopping, and Games. Steve Case, the CEO of AOL, has worked for the last decade to build an accessible network system for the average computer user to browse the Internet and communicate. His vision was to bring the computer world, with its overwhelming amount of information, to the general population. Before AOL, much of the Internet was complicated and unknown to most people, other than "technology junkies." Steve Case wanted to make the services available to everyone and organize the information in such a way that people would want to use the system.

AOL has been around for a while, but the company is seeing a boom in business recently, due to wise business decisions and an understanding of the market and its consumers. The number of Internet users is growing, which is good news for AOL. The Internet is increasingly being used in schools to educate children. Middle-aged working people and the older generation are finding the new technology exciting, informative, and useful.

AOL went public in 1992 with an email service, connection to the World Wide Web, and chat rooms for live communication via computer. The marketing staff at AOL devised a hard-core marketing ploy to let the general public know what AOL had to offer and let the public try the service free for a limited time. People received mailings from AOL that consisted of software to set up the online service in a quick and easy manner. This ploy was immensely successful—the membership on AOL from 155,000 in 1992 to 4.6 million at the beginning of 1996. The Internet and AOL were intertwined, and the public found it a great forum to discover the Internet and online services.

The increase in membership also brought with it the need for a lot of expansion in AOL's networking system. AOL was not equipped to handle this rapid growth and found it was struggling to make profits as well as keep up with the demands of its customers. Systems were overloaded and customers were not getting the technical support they needed. But, even with this, people continued to sign on and become part of the AOL family.

Steve Case knew that he needed to get control of his organization, including his employees, his product, and the marketing. The company was overspending and not seeing the profits that it expected. The competition in online service is intense and volatile. Revenue needed to come from another source other than memberships. As he struggled to find help with the business aspect of the company, he realized that he had impacted American life in a significant way—AOL (and the Internet) was a part of many people's everyday life. Its popularity was the reason for the membership increase and, with it, the distress of the cusomters due to the lack of access. He needed to improve his service to keep the customers content. But the impact that his online service had made was impressive.

The next phase of the organization was intense cost-cutting. This helped to turn things around for AOL, but the organization needed to do more than cut costs. It needed sponsors—companies that would buy portions or rights to AOL to "set up shop." Many deals were made that gave the companies exclusive access within AOL to offer their services. AOL had a membership that reached far and wide in the United States; many companies, like Tel-Save, wanted to reach out to the millions of users of AOL. Tel-Save was the first to make a deal with AOL to get exclusive access to its users over a three-year period for $100 million. Deals such as these followed from many small and large companies—CUC International (discount shopping), Preview Travel, N2K (music retailer), and Barnes & Noble, to name a few. This has seemingly not only been good for AOL, but also for the companies—N2K sold 750 copies of the *Titanic* CD in twenty minutes with an online advertisement on AOL.

Suddenly, AOL could invest in the access networks to improve the speed of the online service as well as the technical support for the program. It bought out the competition of CompuServe and Prodigy. And yet, Steve Case is not fully satisfied with the boom that AOL is seeing. He knows that AOL will not remain on top unless it simplifies the system even more—he calls AOL complicated even now, while hard-core computer users call it the "Internet on training-wheels."

1. If a company designs a popular product, what are some of the problems that it might encounter?

2. Why do you think AOL's marketing ploy of sending out free software was successful?

3. Whom do you think AOL considers its main "target" customers? What are their characteristics?

4. Why was N2K's sale of the *Titanic* CD on AOL so successful?

Internet Exercise

Now that you've heard about America Online, access this for yourself and determine what you think. First access the Internet, and if you haven't used America Online, type in:

www.aol.com

1. What do you like about the way the site is set up?

_____

_____

_____

2. What could be improved?

_____

_____

_____

3. Find the category **Business and Careers,** and click on this. Briefly report on one of the articles you find interesting.

_____

_____

_____

_____

_____

Name _____   Date _____

Journal

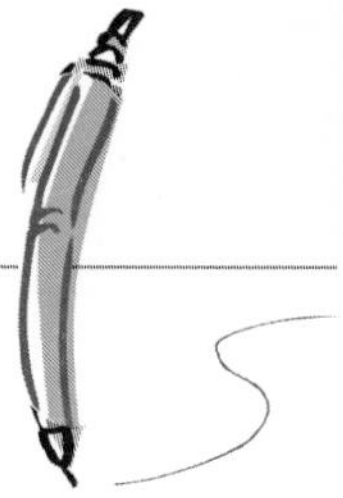

Journal

Name _____ Date _____

Reading and Studying

Maximizing Written Resources

The society we live in revolves around the written word. As the *Condition of Education 1996* report states, "In recent years, literacy has been viewed as one of the fundamental tools necessary for successful economic performance in industrialized societies. Literacy is no longer defined merely as a basic threshold of reading ability, but rather as the ability to understand and use printed information in daily activities, at home, at work, and in the community."[1]

If you read thoroughly and understand what you read, and if you achieve your study goals, you can improve your capacity to learn and understand. In this chapter, you will learn how you can overcome barriers to successful reading and benefit from defining a purpose each time you read. You will explore the PQ3R study technique and see how critical reading can help you maximize your understanding of any text. Finally, the chapter will provide an overview of your library's resources.

In this chapter, you will explore answers to the following questions:

◆ What are some challenges of reading?

◆ Why define your purpose for reading?

◆ How can PQ3R help you study reading materials?

◆ How can you read critically?

◆ What does your library offer?

WHAT ARE SOME CHALLENGES OF READING?

Whatever your skill level, you will encounter challenges that make reading more difficult, such as an excess of reading assignments, difficult texts, distractions, a lack of speed and comprehension, and insufficient vocabulary. Following are some ideas about how to meet these challenges. Note that if you have a reading disability, if English is not your primary language, or if you have limited reading skills, you may need additional support and guidance. Most colleges provide services for students through a reading center or tutoring program. Take the initiative to seek help if you need it. Many accomplished learners have benefited from help in specific areas.

Dealing With Reading Overload

Reading overload is part of almost every college experience. On a typical day, you may be faced with reading assignments that look like this:

◆ An entire textbook chapter on torts (business law)

◆ An original research study on the stages of sleep (psychology)

◆ Pages 1–50 in Arthur Miller's play *Death of a Salesman* (American literature)

Reading all this and more leaves little time for anything else unless you read selectively and skillfully. You can't control your reading load. You can, however, improve your reading skills. The material in this chapter will present techniques that can help you read and study as efficiently as you possibly can, while still having time left over for other things.

Working Through Difficult Texts

While many textbooks are useful teaching tools, some can be poorly written and organized. Students using texts that aren't well written may blame themselves for the difficulty they're experiencing. Because texts are often written with the purpose of challenging the intellect, even well-written and organized texts may be difficult and dense to read. Generally, the further you advance in your education, the more complex your required reading is likely to be. For example, your sociology professor may assign a chapter on the dynamics of social groups, including those of dyads and triads. When is the last time you heard the terms *dyads* and *triads* in normal conversation? You may feel at times as though you are reading a foreign language as you encounter new concepts, words, and terms.

Assignments can also be difficult when the required reading is from primary sources rather than from texts. *Primary sources* are original documents rather than another writer's interpretation of these documents. They include:

- ◆ Historical documents
- ◆ Works of literature (novels, poems, and plays)
- ◆ Business reports
- ◆ Journal articles

The academic writing found in journal articles and business reports is different from other kinds of writing. Some academic writers assume that readers understand sophisticated concepts. They may not define basic terms, provide background information, or supply a wealth of examples to support their ideas. As a result, concepts may be difficult to understand.

Making your way through poorly written or difficult reading material is hard work that can be accomplished through focus, motivation, commitment, and skill. The following strategies may help.

Approach your reading assignments head-on. Be careful not to prejudge them as impossible or boring before you even start to read.

Accept the fact that some texts may require some extra work and concentration. Set a goal to make your way through the material and learn, whatever it takes.

When a primary source discusses difficult concepts that it does not explain, put in some extra work to define such concepts on your own. Ask your instructor or other students for help. Consult reference materials in that particular subject area, other class materials, dictionaries, and encyclopedias. You may want to make this process more convenient by creating your own mini-library at home. Collect reference materials that you use often, such as a dictionary, a thesaurus, a writer's style handbook, and maybe an atlas or computer manual. You may also benefit from owning reference materials in your particular areas of study. "If you find yourself going to the library to look up the same reference again and again, consider purchasing that book for your personal or office library," advises library expert Sherwood Harris.[2]

"No barrier of the senses shuts me out from the sweet, gracious discourse of my book friends. They talk to me without embarrassment or awkwardness."
HELEN KELLER

Look for order and meaning in seemingly chaotic reading materials. The information you will find in this chapter on the PQ3R reading technique and on critical reading will help you discover patterns and achieve a greater depth of understanding. Finding order within chaos is an important skill, not just in the mastery of reading but also in life. This skill can give you power by helping you "read" (think through) work dilemmas, personal problems, and educational situations.

REAL WORLD PERSPECTIVE

How can I cope with a learning disability?

Clacy Albert, Washington State University, Pullman, Washington

All my life I've felt different. I just couldn't seem to learn the way other kids did. I felt stupid and afraid that other people would think I couldn't do anything right. I wouldn't raise my hand in class because I was afraid of being laughed at. I wouldn't volunteer for games because I was afraid I'd let my team down. Study groups were impossible for me. I didn't want anyone to know that I was different. Because of this, my self-esteem really suffered. I became very quiet.

It wasn't until I was a sophomore in high school that a teacher recognized something was wrong with the way I learned. It was my math teacher who saw that I couldn't recognize certain patterns. I would see things in reverse or not be able to recognize a pattern at all. He sat down with my parents and helped them understand something was wrong. Unfortunately, the school I attended didn't have any testing for learning disabilities, so I let it go until I was in college. When I enrolled at WSU, they told us about the learning disability resource center. My mom suggested I finally get the testing I needed. I'm glad I did because now I know that I have dyslexia and need special assistance to handle my studies. I wish there was mandatory testing for this disability in grade school. If there had been, I wouldn't have suffered so deeply all these years. What suggestions do you have for helping me cope with this disability?

Edith Hall, Senior Sales Representative, Prentice Hall

I have a different disability but one that causes similar problems. I have attention deficit hyperactivity disorder, and the fact that it was undiagnosed and untreated for many years has caused lots of problems in my life. It wasn't until I was six years out of college that I was diagnosed ADHD. And the great thing about it is I don't feel crazy anymore. Now I know why I can't sit still for long periods and why I can't complete large and/or long projects like other non-ADHD people can.

I think acknowledging that I had a disorder and then accepting it were the biggest steps to coping and living with this disorder. The other thing I have done is to get educated. I have read almost everything I can get my hands on. I am also involved in a support group. Having other people I can talk with about how my brain affects my behavior and my life truly is one of the best coping strategies I know.

Having a disability or disorder is not a bad thing. Ennis Cosby, slain son of comedian Bill Cosby, said of his dyslexia, "The day I found out I had dyslexia was the best day of my life." Finding out he had dyslexia relieved him of the belief that he was dumb or stupid or slow. For me, like Ennis Cosby, finding out I had ADHD was a great day in my life because I now had tools and help to be different . . . and I no longer felt alone.

Managing Distractions

With so much happening around you, it's often hard to keep your mind on what you are reading. Distractions take many forms. Some are external: the sound of a telephone, a friend who sits next to you at lunch and wants to talk, a young child who asks for help with homework. Other distractions come from within. As you try to study, you may be thinking about your parent's health, an argument you had with a friend or partner, a paper due in art history, or a site on the Internet that you want to visit.

Identify the Distraction and Choose a Suitable Action

Pinpoint what's distracting you before you decide what kind of action to take. If the distraction is *external* and *out of your control*, such as construction outside your building or a noisy group in the library, try to move away from it. If the distraction is *external* but *within your control*, such as the television, telephone, or children, take action. For example, if the television or phone is a problem, turn off the TV or unplug the phone for an hour.

If the distraction is *internal*, there are a few strategies to try that may help you clear your mind. You may want to take a break from your studying and tend to one of the issues that you are worrying about. Physical exercise may relax you and bring back your ability to focus. For some people, studying while listening to music helps to quiet a busy mind. For others, silence may do the trick. If you need silence to read or study and cannot find a truly quiet environment, consider purchasing sound-muffling headphones or even earplugs.

Find the Best Place and Time to Read

Any reader needs focus and discipline in order to concentrate on the material. Finding a place and time that minimize outside distractions will help you achieve that focus. Here are some suggestions:

Read alone unless you are working with other readers. Family members, friends, or others who are not in a study mode may interrupt your concentration. If you prefer to read alone, establish a relatively interruption-proof place and time, such as an out-of-the-way spot at the library or an after-class hour in an empty classroom. If you study at home and live with other people, you may want to place a "Quiet" sign on the door. Some students benefit from reading with one or more other students. If this helps you, plan to schedule a group reading meeting where you read sections of the assigned material and then break to discuss them.

Find a comfortable location. Many students study in the library on a hard-backed chair. Others prefer a library easy chair, a chair in their room, or even the floor. The spot you choose should be comfortable enough for hours of reading, but not so comfortable that you fall asleep. Also, make sure that you have adequate lighting and aren't too hot or too cold.

Choose a regular reading place and time. Choose a spot or two you like and return to them often. Also, choose a time when your mind is alert and focused. Some students prefer to read just before or after the class for which the reading is assigned. Eventually, you will associate preferred places and times with focused reading.

If it helps you concentrate, listen to soothing background music. The right music can drown out background noises and relax you. However, the wrong music can make it impossible to concentrate; for some people, silence is better. Experiment to learn what you prefer; if music helps, stick with the type that works best. A personal headset makes listening possible no matter where you are.

Turn off the television. For most people, reading and TV don't mix.

Building Comprehension and Speed

Most students lead busy lives, carrying heavy academic loads while perhaps working a job or even caring for a family. It's difficult to make time to study at all, let alone handle the enormous reading assignments for your different classes. Increasing your reading comprehension and speed will save you valuable time and effort.

Rapid reading won't do you any good if you can't remember the material or answer questions about it. However, reading too slowly can be equally inefficient because it often eats up valuable study time and gives your mind space to wander. Your goal is to read for maximum speed *and* comprehension. Focus on comprehension first because greater comprehension is the primary goal and also promotes greater speed.

Methods for Increasing Reading Comprehension

Following are some specific strategies for increasing your understanding of what you read:

Continually build your knowledge through reading and studying. More than any other factor, what you already know before you read a passage will determine your ability to understand and remember important ideas. Previous knowledge, including vocabulary, facts, and ideas, gives you a context for what you read.

TERMS

Context
Written or spoken knowledge that can help to illuminate the meaning of a word or passage.

Establish your purpose for reading. When you establish what you want to get out of your reading, you will be able to determine what level of understanding you need to reach and, therefore, what you need to focus on.

Remove the barriers of negative self-talk. Instead of telling yourself that you cannot understand, think positively. Tell yourself: *I can learn this material. I am a good reader.*

Think critically. Ask yourself questions. Do you understand the sentence, paragraph, or chapter you just read? Are ideas and supporting examples clear to you? Could you clearly explain what you just read to someone else?

Methods for Increasing Reading Speed

The following suggestions will help increase your reading speed:

- Try to read groups of words rather than single words.
- Avoid pointing your finger to guide your reading, since this will slow your pace.

◆ Try swinging your eyes from side to side as you read a passage, instead of stopping at various points to read individual words.

◆ When reading narrow columns, focus your eyes in the middle of the column and read down the page. With practice, you'll be able to read the entire column width.

◆ Avoid vocalization when reading.

◆ Avoid thinking each word to yourself as you read it, a practice known as *subvocalization.* Subvocalization is one of the primary causes of slow reading speed.

TERMS

Vocalization
The practice of speaking the words and/or moving your lips while reading.

Facing the challenges of reading is only the first step. The next important step is to examine why you are reading any given piece of material.

WHY DEFINE YOUR PURPOSE FOR READING?

As with all other aspects of your education, asking important questions will enable you to make the most of your efforts. When you define your purpose, you ask yourself *why* you are reading a particular piece of material. One way to do this is by completing this sentence: "In reading this material, I intend to define/learn/answer/achieve . . ." With a clear purpose in mind, you can decide how much time and what kind of effort to expend on various reading assignments. Nearly 375 years ago, Francis Bacon, the English philosopher, recognized that

> Some books are to be tasted, others to be swallowed, and some few to be chewed and digested; that is, some books are to be read only in parts, others to be read but not curiously; and some few to be read wholly, and with diligence and attention.

Achieving your reading purpose requires adapting to different types of reading materials. Being a flexible reader—adjusting your reading strategies and pace—will help you to adapt successfully.

Purpose Determines Reading Strategy

With purpose comes direction; with direction comes a strategy for reading. Following are four reading purposes, examined briefly. You may have one or more for each piece of reading material you approach.

Purpose 1: Read to Evaluate Critically

Critical evaluation involves approaching the material with an open mind, examining causes and effects, evaluating ideas, and asking questions that test the strength of the writer's argument and that try to identify assumptions. Critical reading is essential for you to demonstrate an understanding of material that goes beyond basic recall of information. You will read more about critical reading later in the chapter.

Purpose 2: Read for Comprehension

Much of the studying you do involves reading for the purpose of comprehending the material. The two main components of comprehension are *general ideas* and *specific facts/examples*. These components depend on one another. Facts and examples help to explain or support ideas, and ideas provide a framework that helps the reader to remember facts and examples.

General ideas. General-idea reading is rapid reading that seeks an overview of the material. You may skip entire sections as you focus on headings, subheadings, and summary statements in search of general ideas.

"In books, I could travel anywhere, be anybody, understand worlds long past and imaginary colonies of the future."

RITA DOVE

Specific facts/examples. At times, readers may focus on locating specific pieces of information—for example, the stages of intellectual development in young children. Often, a reader may search for examples that support or explain more general ideas—for example, the causes of economic recession. Because you know exactly what you are looking for, you can skim the material at a rapid rate. Reading your texts for specific information may help before taking a test.

Purpose 3: Read for Practical Application

A third purpose for reading is to gather usable information that you can apply toward a specific goal. When you read a computer software manual, an instruction sheet for assembling a gas grill, or a cookbook recipe, your goal is to learn how to do something. Reading and action usually go hand in hand.

Purpose 4: Read for Pleasure

Some materials you read for entertainment, such as *Sports Illustrated* magazine or the latest John Grisham courtroom thriller. Entertaining reading may also go beyond materials that seem obviously designed to entertain. Whereas some people may read a Jane Austen novel for comprehension, as in a class assignment, others may read Austen books for pleasure.

Purpose Determines Pace

George M. Usova, Senior Education Specialist and Graduate Professor at Johns Hopkins University, explains: "Good readers are flexible readers. They read at a variety of rates and adapt them to the reading *purpose* at hand, the *difficulty* of the material, and their *familiarity* with the subject area."[3] As Table 5-1 shows, good readers link the pace of reading to their reading purpose.

So far, this chapter has focused on reading. Recognizing obstacles to effective reading and defining the various purposes for reading lay the groundwork for effective *studying*—the process of mastering the concepts and skills contained in your texts.

TYPE OF MATERIAL	READING PURPOSE	PACE
Academic readings ◆ Textbooks ◆ Original sources ◆ Articles from scholarly journals ◆ Online publications for academic readers ◆ Lab reports ◆ Required fiction	◆ Critical analysis ◆ Overall mastery ◆ Preparation for tests	◆ Slow, especially if the material is new and unfamiliar
Manuals ◆ Instructions ◆ Recipes	◆ Practical application	◆ Slow to medium
Journalism and nonfiction for the general reader ◆ Nonfiction books ◆ Newspapers ◆ Magazines ◆ Online publications for the general public	◆ Understanding of general ideas, key concepts, and specific facts for personal understanding and/or practical application	◆ Medium to fast
Nonrequired ◆ Fiction	◆ Understanding of general ideas, key concepts, and specific facts for enjoyment	◆ Variable, but tending toward the faster speeds

Table 5-1

Linking purpose to pace.

Source: Adapted from Nicholas Reid Schaffzin, *The Princeton Review Reading Smart*. New York: Random House, 1996, p. 15.

HOW CAN PQ3R HELP YOU STUDY READING MATERIALS?

When you study, you take ownership of the material you read. You learn it well enough to apply it to what you do. For example, by the time students studying to be computer-hardware technicians complete their course work, they should be able to assemble various machines and analyze hardware problems that lead to malfunctions.

Studying also gives you mastery over *concepts*. For example, a dental hygiene student learns the causes of gum disease, a biology student learns what happens during photosynthesis, and a business student learns about marketing research.

This section will focus on a technique that will help you learn and study more effectively as you read your college textbooks.

Preview-Question-Read-Recite-Review (PQ3R)

PQ3R is a technique that will help you grasp ideas quickly, remember more, and review effectively and efficiently for tests. The symbols P-Q-3-R stand for *preview, question, read, recite,* and *review*—all steps in the studying process. Developed more than fifty-five years ago by Francis Robinson, the technique is still being used today because it works.[4] It is particularly helpful for studying texts. When reading literature, read the work once from beginning to end to appreciate the story and language. Then, reread it using PQ3R to master the material.

Moving through the stages of PQ3R requires that you know how to skim and scan. Skimming involves rapid reading of various chapter elements, including introductions, conclusions, and summaries; the first and last lines of paragraphs; boldface or italicized terms; pictures, charts, and diagrams. In contrast, scanning involves the careful search for specific facts and examples. You will probably use scanning during the *review* phase of PQ3R when you need to locate and remind yourself of particular information. In a chemistry text, for example, you may scan for examples of how to apply a particular formula.

TERMS

Skimming
Rapid, superficial reading of material that involves glancing through to determine central ideas and main elements.

TERMS

Scanning
Reading material in an investigative way, searching for specific information.

Preview

The best way to ruin a "whodunit" novel is to flip through the pages to find out how everything turned out. However, when reading textbooks, previewing can help you learn and is encouraged. *Previewing* refers to the process of surveying, or prereading, a book before you actually study it. Most textbooks include devices that give students an overview of the text as a whole as well as of the contents of individual chapters. As you look at Figure 5-1, think about how many of these devices you already use.

Question

Your next step is to examine the chapter headings and, on your own paper, write questions linked to those headings. These questions will focus your attention and increase your interest, helping you relate new ideas to what you already know and building your comprehension. You can take questions from the textbook or from your lecture notes, or come up with them on your own when you preview, based on what ideas you think are most important.

Here is how this technique works. In Figure 5.2, the column on the left contains primary- and secondary-level headings from a section of *Business,* an introductory text by Ricky W. Griffin and Ronald J. Ebert. The column on the right rephrases these headings in question form.

There is no "correct" set of questions. Given the same headings, you would create your own particular set of questions. The more useful kinds of questions are ones that engage the critical-thinking mind actions and processes found in Chapter 4.

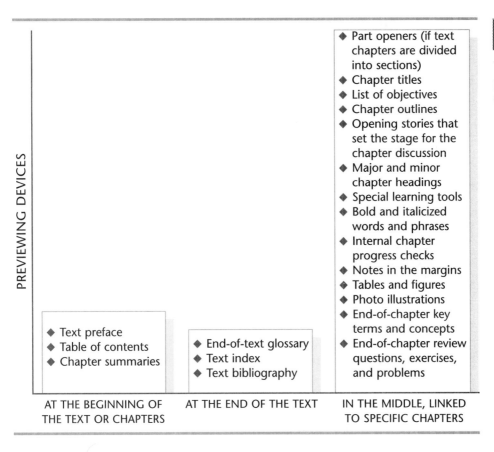

Figure 5-1

Text and chapter previewing devices.

PREVIEWING DEVICES		
		◆ Part openers (if text chapters are divided into sections) ◆ Chapter titles ◆ List of objectives ◆ Chapter outlines ◆ Opening stories that set the stage for the chapter discussion ◆ Major and minor chapter headings ◆ Special learning tools ◆ Bold and italicized words and phrases ◆ Internal chapter progress checks ◆ Notes in the margins ◆ Tables and figures ◆ Photo illustrations ◆ End-of-chapter key terms and concepts
◆ Text preface ◆ Table of contents ◆ Chapter summaries	◆ End-of-text glossary ◆ Text index ◆ Text bibliography	◆ End-of-chapter review questions, exercises, and problems
AT THE BEGINNING OF THE TEXT OR CHAPTERS	AT THE END OF THE TEXT	IN THE MIDDLE, LINKED TO SPECIFIC CHAPTERS

Figure 5-2

Creating questions.

I. THE CONSUMER BUYING PROCESS	I. WHAT IS THE CONSUMER BUYING PROCESS?
A. Problem/Need Recognition	A. Why must consumers first recognize a problem or need before they buy a product?
B. Information Seeking	B. What is information seeking and who answers consumers' questions?
C. Evaluation of Alternatives	C. How do consumers evaluate different products to narrow their choices?
D. Purchase Decision	D. Are purchasing decisions simple or complex?
E. Postpurchase Evaluations	E. What happens after the sale?

Read

Your questions give you a starting point for *reading*, the first R in PQ3R. Read the material with the purpose of answering each question you raised. Pay special attention to the first and last lines of every paragraph, which should tell you what the paragraph is about. As you read, record key words, phrases, and concepts in your notebook. Some students divide the notebook into two columns, writing questions on the left and answers on the right. This method, known as the Cornell note-taking system, is described in more detail in Chapter 6.

If you own the textbook, marking it up—in whatever ways you prefer—is a must. The notations that you make will help you to interact with the material and make sense of it. You may want to write notes in the margins, circle key ideas, or highlight key sections. Some people prefer to underline, although underlining adds more ink to the lines of text and may overwhelm your eye. Although writing in a textbook makes it difficult to sell it back to the bookstore, the increased depth of understanding you can gain is worth the investment.

Highlighting may help you pinpoint material to review before an exam. Here are some additional tips on highlighting:

Get in the habit of marking the text *after* you read the material. If you do it while you are reading, you may wind up marking less important passages.

Highlight key terms and concepts. Mark the examples that explain and support important ideas. You might try highlighting ideas in one color and examples in another.

Highlight figures and tables. They are especially important if they summarize text concepts.

Avoid overmarking. A phrase or two is enough in most paragraphs. Set off long passages with brackets rather than marking every line.

Write notes in the margins with a pen or pencil. Comments like "main point" and "important definition" will help you find key sections later on.

Be careful not to mistake highlighting for learning. You will not necessarily learn what you highlight unless you review it carefully. You may benefit from writing the important information you have highlighted into your lecture notes.

One final step in the reading phase is to divide your reading into digestible segments. Many students read from one topic heading to the next, then stop. Pace your reading so that you understand as you go. If you find you are losing the thread of the ideas you are reading, you may want to try smaller segments, or you may need to take a break and come back to it later.

Recite

Once you finish reading a topic, stop and answer the questions you raised about it in the Q stage of PQ3R. You may decide to recite each answer aloud, silently speak the answers to yourself, tell the answers to another person as though you were teaching him or her, or write your ideas and answers in brief notes. Writing is often the most effective way to solidify what you have read. Use whatever techniques best suit your learning-style profile (see Chapter 2).

After you finish one section, move on to the next. Then repeat the question-read-recite cycle until you complete the entire chapter. If during this process you find yourself fumbling for thoughts, it means that you do not yet "own" the ideas. Reread the section that's giving you trouble until you master its contents. Understanding each section as you go is crucial because the material in one section often forms a foundation for the next.

Review

Review soon after you finish a chapter. Here are some techniques for reviewing:

◆ Skim and reread your notes. Then try summarizing them from memory.

◆ Answer the text's end-of-chapter review, discussion, and application questions.

◆ Quiz yourself, using the questions you raised in the *Q* stage. If you can't answer one of your own or one of the text's questions, go back and scan the material for answers.

◆ Review and summarize in writing the sections and phrases you have highlighted.

◆ Create a chapter outline in standard outline form or think-link form.

◆ Reread the preface, headings, tables, and summary.

◆ Recite important concepts to yourself, or record important information on a cassette tape and play it on your car's tape deck or your Walkman.

◆ Make flash cards that have an idea or word on one side and examples, a definition, or other related information on the other. Test yourself.

◆ Think critically: Break ideas down into examples, consider similar or different concepts, recall important terms, evaluate ideas, and explore causes and effects.

◆ Make think links that show how important concepts relate to one another.

Remember that you can ask your instructor if you need help clarifying your reading material. Your instructor is an important resource. Pinpoint the material you want to discuss, schedule a meeting with him or her during office hours, and come prepared with a list of questions. You may also want to ask what materials to focus on when you study for tests.

If possible, you should review both alone and with study groups. Reviewing in as many different ways as possible increases the likelihood of retention. Figure 5-3 shows some techniques that will help a study group maximize its time and efforts.

Repeating the review process renews and solidifies your knowledge. That is why it is important to set up regular review sessions—for example, once a week. As you review, remember that refreshing your knowledge is easier and faster than learning it the first time.

As you can see in Table 5-2 on page 133, using PQ3R is part of being an active reader. Active reading involves the specific activities that help you retain what you learn.

HOW CAN YOU READ CRITICALLY?

Your textbooks will often contain features that highlight important ideas and help you determine questions to ask while reading. As you advance in your education, however, many reading assignments will not be so clearly marked, especially if they are primary sources. You will need critical-reading skills in

Figure 5-3   Study group techniques.

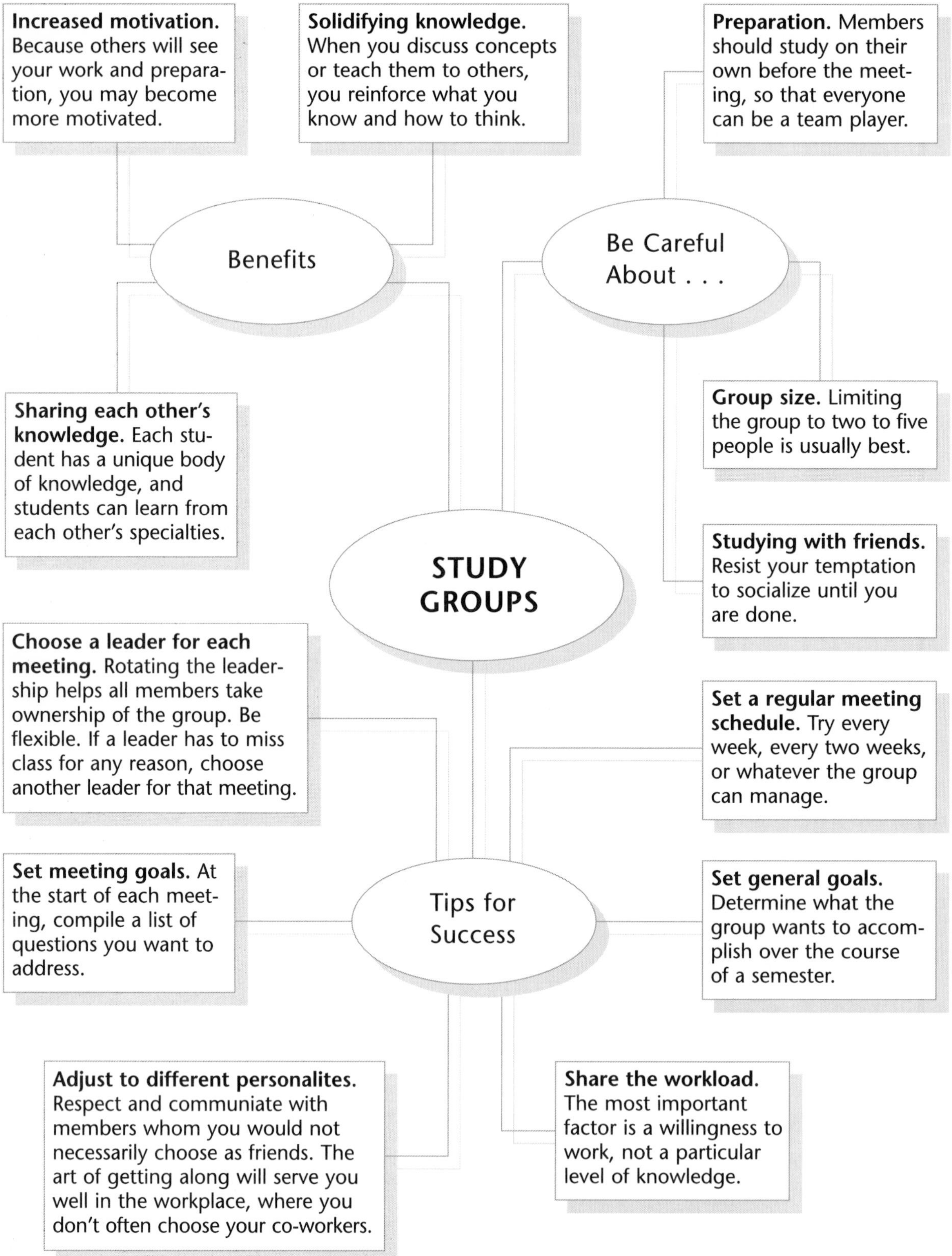

Increased motivation. Because others will see your work and preparation, you may become more motivated.

Solidifying knowledge. When you discuss concepts or teach them to others, you reinforce what you know and how to think.

Preparation. Members should study on their own before the meeting, so that everyone can be a team player.

Benefits

Be Careful About . . .

Sharing each other's knowledge. Each student has a unique body of knowledge, and students can learn from each other's specialties.

Group size. Limiting the group to two to five people is usually best.

STUDY GROUPS

Studying with friends. Resist your temptation to socialize until you are done.

Choose a leader for each meeting. Rotating the leadership helps all members take ownership of the group. Be flexible. If a leader has to miss class for any reason, choose another leader for that meeting.

Set a regular meeting schedule. Try every week, every two weeks, or whatever the group can manage.

Set meeting goals. At the start of each meeting, compile a list of questions you want to address.

Tips for Success

Set general goals. Determine what the group wants to accomplish over the course of a semester.

Adjust to different personalites. Respect and communiate with members whom you would not necessarily choose as friends. The art of getting along will serve you well in the workplace, where you don't often choose your co-workers.

Share the workload. The most important factor is a willingness to work, not a particular level of knowledge.

ACTIVE READERS TEND TO . . .		Table 5-2
Divide material into manageable sections	Answer end-of-chapter questions and applications	Use PQ3R to become an active reader.
Write questions	Create chapter outlines	
Answer questions through focused note taking	Create think links that map concepts in a logical way	
Highlight key concepts	Make flash cards and study them	
Recite, verbally and in writing, the answers to questions	Recite what they learned into a tape recorder and play the tape back	
Focus on main ideas found in paragraphs, sections, and chapters	Rewrite and summarize notes and highlighted materials from memory	
Recognize summary and support devices	Explain what they read to a family member or friend	
Analyze tables, figures, and photos	Form a study group	

order to select the important ideas, identify examples that support them, and ask questions about the text without the aid of any special features or tools.

Critical reading enables you to consider reading material carefully, developing a thorough understanding of it through evaluation and analysis. A critical reader is able to discern what in a piece of reading material is true or useful, such as when using material as a source for an essay. A critical reader can also compare one piece of material to another and evaluate which makes more sense, which proves its thesis more successfully, or which is more useful for the reader's purpose.

Critical reading is reading that transcends taking in and regurgitating material. You can read critically by using PQ3R to get a basic idea of the material, asking questions based on the critical-thinking mind actions, shifting your perspective, and seeking understanding.

Use PQ3R to "Taste" Reading Material

Sylvan Barnet and Hugo Bedau, authors of *Critical Thinking, Reading, and Writing—A Brief Guide to Argument*, suggest that the active reading of PQ3R will help you form an initial idea of what a piece of reading material is all about. Through previewing, skimming for ideas and examples, highlighting and writing comments and questions in the margins, and reviewing, you can develop a basic understanding of its central ideas and contents.[5]

Summarizing, part of the review process in PQ3R, is one of the best ways to develop an understanding of a piece of reading material. To construct a summary, focus on the central ideas of the piece and the main examples that support those ideas. A summary does *not* contain any of your own ideas or your evaluation of the material. It simply condenses the material, making it

TERMS

Summary
A concise restatement of the material, in your own words, that covers the main points.

easier for you to focus on the structure of the piece and its central ideas when you go back to read more critically. At that point, you can begin to evaluate the piece and introduce your own ideas. Using the mind actions will help you.

Ask Questions Based on the Mind Actions

The essence of critical reading, as with critical thinking, is asking questions. Instead of simply accepting what you read, seek a more thorough understanding by questioning the material as you go along. Using the mind actions of the Thinktrix to formulate your questions will help you understand the material.

What parts of the material you focus on will depend on your purpose for reading. For example, if you are writing a paper on the causes of World War II, you might spend your time focusing on how certain causes fit your thesis. If you are comparing two pieces of writing that contain opposing arguments, you may focus on picking out their central ideas and evaluating how well the writers use examples to support these ideas.

You can question any of the following components of reading material:

- The central idea of the entire piece
- A particular idea or statement
- The examples that support an idea or statement
- The proof of a fact
- The definition of a concept

Following are some ways to critically question your reading material, based on the mind actions. Apply them to any component you want to question by substituting the component for the words "it" and "this."

 Similarity: What does this remind me of, or how is it similar to something else I know?

 Difference: What different conclusions are possible?

How is this different from my experience?

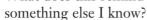 Cause and Effect: Why did this happen, or what caused this?

What are the effects or consequences of this?

What effect does the author want to have, or what is the purpose of this material?

What effects support a stated cause?

 Example to Idea: How would I classify this, or what is the best idea to fit this example(s)?

How would I summarize this, or what are the key ideas?

What is the thesis or central idea?

 Idea to Example: What evidence supports this, or what examples fit this idea?

Evaluation: How would I evaluate this? Is it valid or pertinent?
Does this example support my thesis or central idea?

Shift Your Perspective

Your understanding of perspective will help you understand that many reading materials are written from a particular perspective. Perspective often has a strong effect on how the material is presented. For example, if a recording artist and a music censorship advocate were to each write a piece about a controversial song created by that artist, their different perspectives would result in two very different pieces of writing.

To analyze perspective, ask questions like the following:

What perspective is guiding this? What are the underlying ideas that influence this material?

Who wrote this, and what may be the author's perspective? For example, a piece on a new drug written by an employee of the drug manufacturer may differ from a doctor's evaluation of the drug.

What does the title of the material tell me about its perspective? For example, a piece titled "New Therapies for Diabetes" may be more informational, and "What's Wrong With Insulin Injections" may intend to be persuasive.

How does the material's source affect its perspective? For example, an article on health management organizations (HMOs) published in an HMO newsletter may be more favorable and one-sided than one published in *The New York Times*.

Seek Understanding

Reading critically allows you to investigate what you read so that you can reach the highest possible level of understanding. Think of your reading process as an archaeological dig. The first step is to excavate a site and uncover the artifacts. In reading, that corresponds to your initial preview and reading of the material. As important as the excavation is, the process would be incomplete if you stopped there and just took home a bunch of items covered in dirt. The second half of the process is to investigate each item, evaluate what all of those items mean, and derive new knowledge and ideas from what you discover. Critical reading allows you to complete that crucial second half of the process.

As you work through all of the different requirements of critical reading, remember that critical reading takes *time* and *focus*. Finding a time, place, and purpose for reading, covered earlier in the chapter, is crucial to successful critical reading. Give yourself a chance to gain as much as possible from what you read.

No matter where or how you prefer to study, your school's library (or libraries) can provide many useful services to help you make the most of classes, reading, studying, and assignments.

W HAT DOES YOUR LIBRARY OFFER?

Your library can help you search for all kinds of information. First, learn about your library, its resources, and its layout. While some schools have only one library, other schools have a library network that includes one or more central libraries and smaller, specialized libraries that focus on specific academic areas. Take advantage of library tours, training sessions, and descriptive pamphlets. Spend time walking around the library on your own. If you still have questions, ask a librarian. A simple question can save hours of searching. The following sections will help you understand how your library operates.

General Reference Works

"With one day's reading a man may have the key in his hands."

EZRA POUND

General reference works give you an overview and lead you to more specific information. These works cover topics in a broad, nondetailed way. General reference guides are found in the front of most libraries and are often available on CD-ROM, a compact disk that contains millions of words and images. You access this information by inserting the disk into a specially designed computer. Among the works that fall into this category are:

- Encyclopedias—for example, the multivolume *Encyclopedia Britannica*
- Almanacs—*The World Almanac and Book of Facts*
- Dictionaries—*Webster's New World College Dictionary*
- Biographical reference works—*Webster's Biographical Dictionary*
- Bibliographies—*Books in Print*

Specialized Reference Works

Look at *specialized reference works* to find more specific facts. Specialized reference works include encyclopedias and dictionaries that focus on a narrow field. The short summaries you will find there focus on critical ideas. Bibliographies that accompany the articles point you to the names and works of recognized experts. Examples of specialized references include the *International Encyclopedia of Film*, the *Encyclopedia of Computer Science and Technology*, and the *Dictionary of Education*.

Book Catalog

Found near the front of the library, the *book catalog* lists every book the library owns. The listings usually appear in three separate categories: authors' names, book titles, and subjects. Not too long ago, most libraries stored their book catalog on index-sized cards in hundreds of small drawers. Today, many libraries have replaced these cards with computers. Using a terminal that has access to the library's computer records, you can search by specific author, title, and subject.

The computerized catalog in your college library is probably connected to the holdings of other college and university libraries. This gives you an online search capacity, which means that if you don't find the book you want in your local library, you can track it down in another library and request it through an interlibrary loan. *Interlibrary loan* is a system used by many colleges to allow students to borrow materials from a library other than the one at their school. Students request materials through their own library, where the materials are eventually delivered by the outside library. When you are in a rush, keep in mind that an interlibrary loan may take a substantial amount of time.

Periodical Indexes

Periodicals are magazines, journals, and newspapers that are published on a regular basis throughout the year. Examples include *Time, Business Week,* and *Science.* Many libraries display periodicals that are a year or two old and convert older copies to microfilm or microfiche (photocopies of materials reduced greatly in size and printed on film readable in a special reading machine—*microfilm* is a strip of film, and *microfiche* refers to individual leaves of film). Finding articles in publications involves a search of periodical indexes. The most widely used general index is the *Reader's Guide to Periodical Literature,* which is available on CD-ROM and in book form. The *Reader's Guide* indexes articles in more than 100 general-interest magazines and journals.

Electronic Research

You will also find complete source material through a variety of electronic sources, including the Internet, online services, and CD-ROM. Here is a sampling of the kind of information you will find:

- Complete articles from thousands of journals and magazines
- Complete articles from newspapers around the world
- Government data on topics as varied as agriculture, transportation, and labor
- Business documents, including corporate annual reports

Your library is probably connected to the *Internet,* a worldwide computer network that links government, university, research, and business computers along the information superhighway. Tapping into the *World Wide Web*—a tool for searching the huge libraries of information stored on the Internet—gives you access to billions of written words and graphic images. The Internet is so vast that there are many books about Internet research to help you explore it. If your college has its own Internet home page, start by spending some time browsing through it.

Although most libraries do not charge a fee to access the Internet, they may charge when you connect to commercial online services, including Nexis, CompuServe, and Prodigy. Ask your librarian about all fees and restrictions. Libraries also have electronic databases on CD-ROM. A database is a collection of data—or, in the case of most libraries, a list of related resources that all focus on one specific subject area—arranged so that you can search through it and retrieve specific items easily. For example, the DIA-

LOG Information System includes hundreds of small databases in specialized areas. CD-ROM databases are generally smaller than online databases and are updated less frequently. However, there is never a user's fee.

читать

This word may look completely unfamiliar to you, but anyone who can read the Russian language and alphabet will know that it means "read." People who read languages that use different kinds of characters, such as Russian, Japanese, or Greek, learn to process those characters as easily as you process the letters of your native alphabet. Your mind learns to individually process each letter or character you see. This ability enables you to move to the next level of understanding—making sense of those letters or characters when they are grouped to form words, phrases, and sentences.

Think of this concept when you read. Remember that your mind is an incredible tool, processing unmeasurable amounts of information so that you can understand the concepts on the page. Give it the best opportunity to succeed by reading as often as you can and by focusing on all of the elements that help you read to the best of your ability.

Success in the Real World

Carol Walton

Carol Walton, Director of the Tiputini Biodiversity Station, never thought she would need to know about business when she left for the Amazon rain forest. However, even while in the rain forest, she had to become an international marketer, accountant, and logistical expert.

Carol's background is in veterinary medicine, although she had always tried to spend as much time as possible in the jungle during school. She loved the outdoors and teaching people about nature. She volunteered to lead tours during summer vacations and would save her vacation time to spend it in the rain forests.

By taking some time to seriously analyze her life, and developing a strategic plan of sorts for herself, she discovered that she was most happy outdoors in the jungle. She had not thought of making a career out of this because she had been tied to her ideas of living a typical, responsible life. She sat down and wrote out everything she wanted to be doing. She wrote the story in the present tense as if she were already doing it. She then wrote out twenty steps that she needed to take to make the story a reality.

Getting to her ultimate goal required sacrifice. She had to give up her lifestyle in the United States, complete with all the comforts and the income of her veterinary practice, and work as a guide for $25 a day in South America. She was definitely afraid to do this but knew that by working for a short time as a guide, she would soon be able to take advantage of other opportunities. She saw her ultimate goal and had to follow along the path to get there.

While working as a guide, Carol strategically made numerous contacts. Soon she was approached by a private university, Universidad San Francisco, and asked to be in charge of building and managing a research station in the jungle. For the next two years, she dedicated herself to building the best possible station. She analyzed other stations, evaluated how to minimize the ecological impact, worked with architects, and purchased all supplies. She set up a marketing effort to attract researchers, students, and ecologically minded tourists. The business skills she uses all the time now include logistical management (determining how to get supplies and people to the remote location), time management, budgeting, marketing, advertising, finance, accounting, and management. The station is running full-force, and Carol continues to manage the operations and marketing efforts. The station is more successful than anyone originally thought possible. By having a lot of initiative and through careful planning, Carol has achieved what she set out to do and is completely fulfilled in her career. She just ran across the story she had written years ago and was amazed that it all had come true.

Carol defines success as living a life so that you feel fulfilled, doing something you feel is worthwhile and helping the world in whatever way you can. She believes that everyone, at some point in their lives, should spend some time away from their home and family because they will appreciate them much more and gain invaluable experience. She thinks that, although not everyone is going to agree with what you're doing, you'll be all right if you stay focused on what's important to you and the people who are important to you.

People sometimes live their lives as though they are just going through the motions; Carol advises students to be conscious of the decisions they make because life is not a dress rehearsal:

> "Try to find something important to you. Learn how to find the humor in everything, even in the tough times. And love as much as possible. That's all there is to life!"

Chapter 5   Applications

Name _____   Date _____

KEY INTO YOUR LIFE
Opportunities to Apply What You Learn

 Studying a Text Page

Read the following excerpt from the Groups and Organizations chapter in the sixth edition of John J. Macionis's *Sociology*, a Prentice Hall text.[6] Using what you learned in this chapter about study techniques, complete the questions on the following page.

SOCIAL GROUPS

Virtually everyone moves through life with a sense of belonging; this is the experience of group life. A **social group** refers to *two or more people who identify and interact with one another.* Human beings continually come together to form couples, families, circles of friends, neighborhoods, churches, businesses, clubs, and numerous large organizations. Whatever the form, groups encompass people with shared experiences, loyalties, and interests. In short, while maintaining their individuality, the members of social groups also think of themselves as a special "we."

Groups, Categories, and Crowds

People often use the term "group" imprecisely. We now distinguish the group from the similar concepts of category and crowd.

Category

A *category* refers to people who have some status in common. Women, single fathers, military recruits, homeowners, and Roman Catholics are all examples of categories.

Why are categories not considered groups? Simply because, while the individuals involved are aware that they are not the only ones to hold that particular status, the vast majority are strangers to one another.

Crowd

A *crowd* refers to a temporary cluster of individuals who may or may not interact at all. Students sitting in a lecture hall do engage one another and share some common identity as college classmates; thus, such a crowd might be called a loosely formed group. By contrast, riders hurtling along on a subway train or bathers enjoying a summer day at the beach pay little attention to one another and amount to an anonymous aggregate of people. In general, then, crowds are too transitory and impersonal to qualify as social groups.

The right circumstances, however, could turn a crowd into a group. People riding in a subway train that crashes under the city streets generally become keenly aware of their common plight and begin to help one another. Sometimes such extraordinary experiences become the basis for lasting relationships.

Primary and Secondary Groups

Acquaintances commonly greet one another with a smile and the simple phrase, "Hi! How are you?" The response is usually a well scripted "Just fine, thanks. How about you?" This answer, of course, is often more formal than truthful. In most cases, providing a detailed account of how you are *really* doing would prompt the other person to beat a hasty and awkward exit.

Sociologists classify social groups by measuring them against two ideal types based on members' genuine level of personal concern. This variation is the key to distinguishing *primary* from *secondary* groups.

According to Charles Horton Cooley (1864–1929), who is introduced in the box, a **primary group** is *a small social group whose members share personal and enduring relationships*. Bound together by primary relationships, individuals in primary groups typically spend a great deal of time together, engage in a wide range of common activities, and feel that they know one another well. Although not without periodic conflict, members of primary groups display sincere concern for each other's welfare. The family is every society's most important primary group.

Cooley characterized these personal and tightly integrated groups as *primary* because they are among the first groups we experience in life. In addition, the family and early play groups also hold primary importance in the socialization process, shaping attitudes, behavior, and social identity.

Source: Sociology, 6/E by John J. Macionis, © 1997. Reprinted by permission of Prentice-Hall, Inc., Upper Saddle River, NJ.

1. Identify the headings on the page and the relationship among them. Which headings are primary-level headings; which are secondary; which are tertiary (third-level heads)? Which heading serves as an umbrella for the rest?

2. What do the headings tell you about the content of the page?

3. Identify the boldface and italicized terms. How do boldface terms differ from italicized terms?

4. After reading the excerpt headings, write three study questions. List the questions below:

5. Using a marker pen, highlight key phrases and sentences. Write short marginal notes to help you review the material at a later point.

6. After reading the excerpt, list four key concepts that you will need to study:

   a.

   b.

   c.

   d.

5.2 *Focusing on Your Purpose for Reading*

Read the following paragraphs on electronic commerce taken from *The Internet Guide for Accountants* by Kogan, Sudit, and Vasarhelyi. Then answer the questions that follow.

ELECTRONIC COMMERCE

Electronic commerce (EC) is a broad term encompassing electronically conducted business activities and transactions. Through the use of computer technology and standards, the flow of business information and the conduct of commercial activities can be remote, automatic, and electronic.

The WWW greatly facilitated the growth of electronic commerce over the Internet by bringing point-and-click usage and a simple publishing language (HTML) to the Internet, so that millions of users with only basic computer literacy could conduct business on the Internet easily and with low cost. In this chapter the present scope of electronic commerce and its major manifestation and practices are reviewed, future prospects and opportunities are contemplated, and implications for the accounting profession are discussed.

For Internet purposes it is useful to classify goods as *bitable* (soft goods) and *nonbitable*. The first can be delivered through the net (e.g., software, information, or money), while the second class requires physical delivery of goods (such as shoes or automobiles). Apart from the physical delivery of the goods, the entire sales process can be completed over the net in both categories.

It is also useful to classify goods as *commodity* or *noncommodity* goods. For Internet purposes the former are the goods that the consumer does not need to see, try, touch, smell, or taste in order to buy. The latter are less appropriate for electronic commerce as direct contact is necessary. With consumer experience, goods can evolve to commodity from noncommodity items. Bitable commodity items are the best prospects for electronic commerce.

Even commodity items have *bitable attributes*. Progressively, with the customer's experience the shopping decision may reduce a noncommodity item to a commodity item through experience and judicious understanding of some of its attributes. For example, after trying and purchasing a few times, a customer may realize that female Levis jeans are a good fit with a waist size of 28 and a length of 30. The decision will then be based on price (a bitable attribute) and size (a bit-describable attribute).

Electronic commerce on the Internet can be currently viewed as consisting of the following two areas:

♦ Direct selling over the Internet.
♦ Using the Internet for activities that support and facilitate commerce (e.g., electronic marketing, transaction processing, and electronic finance).

Most opportunities in the second area will present themselves through advertising, subscription services, and transaction processing.

Subscription services are technologically related to the concept of micropayments, and while the security and standards of payments over the net are evolving, electronic commerce has started slowly. Subscription services will allow the user to buy access to valuable information for his/her activities (e.g., stock prices, analyst reports, test results, etc.).

Transaction services will progressively take care of the "back office" functions of many businesses, use the Internet as the virtual private network, and allow for substantial buying and selling over the Internet.

Advertising on the Internet is in its embryonic stages.* According to the *Los Angeles Times*

* Behal, Bob, Menachen, Lauren & Nymberg, Hogan, "Advertising on the Internet," unpublished manuscript, 1996.

(June 10, 1996), out of $125 billion, U.S. advertising market on-line advertisement in 1995 was about $80 million. At the same time, the newspaper cites Jupiter Communications projections of on-line ads growing from about $340 million in 1996 to $5 billion in 2000. This rapid growth indicates a promising future for Web advertising. Some of the largest U.S. advertisers seem to be convinced. In April 1996, Proctor and Gamble (with an annual advertising budget in excess of $3 billion) signed a deal with Yahoo (http://www.yahoo.com)—the most common popular Internet directory.

Differentiating Business to Business from Person to Business

While most current discussion of electronic commerce revolves around consumer-oriented commerce, a large portion of EC will be of the business-to-business variety. This variety involves a mutation from EDI (electronic data interchange) concepts to a wider set of activities formalized initially through mutual agreements and progressively developing industry standards that will eventually lead to purely blind, automatic transactions, where no specific deals and agreements between the parties are necessary.

Possibilities With Electronic Commerce

- What if you were able to make changes to any technical drawing from a computer and then immediately share the modifications with all end users instantaneously through the usage of groupware associated with the Internet?

- Imagine bidding for and winning a contract without extensive procurement of RFPs, handling reams of paper, leaving telephone messages, and waiting indefinitely for answers.

- Consider using a computer to find, immediately, all the information needed to prepare a competitive bid.

- Suppose you were able to access data instantly, from old billing information to complex technical specifications—no more searching through stuffed filing cabinets only to find a faded, dirty, unusable original.

- Think of your management or auditors being able to trace instantaneously all the steps of a transaction by a client.

- Think of your security officers identifying fraud while someone is trying to break into a system.

- Now imagine customer involvement with the development or improvement of a product or service: Consider what it would be like if companies could come together to share talents and unite resources to go after opportunities normally beyond the realm of any of the individual companies. Picture an environment where a company is not only electronically linked internally but also linked externally to any location in the world.

These are some selected activities being facilitated by the combination of computer and electronic commerce technologies. The trend in electronic commerce is to mold the vast network of small businesses, government agencies, large corporations, and independent contractors into a single-business community with the ability to communicate with one another seamlessly across any computer platform.

Integration means more than coming together externally—it also encompasses internal integration. In an internally integrated organization, incoming orders are received electronically, and the information goes not only to production but also to shipping, billing, and inventory systems automatically—without any human intervention. Internal integration also means that critical data are stored digitally in formats and on media that permit instantaneous retrieval and electronic transmission.

While technology is important to integration, human resources are indispensable. Electronic commerce principles require coworkers, customers, and even former competitors to work together to solve problems, improve services, create new products, and pursue new markets. One essential feature of electronic commerce is data continuity, which is the concept of having data created, modified, and saved in such a way that it can be used throughout the life cycle of a manufactured product, as well as through the value chain* of complementary products. The understanding of the value chain, and the increased connectivity of the value chain facilitated by internetworking, can provide substantive competitive advantage. Figure 1 displays a visualization of how the value chain can benefit from partners sharing intranets (Extranets), the corporation with its own intranet, and the buyers from access through the Internet.

*Michael E. Porter and Victor E. Millar, "How Information Gives You Competitive Advantage," *Harvard Business Review,* July–August 1985.

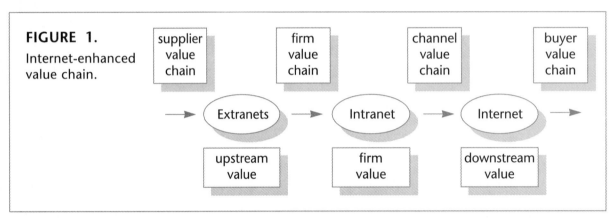

FIGURE 1.
Internet-enhanced value chain.

Source: From *The Internet Guide for Accountants* by Kogan, Sudit, and Vasarhelyi. Copyright © 1998 by Prentice-Hall, Inc. Upper Saddle River, NJ. Used by permission.

1. *Reading for critical evaluation.* Evaluate the material by answering these questions:

   a. Were the ideas clearly supported by examples? If you feel one or more were not supported, give an example.

   _____

   _____

   _____

   _____

   b. Did the authors make any assumptions that weren't examined? If so, name one or more.

   _____

   _____

   _____

   _____

   c. Do you disagree with any part of the material? If so, which part, and why?

   _____

   _____

   _____

   _____

d. Do you have any suggestions for how the material could have been presented more effectively?

_____

_____

_____

2. *Reading for practical application.* Imagine you have to give a presentation on this material the next time the class meets. On a separate sheet of paper, create an outline or think link that maps out the key elements you would discuss.

3. *Reading for comprehension.* Briefly summarize the article.

_____

_____

_____

_____

_____

Internet Exercise

There are many newspapers and popular magazines on the Internet. Although you will not have access to every article unless you pay for a subscription, there are still many articles you may read free of charge. Skimming articles on the Internet is a quick way to keep up on current events and business news.

1. Access the following magazines and select one article (print a copy for this assignment):

Fortune magazine—**www.fortune.com**

Time magazine—**www.time.com**

Newsweek magazine—**www.newsweek.com**

2. Use the PQ3R technique on the article you selected:

a. Preview. Skim the article (headings, introduction, conclusion/summary, first and second lines of the paragraphs).

b. Question. Jot down 3 or 4 questions, based on your skimming:

(1) _____

_____

(2) _____

_____

(3) _____

_____

(4) _____

_____

      c. Read the article.

      d. Recite the answers to the questions you formed above.

      e. Review by writing a one-paragraph summary:

_____

_____

_____

_____

_____

_____

_____

3. Find another magazine or journal that interests you on the Internet. What is the magazine? Briefly report on one of the articles.

_____

_____

_____

_____

_____

_____

_____

_____

_____

_____

_____

Journal

Name _____   Date _____

Journal

Name _____ Date _____

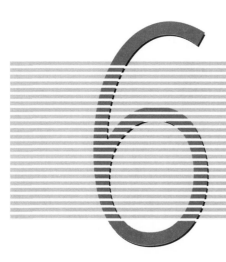

Note Taking and Writing

Harnessing the Power of Words and Ideas

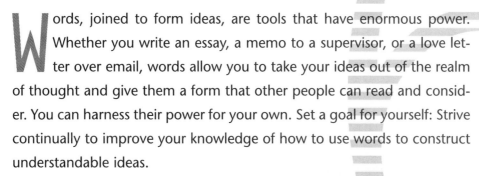

Words, joined to form ideas, are tools that have enormous power. Whether you write an essay, a memo to a supervisor, or a love letter over email, words allow you to take your ideas out of the realm of thought and give them a form that other people can read and consider. You can harness their power for your own. Set a goal for yourself: Strive continually to improve your knowledge of how to use words to construct understandable ideas.

This chapter will teach you the note-taking skills you need to record information successfully. It will show you how to express your written ideas completely and how good writing is linked to clear thinking. In class or at work, taking notes and writing well will help you stand out from the crowd.

In this chapter, you will explore answers to the following questions:

◆ How does taking notes help you?

◆ What note-taking system should you use?

◆ How can you write faster when taking notes?

◆ Why does good writing matter?

◆ What are the elements of effective writing?

◆ What is the writing process?

HOW DOES TAKING NOTES HELP YOU?

Notes help you learn when you are sitting in class, doing research, or studying. Since it is virtually impossible to take notes on everything you hear or read, the act of note taking encourages you to decide what is worth remembering. The positive effects of note taking include:

◆ Your notes provide material that helps you study information and prepare for tests.

◆ When you take notes, you become an active, involved listener and learner.

◆ Notes help you think critically and organize ideas.

◆ The information you learn in class may not appear in any text; you will have no way to study it without writing it down.

◆ If it is difficult for you to process information while in class, having notes to read and make sense of later can help you learn.

◆ Note taking is a skill for life that you will use on the job and in your personal life.

Recording Information in Class

Your notes have two purposes: First, they should reflect what you heard in class; second, they should be a resource for studying, writing, or comparing with your text material.

Prepare to Take Class Notes

Taking good class notes depends on good preparation, including the following:

◆ If your instructor assigns reading on a lecture topic, you may choose to complete the reading before class so that the lecture becomes more of a review than an introduction.

◆ Use separate pieces of 8½-by-11-inch paper for each class. If you use a three-ring binder, punch holes in papers your instructor hands out and insert them immediately following your notes for that day.

◆ Take a comfortable seat where you can easily see and hear, and be ready to write as soon as the instructor begins speaking.

◆ Choose a note-taking system that helps you handle the instructor's speaking style. While one instructor may deliver organized lectures at a normal speaking rate, another may jump from topic to topic or talk very quickly.

◆ Set up a support system with a student in each class. That way, when you are absent, you can get the notes you missed.

What to Do During Class

Because no one has the time to write down everything he or she hears, the following strategies will help you choose and record what you feel is important, in a format that you can read and understand later.

◆ Date each page. When you take several pages of notes during a lecture, add an identifying letter or number to the date on each page: 11/27 A, 11/27 B, . . . or 11/27—1 of 3, 11/27—2 of 3.

◆ Add the specific topic of the lecture at the top of the page. For example:

11/27A—Accrual Accounting vs. Cash Accounting

◆ If your instructor jumps from topic to topic during a single class, try starting a new page for each new topic.

◆ Ask yourself critical-thinking questions as you listen: Do I need this information? Is the information important, or is it just a digression? Is the information fact or opinion? If it is opinion, is it worth remembering? (Chapter 4 offers ideas about how to distinguish between fact and opinion.)

◆ Record whatever an instructor emphasizes (see Figure 6-1 for details).

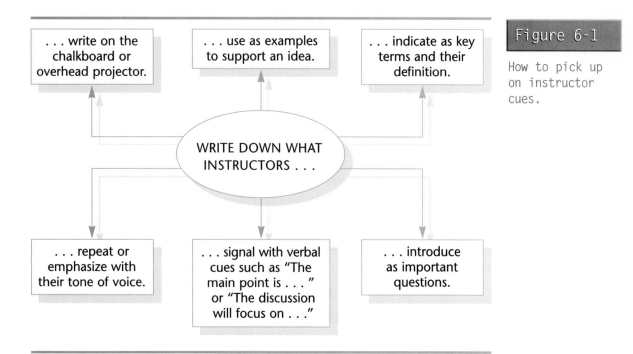

Figure 6-1

How to pick up on instructor cues.

. . . write on the chalkboard or overhead projector.

. . . use as examples to support an idea.

. . . indicate as key terms and their definition.

WRITE DOWN WHAT INSTRUCTORS . . .

. . . repeat or emphasize with their tone of voice.

. . . signal with verbal cues such as "The main point is . . . " or "The discussion will focus on . . ."

. . . introduce as important questions.

◆ Continue to take notes during class discussions and question-and-answer periods. What your fellow students ask about may help you as well.

◆ Leave one or more blank spaces between points. This white space will help you review your notes because information will appear in self-contained sections.

◆ Draw pictures and diagrams that help illustrate ideas.

◆ Indicate material that is especially important with a star, with underlining, with a highlighter pen, or with words in capital letters.

◆ If you cannot understand what the instructor is saying, leave a space and place a question mark in the margin. Then ask the instructor to explain it again after class, or discuss it with a classmate. Fill in the blank when the idea is clear.

◆ Take notes until the instructor stops speaking. Students who stop writing a few minutes before the class is over can miss critical information.

◆ Make your notes as legible, organized, and complete as possible. Your notes are only useful if you can read and understand them.

Make Notes a Valuable After-Class Reference

Class notes are a valuable study tool when you review them regularly. Try to begin your review within a day of the lecture. Read over the notes to learn the information, clarify abbreviations, fill in missing information, and underline or highlight key points. Try to review each week's notes at the end of that week. Think critically about the material in writing, study group discussions, or quiet reflective thought. You might also try summarizing your notes, either while reviewing them or doing it from memory.

You can take notes in many ways. Different note-taking systems suit different people and situations. Explore each system and choose what works for you.

WHAT NOTE-TAKING SYSTEM SHOULD YOU USE?

You will benefit most from the system that feels most comfortable to you. As you consider each system, remember the learning-styles profile you compiled in Chapter 2. The most common note-taking systems include outlines, the Cornell system, and think links.

Taking Notes in Outline Form

When a reading assignment or lecture seems well organized, you may choose to take notes in outline form. *Outlining* shows the relationships among ideas and their supporting examples through the use of line-by-line phrases set off by varying indentations.

Formal outlines indicate ideas and examples using Roman numerals, capital and lowercase letters, and numbers. When you are pressed for time, such as during class, you can use an informal system of consistent indenting and dashes instead. Formal outlines also require at least two headings on the same level—that is, if you have a II A, you must also have a II B. Figure 6-2 shows an outline on civil rights legislation.

Guided Notes

From time to time, an instructor may give you a guide, usually in the form of an outline, to help you take notes in the class. This outline may be on a page that you receive at the beginning of the class, on the board, or on an overhead projector.

Although *guided notes* help you follow the lecture and organize your thoughts during class, they do not replace your own notes. Because they are more of a basic outline of topics than a comprehensive coverage of informa-

Figure 6-2

Sample formal outline.

Civil Rights Legislation: 1860–1968

I. Post–Civil War Era
   A. Fourteenth Amendment, 1868: equal protection of the law for all citizens
   B. Fifteenth Amendment, 1870: constitutional rights of citizens regardless of race, color, or previous servitude
II. Civil Rights Movement of the 1960s
   A. National Association for the Advancement of Colored People (NAACP)
      1. Established in 1910 by W.E.B. DuBois and others
      2. Legal Defense and Education fund fought school segregation.
   B. Martin Luther King Jr., champion of nonviolent civil rights action
      1. Led bus boycott 1955–1956
      2. Marched on Washington D.C.: 1963
      3. Awarded NOBEL PEACE PRIZE: 1964
      4. Led voter registration drive in Selma, Alabama: 1965
   C. Civil Rights Act of 1964: prohibited discrimination in voting, education, employment, and public facilities
   D. Voting Rights Act of 1965: gave the government power to enforce desegregation.
   E. Civil Rights Act of 1968: prohibited discrimination in the sale or rental of housing

tion, they require that you fill in what they do not cover in detail. If you tune out in class because you think that the guided notes are all you need, you will most likely miss important information.

When you receive guided notes on paper, write directly on the paper if there is room. If not, use a separate sheet and write on it the outline categories that the guided notes suggest. If the guided notes are on the board or overhead, copy them down, leaving plenty of space in between for your own notes.

Using the Cornell Note-Taking System

The *Cornell note-taking system*, also known as the T-note system, was developed more than forty-five years ago by Walter Pauk at Cornell University.[1] The system is successful because it is simple—and because it works. It consists of three sections on ordinary note paper:

- ◆ *Section 1*, the largest section, is on the right. Record your notes here in informal outline form.
- ◆ *Section 2*, to the left of your notes, is the *cue column*. Leave it blank while you read or listen; then fill it in later as you review. You might fill it with comments that highlight main ideas, clarify meaning, suggest examples, or link ideas and examples. You can even draw diagrams.
- ◆ *Section 3*, at the bottom of the page, is the *summary area*, where you summarize the notes on the page. When you review, use this section to reinforce concepts and provide an overview.

When you use the Cornell system, create the note-taking structure before class begins. Picture an upside-down letter T and use Figure 6-3 as your guide. Make the cue column about $2\frac{1}{2}$ inches wide and the summary area 2 inches tall. Figure 6-3 shows how a student used the Cornell system to take notes in an introduction to business course.

Creating a Think Link

A *think link*, also known as a mind map, is a visual form of note taking. When you draw a think link, you diagram ideas using shapes and lines that link ideas and supporting details and examples. The visual design makes the connections easy to see, and the use of shapes and pictures extends the material beyond just words. Many learners respond well to the power of visualization. You can use think links to brainstorm ideas for paper topics as well.

One way to create a think link is to start by circling your topic in the middle of a sheet of unlined paper. Next, draw a line from the circled topic and write the name of the first major idea at the end of that line. Circle the idea also. Then jot down specific facts related to the idea, linking them to the idea with lines. Continue the process, connecting thoughts to one another using circles, lines, and words.

A think link may be difficult to construct in class, especially if your instructor talks quickly. In this case, use another note-taking system during

TERMS

Visualization
The interpretation of verbal ideas through the use of mental visual images.

class. Then make a think link as you review. Figure 6-4 shows a think link on a sociology concept called *social stratification*.

Once you choose a note-taking system, your success will depend on how well you use it. Personal shorthand will help you make the most of whatever system you choose.

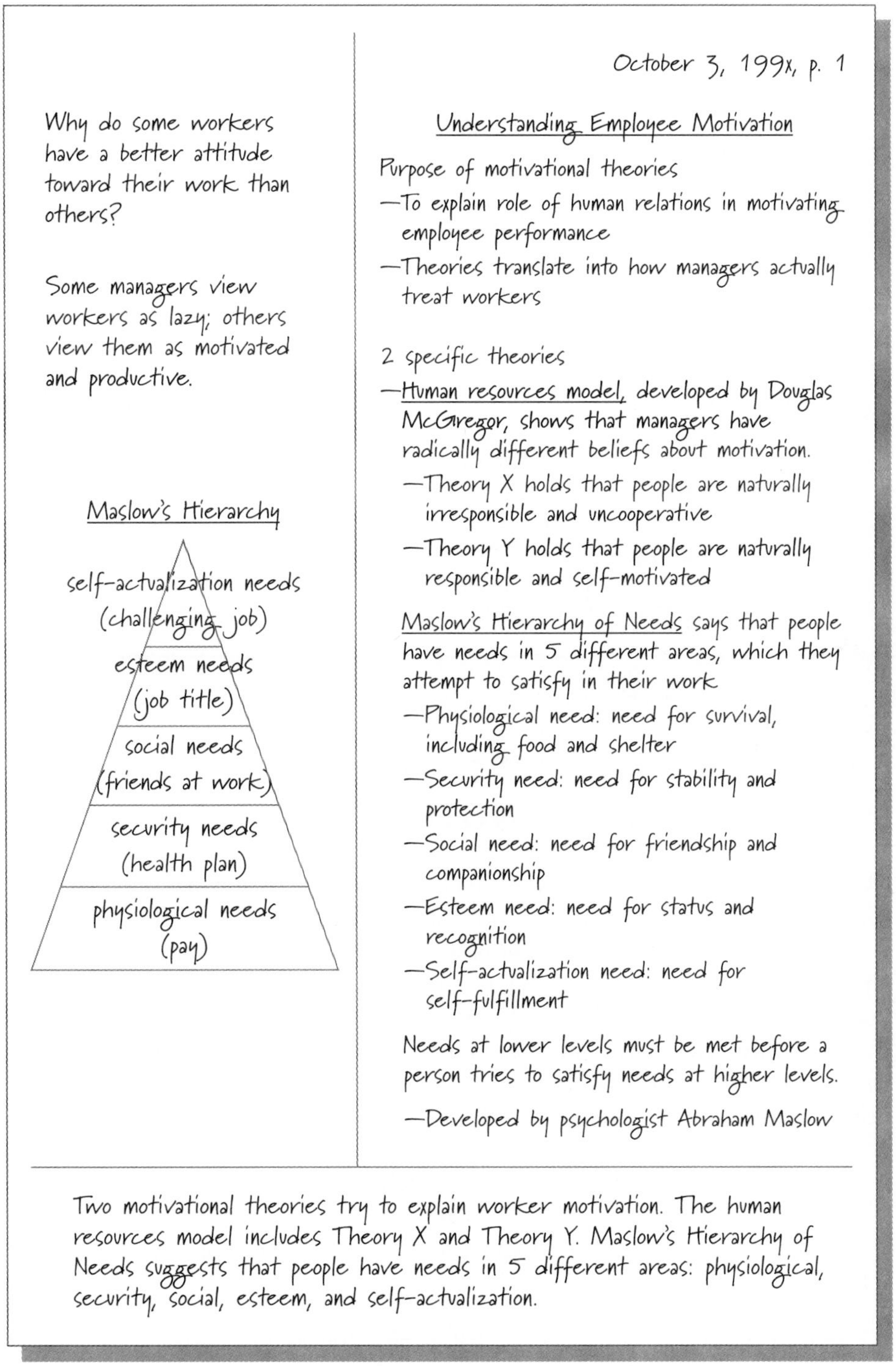

Figure 6-3

Notes taken
using the
Cornell System.

October 3, 199x, p. 1

<u>Understanding Employee Motivation</u>

Why do some workers have a better attitude toward their work than others?

Some managers view workers as lazy; others view them as motivated and productive.

Purpose of motivational theories
—To explain role of human relations in motivating employee performance
—Theories translate into how managers actually treat workers

2 specific theories
—<u>Human resources model</u>, developed by Douglas McGregor, shows that managers have radically different beliefs about motivation.
  —Theory X holds that people are naturally irresponsible and uncooperative
  —Theory Y holds that people are naturally responsible and self-motivated

<u>Maslow's Hierarchy</u>

self-actualization needs (challenging job)

esteem needs (job title)

social needs (friends at work)

security needs (health plan)

physiological needs (pay)

<u>Maslow's Hierarchy of Needs</u> says that people have needs in 5 different areas, which they attempt to satisfy in their work
—Physiological need: need for survival, including food and shelter
—Security need: need for stability and protection
—Social need: need for friendship and companionship
—Esteem need: need for status and recognition
—Self-actualization need: need for self-fulfillment

Needs at lower levels must be met before a person tries to satisfy needs at higher levels.

—Developed by psychologist Abraham Maslow

Two motivational theories try to explain worker motivation. The human resources model includes Theory X and Theory Y. Maslow's Hierarchy of Needs suggests that people have needs in 5 different areas: physiological, security, social, esteem, and self-actualization.

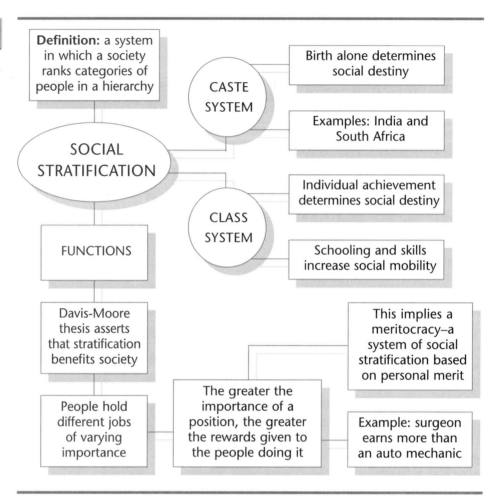

Figure 6-4

Sample think
link.

HOW CAN YOU WRITE FASTER WHEN TAKING NOTES?

When taking notes, many students feel they can't keep up with the instructor. Using some personal shorthand (not standard secretarial shorthand) can help to push the pen faster. *Shorthand* is writing that shortens words or replaces them with symbols. Because you are the only intended reader, you can misspell and abbreviate words in ways that only you understand.

The only danger with shorthand is that you might forget what your writing means. To avoid this problem, review your shorthand notes while your abbreviations and symbols are fresh in your mind. If there is any confusion, spell out words as you review.

Here are some suggestions that will help you master this important skill:

1. Use the following standard abbreviations in place of complete words:

w/	with	cf	compare, in comparison to
w/o	without	ff	following
→	means; resulting in	Q	question

←	as a result of	p.	page
↑	increasing	*	most importantly
↓	decreasing	<	less than
∴	therefore	>	more than
∵	because	=	equals
≈	approximately	%	percent
+ or &	and	△	change
–	minus; negative	2	to; two; too
NO. or #	number	vs	versus; against
i.e.	that is,	eg	for example
etc.	and so forth	c/o	care of
ng	no good	lb	pound

2. Shorten words by removing vowels from the middle of words:

   prps   =   purpose

   Crvtte   =   Corvette (as on a vanity license plate for a car)

3. Substitute word beginnings for entire words:

   assoc   =   associate; association

   info   =   information

4. Form plurals by adding s:

   prblms   =   problems

   prntrs   =   printers

5. Make up your own symbols and use them consistently:

   b/4   =   before

   2thake   =   toothache

6. Learn to rely on key phrases instead of complete sentences ("German— nouns capitalized" instead of "In the German language, all nouns are capitalized").

   While note taking focuses on taking in ideas, writing focuses on expressing them. Next you will explore the roles that writing can play in your life.

WHY DOES GOOD WRITING MATTER?

Good writing depends upon and reflects clear thinking. Therefore, a clear thought process is the best preparation for a well-written document, and a well-written document shows the reader a clear thought process. Good writing also depends on reading. The more you expose yourself to the work of other writers, the more you will develop your ability to express yourself well. Not only will you learn more words and ideas, but you will also learn about all the different ways a writer can put words together in order to express ideas. In addition, critical reading generates new ideas inside your mind, ideas you can use in your writing.

In school, almost any course you take will require you to write essays or papers in order to communicate your knowledge and thought process. In order to express yourself successfully in those essays and papers, you need good writing skills. Knowing how to write and express yourself is essential outside of school as well.

Instructors, supervisors, and other people who see your writing judge your thinking ability based on what you write and how you write it. Over the next few years you may write papers, essays, answers to essay test questions, job application letters, résumés, business proposals and reports, memos to co-workers, and letters to customers and suppliers. Good writing skills will help you achieve the goals you set out to accomplish with each writing task.

WHAT ARE THE ELEMENTS OF EFFECTIVE WRITING?

Every writing situation is different, based upon three elements. Your goal is to understand each element before you begin to write:

◆ *Your purpose:* What do you want to accomplish with this particular piece of writing?
◆ *Your topic:* What is the subject about which you will write?
◆ *Your audience:* Who will read your writing?

Figure 6-5 shows how these elements are interdependent. As a triangle needs three points to be complete, a piece of writing needs these three elements.

Writing Purpose

Writing without having set your purpose first is like driving without deciding where you want to arrive. You'll get somewhere, but chances are it won't be where you needed to go. Therefore, when you write, always define what you want to accomplish before you start.

There are many different purposes for writing. However, the two purposes you will most commonly use in classwork and on the job are to inform and to persuade.

Figure 6-5

The three elements of writing.

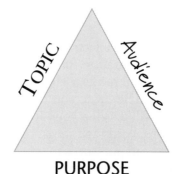

The purpose of *informative writing* is to present and explain ideas. A research paper on how hospitals use donated blood to save lives informs readers without trying to mold opinion. The writer presents facts in an unbiased way, without introducing a particular point of view. Most newspaper articles, except on the opinion and editorial pages, are examples of informative writing.

Persuasive writing has the purpose of convincing readers that your point of view is correct. Often, persuasive writing seeks to change the mind of the reader. For example, as a member of the student health committee, you write a newspaper column attempting to persuade readers to give blood. Examples of persuasive writing include newspaper editorials, business proposals, and books and magazine articles with a point of view.

Additional possible writing purposes include *entertaining* the reader and *narrating* (describing an image or event to the reader). Although most of your writing in school will inform or persuade, you may occasionally need to entertain or narrate as well. Sometimes purposes will even overlap—you might write an informative essay that entertains at the same time.

Knowing Your Audience

In almost every case, a writer creates written material so that it can be read by others. The two partners in this process are the writer and the audience. Knowing who your audience is will help you communicate successfully.

Key Questions About Your Audience

In school, your primary audience is your instructors. For many assignments, instructors will want you to assume that they are typical readers rather than informed instructors. Writing for typical readers usually means that you should be as complete as possible in your explanations.

At times you may write papers that intend to address informed instructors or a specific reading audience other than your instructors. In such cases, you may ask yourself some or all of the following questions, depending on which are relevant to your topic:

◆ What are my readers' ages, cultural backgrounds, interests, and experiences?

◆ What are their roles? Are they instructors, students, employers, customers?

◆ How much do they know about my topic? Are they experts or beginners in the field?

◆ Are they interested, or do I have to convince them to read what I write?

◆ Can I expect my audience to have an open or closed mind?

After you answer the questions about your audience, take what you have discovered into consideration as you write.

Your Commitment to Your Audience

Your goal is to organize your ideas so that readers can follow them. Suppose, for example, you are writing an informative research paper for a nonexpert

▲ TERMS

Audience
The reader or readers of any piece of written material.

audience on using online services to get a job. One way to accomplish your goal is to first explain what these services are and the kinds of help they offer, then describe each service in detail, and finally conclude with how these services will change job hunting in the twenty-first century.

Effective and successful writing involves following the steps of the *writing process*.

REAL WORLD PERSPECTIVE

How can I improve my writing?

Erica Epstein, Ithaca College, Ithaca, New York

I don't know if it was the school's fault or mine, but by the time I was in high school, I didn't do homework or reading. I just stopped paying attention. The classes were too boring. Fifteen weeks of the same topic was redundant. I think education should be interesting. The material should be tied in with something else so it has meaning. Instead, the teacher feeds you the information so you don't really have to put much effort in. But now, even though I do all right, I have to work really hard to write a good paper. I think if I'd had a better start, I wouldn't have to spend so much time rewriting my papers.

My teachers say the main problem is with my grammar. I tend to go from the past tense to the present tense in the wrong places. I just don't make proper sentences. I also have trouble organizing my material. I jump in and start writing. But I end up starting somewhere in the middle when I should be somewhere else. This is really frustrating. I had to take the writing class twice because I didn't get a high enough score the first time. I passed it this semester. I go to the writing center. They help me outline what I'm going to write. But I still end up rewriting my work before it's what I want. It's been really helpful, but I know I still need to do more. What suggestions do you have?

Tom Smith, University of Wyoming

First of all, just like you, I get help from the writing center at my school. They know a lot about what the different teachers expect of you, particularly the technical stuff like footnote and bibliography requirements. They also give great advice about phrasing and punctuation. I also ask several of my friends to edit my papers. Usually, they'll focus in on the weaker points, and then I can make the changes and strengthen my work. If your papers are sounding too chatty, this would probably be the best thing for you to do. They'll be able to show you where you've gotten off the point. I'm never bothered by their comments. In fact, I'm grateful because it helps my papers be more professional.

By the time three or four people have read my work, I'm usually pretty sure I've handled the problems. I also personally edit my papers about three or four times before I turn them in. I make sure I got my point across. I also try and look at my paper from an opposing perspective or different viewpoint. That way I can be sure my arguments are clear. Finally, if you don't have a reference book for writers, I suggest you go to your college bookstore and get one. And don't forget to use your spell-check and thesaurus. That way you'll be sure your spelling is correct, and you can increase your vocabulary with every paper you write.

W HAT IS THE WRITING PROCESS?

The writing process provides an opportunity for you to state and refine your thoughts until you have expressed yourself as clearly as possible. Critical thinking plays an important role every step of the way. The four main parts of the process are planning, drafting, revising, and editing.

Planning

Planning gives you a chance to think about what to write and how to write it. Planning involves brainstorming ideas, defining and narrowing your topic by using prewriting strategies, conducting research if necessary, writing a thesis statement, and writing a working outline. Although the steps in preparing to write are listed in sequence, in real life the steps overlap one another as you plan your document.

Open Your Mind Through Brainstorming

Whether your instructor assigns a partially defined topic (novelist Toni Morrison) or a general category within which you make your own choice (women authors), you should brainstorm to develop ideas about what you want to write. Brainstorming is a creative technique that involves generating ideas about a subject without making judgments. You may want to look at the section on creativity in Chapter 4 for more details.

First, let your mind wander! Write down anything on the assigned subject that comes to mind, in no particular order. Then, organize that list into an outline or think link that helps you see the possibilities more clearly. To make the outline or think link, separate list items into general ideas or categories and sub-ideas or examples. Then associate the sub-ideas or examples with the ideas they support or fit. Figure 6-6 shows a portion of an outline that the student editor for this book, Michael B. Jackson, constructed from his brainstorming list. The assignment is a five-paragraph essay on a life-changing event. Here, only the subject that Michael eventually chose is shown broken down into different ideas.

Narrow Your Topic Through Prewriting Strategies

When your brainstorming has generated some possibilities, you can narrow your topic. Focus on the sub-ideas and examples from your initial brainstorming session. Because they are relatively specific, they will be more likely to point you toward possible topics.

Choose one or more sub-ideas or examples that you like and explore them using prewriting strategies such as brainstorming, freewriting, and asking journalists' questions.[2] Prewriting strategies will help you decide which of your possible topics you would most like to pursue.

Brainstorming. The same process you used to generate ideas will also help you narrow your topic further. Generate thoughts about the possibility you

> **TERMS**
>
> **Prewriting strategies** Techniques for generating ideas about a topic and finding out how much you already know before you start your research and writing.

Part of a brainstorming outline.

A life-changing event . . .

  —Family

  —Childhood

  →Military

    —travel

    →boot

      —physical conditioning

        • swim tests

        • intensive training

        • <u>ENDLESS</u> push-ups!

      —Chief who was our commander

      —mental discipline

        • military lifestyle

        • perfecting our appearance

      —self-confidence

        • walk like you're in control

        • don't blindly accept anything

have chosen and write them down. Then, organize them into categories, noticing any patterns that appear. See if any of the sub-ideas or examples seem as if they might make good topics.

Freewriting. Another stream-of-consciousness technique that encourages you to put down ideas on paper as they occur to you is called *freewriting*. When you freewrite, you write whatever comes to mind without censoring your ideas or worrying about grammar, spelling, punctuation, or organization. Freewriting helps you think creatively and gives you an opportunity to begin weaving in information that you know. Freewrite on the sub-ideas or examples you have created to see if you want to pursue any of them. The entry below shows a sample of freewriting.

Boot camp for the Coast Guard really changed my life. First of all, I really got in shape. We had to get up every morning at 5 a.m., eat breakfast, and go right into training. We had to do endless military-style push-ups—but we later found out that these have a purpose, to prepare us to hit the deck in the event of enemy fire. We had a lot of aquatic tests, once we were awakened at 3 a.m. to do one in full uniform! Boot camp also helped me to feel confident about myself and be disciplined. Chief Marzloff was the main person who made that happen. He was tough but there was always a reason. He got angry when I used to nod my head whenever he would speak to me, he said that made it seem like I was blindly accepting whatever he said, which was a weakness. From him I have learned to keep an eye on my body's movements when I communicate. I learned a lot more from him too.

Asking journalists' questions. When journalists start working on a story, they ask themselves Who? What? When? Where? Why? and How? You can use these *journalists' questions* to focus your thinking. Ask these questions about any sub-idea or example to discover what you may want to discuss. For example:

Who?	Who was at boot camp? Who influenced me the most?
What?	What about boot camp changed my life? What did we do?
When?	When in my life did I go to boot camp, and for how long? When did we fulfill our duties?
Where?	Where was boot camp located? Where did we spend our day-to-day time?
Why?	Why did I decide to go there? Why was it such an important experience?
How?	How did we train in the camp? How were we treated? How did we achieve success?

As you prewrite, don't forget to focus on the paper length, due date of your assignment, and any other requirements (such as topic area or purpose). These requirements influence your choice of a final topic. For example, if you had a month to write an informative twenty-page paper on learning disabilities, you might choose to discuss the symptoms, diagnosis, effects, and treatment of attention deficit disorder. If you were given a week to write a five-page persuasive essay, you might write about how elementary students with ADD need special training.

Prewriting will help you develop a topic broad enough to give you something with which to work but narrow enough to be manageable. Prewriting also helps you see what you know and what you don't know. If your assignment requires more than you already know, you may need to do research.

Conduct Research

Much of the writing you do in college, such as when you must write a short essay for freshman composition or for an exam, will rely on what you already know about a subject. In these cases, prewriting strategies may generate all the ideas and information you need. In other writing situations, outside sources are necessary. Try doing your research in stages. In the first stage, look for a basic overview that can help you write a thesis statement. In the second stage, go into more depth in your research, tracking down information that will help you fill in the gaps and complete your thoughts.

Write a Thesis Statement

Your work up until this point has prepared you to write a *thesis statement*, the central message you want to communicate. The thesis statement states your subject and point of view, reflects your writing purpose and audience, and acts as the organizing principle of your paper. It tells your readers what they should expect to read. Here is an example from Michael's paper:

Topic	Coast Guard boot camp
Purpose	To inform and narrate
Audience	Instructor with unknown knowledge about the topic
Thesis statement	Chief Marzloff, our Basic Training Company Commander at the U. S. Coast Guard Basic Training Facility, shaped my life through physical conditioning, developing my self-confidence, and instilling strong mental discipline.

A thesis statement is just as important in a short document, such as a letter, as it is in a long paper. For example, when you write a job application letter, a clear thesis statement will help you tell the recruiter why you deserve the job.

Write a Working Outline

The final step in the preparation process involves writing a working outline. Use this outline as a loose guide instead of a finalized structure. As you draft your paper, your ideas and structure may change many times. Only through allowing changes and refinements to happen can you get closer and closer to what you really want to say. Some students prefer a more formal outline structure, while others like to use a think link. Choose whatever form suits you best.

Create a Checklist

Use the checklist in Table 6-1 to make sure your preparation is complete. Under "Date Due," create your own writing schedule, giving each task an intended completion date. Work backwards from the date the assignment is due, and estimate how long it will take to complete each step. Refer to Chapter 3 for time management skills that will help you schedule your writing process.

As you develop your schedule, keep in mind that you'll probably move back and forth between tasks. You might find yourself doing two and even three things on the same day. Stick to the schedule as best you can, while balancing the other demands of your busy life, and check off your accomplishments on the list as you complete them.

Drafting

Some people aim for perfection when they write a first draft. They want to get everything right—from word choice to tone to sentence structure to paragraph organization to spelling, punctuation, and grammar. Try to resist this

DATE DUE	TASK	IS IT COMPLETE?
	Brainstorm	
	Define and narrow	
	Use prewriting strategies	
	Conduct research if necessary	
	Write thesis statement	
	Write working outline	
	Complete research	

Table 6-1

Preparation checklist.

tendency because it may lead you to shut the door on ideas before you even know they are there.

A *first draft* involves putting ideas down on paper for the first time—but not the last! You may write many different versions of the assignment until you like what you see. Each version moves you closer to communicating exactly what you want to say in the way you want to say it. The process is like starting with a muddy pond and gradually clearing the mud away until your last version is a clear body of water, showing the rocks and the fish underneath the surface. Think of your first draft as a way of establishing the pond before you start clearing it up.

The elements of writing a first draft are freewriting, crafting an introduction, organizing the ideas in the body of the paper, formulating a conclusion, and citing sources.

Freewriting Your Draft

If the introduction, body, and conclusion are the three parts of the sandwich, freewriting is the process of searching the refrigerator for the ingredients and laying them all out on the table. Take everything that you have developed in the planning stages and freewrite a very rough draft. Don't censor yourself. For now, don't consciously think about your introduction, conclusion, or structure within the paper body. Focus on getting your ideas out of the realm of thought and onto the paper, in whatever form they prefer to be at the moment.

When you have the beginnings of a paper in your hands, you can start to shape it into something with a more definite form. First, work on how you want to begin your paper.

Writing an Introduction

The introduction tells your readers what the rest of the paper will contain. Including the thesis statement is essential. Here, for example, is a draft of an introduction for Michael's paper about the Coast Guard. The thesis statement is underlined at the end of the paragraph:

"Clear a space for the writing voice. . . . you cannot will this to happen. It is a matter of persistence and faith and hard work. So you might as well just go ahead and get started."

ANNE LAMOTT

Chief Marzloff took on the task of shaping the lives and careers of the youngest, newest members of the U. S. Coast Guard. During my eight weeks in training, he was my father, my instructor, my leader, and my worst enemy. He took his job very seriously and demanded that we do the same. <u>The Chief was instrumental in conditioning our bodies, developing our self-confidence, and instilling mental discipline within us.</u>

When you write an introduction, you might try to draw the reader in with an anecdote—a story that is directly related to the thesis. You can try other hooks, including a relevant quotation, dramatic statistics, and questions that encourage critical thinking. Whatever strategy you choose, be sure it is linked to your thesis statement. In addition, try to state your purpose without referring to its identity as a purpose. For example, in your introductory paragraph, state, "Computer technology is infiltrating every aspect of business" instead of "In this paper, my purpose is to prove that computer technology is infiltrating every aspect of business."

After you have an introduction that seems to set up the purpose of your paper, work on making sure the body fulfills that purpose.

TERMS

Hooks
Elements—including facts, quotes, statistics, questions, stories, or statements—that catch the reader's attention and encourage him or her to want to continue to read.

Creating the Body of a Paper

The body of the paper contains your central ideas and supporting evidence. *Evidence*—proof that informs or persuades—consists of the facts, statistics, examples, and expert opinions that you know or have gathered during research.

Look at the array of ideas and evidence within your draft in its current state. Think about how you might group certain items of evidence with the particular ideas they support. Then, when you see the groups that form, try to find a structure that helps you to organize them into a clear pattern. Here are some strategies to consider:

Arrange ideas by time. Describe events in order or in reverse order.

Arrange ideas according to importance. You can choose to start with the idea that carries the most weight and move to ideas with less value or influence. You can also move from the least important to the most important idea.

Arrange ideas by problem and solution. Start with a specific problem; then discuss one or more solutions.

Writing the Conclusion

Your conclusion is a statement or paragraph that provides closure for your paper. Aim to summarize the information in the body of your paper, as well as to critically evaluate what is important about that information. Try one of the following devices:

- A summary of main points (if material is longer than three pages)
- A story, a statistic, a quote, a question that makes the reader think
- A call to action
- A look to the future

As you work on your conclusion, try not to introduce new facts or restate what you feel you have proved ("I have successfully proven that violent cartoons are related to increased violence in children"). Let your ideas as they are presented in the body of the paper speak for themselves. Readers should feel that they have reached a natural point of completion.

Crediting Authors and Sources

When you write a paper using any materials other than your own thoughts and recollections, the ideas you gathered in your research become part of your own writing. This does not mean that you can claim these ideas as your own or fail to attribute them to someone. You need to credit authors for their ideas and words in order to avoid plagiarism.

To prevent plagiarism, learn the difference between a quotation and a paraphrase. A *quotation* refers to a source's exact words, which are set off from the rest of the text by quotation marks. A *paraphrase* is a restatement of the quotation in your own words, using your own sentence structure. Restatement means to completely rewrite the idea, not just to remove or replace a few words. A paraphrase may not be acceptable if it is too close to the original.

Even an acceptable paraphrase requires a citation of the source of the ideas within it. Take care to credit any source that you quote, paraphrase, or use as evidence. To credit sources, write a footnote or endnote that describes the source. Use the format preferred by your instructor. Writing handbooks, such as the *MLA Handbook*, contain acceptable formats.

TERMS

Plagiarism
The act of using someone else's exact words, figures, unique approach, or specific reasoning without giving appropriate credit.

Revising

When you *revise*, you critically evaluate the word choice, paragraph structure, and style of your first draft to see how it works. Any draft, no matter how good, can always be improved. Be thorough as you add, delete, replace, and reorganize words, sentences, and paragraphs. You may want to print out your draft and then spend time making notes and corrections on that hard copy before you make changes on a typewritten or computer-printed version. Figure 6-7 shows a paragraph from Michael's first draft, with revision comments added.

In addition to revising on your own, some of your classes may include peer review (having students read each other's work and offer suggestions). A peer reviewer can tell you what comes across well and what may be confusing. Having a different perspective on your writing is extremely valuable. Even if you don't have an organized peer-review system, you may want to ask a classmate to review your work as a favor to you.

The elements of revision include being a critical writer, evaluating paragraph structure, and checking for clarity and conciseness.

Being a Critical Writer

Critical thinking is as important in writing as it is in reading. Thinking critically when writing will help you move your papers beyond restating what you have researched and learned. Of course, your knowledge is an important part

Of the changes that ~~happened to us~~, the physical
[military recruits undergo]

transformation is the ~~biggest~~. ~~When we arrived at the~~
[most evident]

~~training facility, it was January, cold and cloudy. At the~~
[Too much]

~~time~~, I was a little thin, but I had been working out and
[Maybe— upon my January arrival at the]

thought that I could physically do anything. Oh boy, was
[training facility,]

I wrong! The Chief said to us right away: "Get down,

maggots!" Upon this command, we all to drop to the
[his trademark phrase]   [were]

ground and do military-style push-ups. Water survival
[endless]

tactics were also part of the training ~~that we had to~~

~~complete~~. Occasionally, my dreams of home were
[unnecessary]

interrupted at 3 a.m. when we had a surprise aquatic

test. Although we ~~didn't feel too happy about~~ this
[resented]

sub-human treatment at the time, we learned to
[mention how chief was involved]

appreciate how the conditioning was turning our bodies

into fine-tuned machines.
[say more about this (swimming in uniform incident?)]

of your writing. What will make your writing even more important and unique, however, is how you use critical thinking to construct your own new ideas and knowledge from what you have learned.

The key to critical writing is asking the question, "So what?" For example, if you were writing a paper on nutrition, you might discuss a variety of good eating habits. Asking "So what?" could lead you into a discussion of *why* these habits are helpful, or what positive effects they have. If you were writing a paper on egg imagery in the novel *All the King's Men* by Robert Penn Warren, you might list all the examples you noticed of that imagery. Then, asking "So what?" could lead you to evaluate why that imagery is so strong and what idea you think those examples convey.

As you revise, ask yourself questions that can help you think through ideas and examples, come up with your own original insights about the material, and be as complete and clear as possible. Use the mind actions to guide you. Here are some examples of questions you may ask:

Are these examples clearly connected to the idea?

Are there any similar concepts or facts I know of that can add to how I support this?

What else can I recall that can help to support this idea?

In evaluating any event or situation, have I clearly indicated the causes and effects?

What new idea comes to mind when I think about these examples or facts?

How do I evaluate any effect/fact/situation? Is it good or bad, useful or not?

What different arguments might a reader think of that I should address here?

Finally, critical thinking can help you evaluate the content and form of your paper. As you start your revision, ask yourself the following questions:

- Will my audience understand my thesis and how I've supported it?
- Does the introduction prepare the reader and capture attention?
- Is the body of the paper organized effectively?
- Is each idea fully developed, explained, and supported by examples?
- Are my ideas connected to one another through logical transitions?
- Do I have a clear, concise, simple writing style?
- Does the paper fulfill the requirements of the assignment?
- Does the conclusion provide a natural ending to the paper?

Checking for Clarity and Conciseness

Aim to say what you want to say in the clearest, most efficient way possible. A few well-chosen words will do your ideas more justice than a flurry of language. Try to eliminate extra words and phrases. Rewrite wordy phrases in a more concise, conversational way. For example, you can write "if" instead of "in the event that," or "now" instead of "this point in time." "Capriciously, I sauntered forth to the entryway and pummeled the door that loomed so majestically before me," might become "I skipped to the door and knocked loudly."

Editing

In contrast to the critical thinking of revising, *editing* involves correcting technical mistakes in spelling, grammar, and punctuation, as well as checking style consistency for elements such as abbreviations and capitalizations. Editing comes last, after you are satisfied with your ideas, organization, and style of

"See revision as 'envisioning again.' If there are areas in your work where there is a blur or vagueness, you can simply see the picture again and add the details that will bring your work closer to your mind's picture."
NATALIE GOLDBERG

writing. If you use a computer, you might want to use the grammar-check and spell-check functions to find mistakes. A spell-checker helps, but you still need to check your work on your own. While a spell-checker won't pick up the mistake in the following sentence, someone who is reading for sense will:

They are not hear on Tuesdays.

Look also for *sexist language*, which characterizes people based on their gender. Sexist language often involves the male pronoun *he* or *his*. For example, "An executive often spends hours each day going through his electronic mail" implies that executives are always men. A simple change will eliminate the sexist language: "Executives often spend hours each day going through their electronic mail," or, "An executive often spends hours each day going through his or her electronic mail." Try to be sensitive to words that leave out or slight women. *Mail carrier* is preferable to *mailman*; use *student* rather than *coed*.

Proofreading is the last stage of editing, occurring when you have a final version of your paper. Proofreading means reading every word and sentence in the final version to make sure they are accurate. Look for technical mistakes, run-on sentences, and sentence fragments. Look for incorrect word usage and references that aren't clear.

Teamwork can be a big help as you edit and proofread because another pair of eyes may see errors that you didn't notice on your own. If possible, have someone look over your work. Ask for feedback on what is clear and what is confusing. Then ask the reader to edit and proofread for errors.

A Final Checklist

You are now ready to complete your revising and editing checklist. All the tasks listed in Table 6-2 should be complete when you submit your final paper.

Your final paper reflects all the hard work you put in during the writing process. Figure 6-8 shows the final version of Michael's paper.

	DATE DUE	TASK	IS IT COMPLETE?
Table 6-2 Revising and editing checklist.		Check the body of the paper for clear thinking and adequate support of ideas	
		Finalize introduction and conclusion	
		Check word spelling and usage	
		Check grammar	
		Check paragraph structure	
		Make sure language is familiar and concise	
		Check punctuation	
		Check capitalization	
		Check transitions	
		Eliminate sexist language	

March 19, 1999
Michael B. Jackson

BOYS TO MEN

His stature was one of confidence, often misinterpreted by others as cockiness. His small frame was lean and agile, yet stiff and upright, as though every move were a calculated formula. For the longest eight weeks of my life, he was my father, my instructor, my leader, and my worst enemy. His name is Chief Marzloff, and he had the task of shaping the lives and careers of the youngest, newest members of the U. S. Coast Guard. As our Basic Training Company Commander, he took his job very seriously and demanded that we do the same. Within a limited time span, he conditioned our bodies, developed our self-confidence, and instilled within us a strong mental discipline.

Of the changes that recruits in military basic training undergo, the physical transformation is the most immediately evident. Upon my January arrival at the training facility, I was a little thin, but I had been working out and thought that I could physically do anything. Oh boy, was I wrong! The Chief wasted no time in introducing me to one of his trademark phrases: "Get down, maggots!" Upon this command, we were all to drop to the ground and produce endless counts of military-style push-ups. Later, we found out that exercise prepared us for hitting the deck in the event of enemy fire. Water survival tactics were also part of the training. Occasionally, my dreams of home were interrupted at about 3 a.m. when our company was selected for a surprise aquatic test. I recall one such test that required us to swim laps around the perimeter of a pool while in full uniform. I felt like a salmon swimming upstream, fueled only by natural instinct. Although we resented this sub-human treatment at the time, we learned to appreciate how the strict guidance of the Chief was turning our bodies into fine-tuned machines.

Beyond physical ability, Chief Marzloff also played an integral role in the development of our self-confidence. He would often declare in his raspy voice, "Look me in the eyes when you speak to me! Show me that you believe what you're saying!" He taught us that anything less was an expression of disrespect. Furthermore, he appeared to attack a personal habit of my own. It seemed that whenever he would speak to me individually, I would nervously nod my head in response. I was trying to demonstrate that I understood, but to him, I was blindly accepting anything that he said. He would roar, "That is a sign of weakness!" Needless to say, I am now conscious of all bodily motions when communicating with others. The Chief also reinforced self-confidence through his own example. He walked with his square chin up and chest out, like the proud parent of a newborn baby. He always gave the appearance that he had something to do, and that he was in complete control. Collectively, all of the methods that the Chief used were successful in developing our self-confidence.   *(continued)*

(continued)

Figure 6-8

Final version of paper.

Figure 6-8

Continued.

Perhaps the Chief's greatest contribution was the mental discipline that he instilled in his recruits. He taught us that physical ability and self-confidence were nothing without the mental discipline required to obtain any worthwhile goal. For us, this discipline began with adapting to the military lifestyle. Our day began promptly at 0500 hours, early enough to awaken the oversleeping roosters. By 0515 hours, we had to have showered, shaved, and perfectly donned our uniforms. At that point, we were marched to the galley for chow, where we learned to take only what is necessary, rather than indulging. Before each meal, the Chief would warn, "Get what you want, but you will eat all that you get!" After making good on his threat a few times, we all got the point. Throughout our stay, the Chief repeatedly stressed the significance of self-discipline. He would calmly utter, "Give a little now, get a lot later." I guess that meant different things to all of us. For me, it was a simple phrase that would later become my personal philosophy on life. The Chief went to great lengths to ensure that everyone under his direction possessed the mental discipline required to be successful in boot camp or in any of life's challenges.

Chief Marzloff was a remarkable role model and a positive influence on many lives. I never saw him smile, but it was evident that he genuinely cared a great deal about his job and all the lives that he touched. This man single-handedly conditioned our bodies, developed our self-confidence, and instilled a strong mental discipline that remains in me to this day. I have not seen the Chief since March 28, 1992, graduation day. Over the years, however, I have incorporated many of his ideals into my life. Above all, he taught us the true meaning of the U. S. Coast Guard slogan, "Semper Peratus" (Always Ready).

Suà

Suà is a Shoshone Indian word, derived from the Uto-Aztecan language, meaning "think." While much of the Native American tradition in the Americas focuses on oral communication, written languages have allowed Native American perspectives and ideas to be understood by readers outside the Native American culture. The writings of Leslie Marmon Silko, N. Scott Momaday, and Sherman Alexis have expressed important insights that all readers can consider.

Think of *suà*, and of how thinking can be communicated to others through writing, every time you begin to write. The power of writing allows you to express your own insights so that others can read them and perhaps benefit from knowing them. Explore your thoughts, sharpen your ideas, and remember the incredible power of the written word.

Success in the Real World

Stuart Scott

With his pearly grin and charismatic personality, 32-year-old Stuart Scott co-hosts ESPN's *SportsCenter.* Termed "El Fuego" (the fire) by a recent article in *Esquire* magazine, Stuart has helped make the somewhat comical sports show just about the hottest thing going. How did this young African American get so big, so fast? Well, according to Stuart, it was a gamble:

> I followed the same path of hard work and serious pursuit that everyone who wants to be a TV sports anchor does. I graduated from the University of North Carolina with a degree in speech communications and radio, television, and motion pictures. I worked at the student radio station, WXYC-FM, as a sports and news reporter. And I played football.

Stuart worked as a sports reporter for WESH-TV in Orlando where in just three short years he had won first-place honors from the Central Florida Press Club for one of his feature stories. He got his big break with ESPN, the world leader in sports coverage, when he was signed on as anchor of the growing ESPN2 network.

It didn't take long for Stuart to become El Fuego and move on to *SportsCenter.* He admits that he faced some serious controversy over his approach and distinctive street-style delivery of sports. In a recent interview with *Esquire* magazine, Stuart commented to his critics, "I have to walk a tighter line. I do recognize that there is an African American audience that relates to me simply because I'm black and because my style is familiar to them. I'm doing it purposefully to prove that you can be diverse and do this job."

Scott's mother was a schoolteacher and his father worked for the postal service in Chicago. Scott knows that they were an important part of his success. They demanded hard work from him and also encouraged him to do anything he wanted to do. It is clear that Stuart's parents instilled the kind of confidence in him that has led to his success at *SportsCenter:*

> I know there are and were people out there who thought, "This guy will never make it," but I knew I could. I also knew I was going to have to work extra hard to do the sportscasts my way. But that's my style and that's part of who I am.

Stuart says you still have to do the hard work to become successful. And he recognizes that he has had just as many bad nights on the show as anyone else. "You have bad nights and you go on," he says. It is apparent that Stuart really has gone on. His popularity only continues to grow and his opportunities seem limitless.

Chapter 6 Applications

Name _____ Date _____

KEY INTO YOUR LIFE
Opportunities to Apply What You Learn

6.1 *Evaluate Your Notes*

Choose one particular class period from the last two weeks. Have a classmate photocopy his or her notes from that class period for you. Then evaluate your notes by comparing them with your classmate's. Think about:

◆ Do your notes make sense?
◆ How is your handwriting?
◆ Do the notes cover everything that was brought up in class?
◆ Are there examples to back up ideas?
◆ What note-taking system is used?
◆ Will these notes help you study?

Write your evaluation here: _____

_____

_____

_____

_____

_____

What ideas or techniques from your classmate's notes do you plan to use in the future? _____

_____

_____

_____

_____

6.2   *Class vs. Reading*

Pick a class for which you have a regular textbook. Choose a set of class notes on a subject that is also covered in that textbook. Read the textbook section that corresponds to the subject of your class notes, taking notes as you go. Compare your reading notes to the notes you took in class.

Did you use a different system with the textbook or the same system as in class? Why? _____

_____

_____

Which notes can you understand better? Why do you think that's true?

_____

_____

_____

What did you learn from your reading notes that you want to bring to your class note-taking strategy? _____

_____

_____

_____

_____

6.3   *Prewriting*

Choose a topic you are interested in and know something about—for example, college sports, handling stress in a stressful world, our culture's emphasis on beauty and youth, or child rearing. Narrow your topic; then use the following prewriting strategies to discover what you already know about the topic and what you would need to learn if you had to write an essay about the subject for one of your classes. (If necessary, continue this prewriting exercise on a separate sheet of paper.)

Brainstorm your ideas: _____

_____

_____

Freewrite: _____

Ask journalists' questions: _____

 ## 6.4 *Writing a Thesis Statement*

Write two thesis statements for each of the following topics. The first statement should try to inform the reader, while the second should try to persuade. In each case, writing a thesis statement will require that you narrow the topic.

◆ *The rising cost of a college education*

Thesis with an informative purpose: _____

Thesis with a persuasive purpose: _____

◆ *Taking care of your body and mind*

Thesis with an informative purpose: _____

Thesis with a persuasive purpose: _____

_____

_____

◆ *Career choice*

Thesis with an informative purpose: _____

_____

_____

Thesis with a persuasive purpose: _____

_____

_____

6.5 *Team-Building Exercise: Collaborative Writing*

In many jobs, you may be asked to work with other employees to produce written documents, including reports, proposals, procedure manuals, and even important letters and memos. Writing in groups, also known as *collaborative writing*, involves planning, drafting, revising, and editing.

To see what collaborative writing is like, join with three classmates and choose a general topic you are all interested in—for example, "What Colleges Can Do to Help Students Juggle School, Work, and Family" or "Teaching Safer Sex in an Age When Sex Isn't Safe." Now imagine that you and the other group members have to write a persuasive paper on some aspect of this topic. Writing the paper involves the following steps:

◆ Each group member should spend an hour in the library to get an overview of the topic so that everyone is able to write about it in general terms.

◆ The group should come together to brainstorm the topic, narrow its focus, and come up with a thesis. Use your research and thesis to write a working outline that specifies what the paper will say and the approach it will take. Divide the writing assignment into parts and assign a part to each group member.

◆ Each group member should *draft* his or her portion of the paper. Each section should be about two to three paragraphs long.

◆ Photocopy each draft and give a copy to each group member. Working independently, each person should use the suggestions in this chapter to *evaluate and revise* each section. Afterwards, come together as a group to hammer out differences and prepare a final, unedited version.

◆ Photocopy this version and distribute it to the group members. Have eveyone *edit* the material, looking for mistakes in spelling, grammar, punctuation, and usage. Incorporate the group's changes into a final version you all agree on, and ask every group member to read it. The group's goal is to produce a finished paper that satisfies the thesis and also looks good.

◆ Working alone, each group member should answer the following questions. Finally, compare your responses with those of the other group members:

1. What do you see as the advantages and disadvantages of collaborative writing? Is it difficult or easy to write as a team member?

   _____

   _____

   _____

2. What part of the collaborative writing project worked best? Where did you encounter problems?

   _____

   _____

   _____

3. What did you learn from this experience that will make you a more effective collaborative writer on the next project?

   _____

   _____

   _____

Case Studies

Soup's On

Campbell Soup Company

When was the last time you ate a home-cooked meal? If you're like many people, it has been awhile, and the Campbell Soup Company wants you to know that it feels your hunger pains. It's spending a lot of money studying America in an attempt to better know how soup might fit into our lifestyle. Soup? Believe it or not, soup is big business—in the United States alone, over $3.5 billion of canned soup is sold annually. So, how does soup fit into the American lifestyle?

As a result of changing lifestyles, Americans are increasingly eating outside the home. Mealtime is no longer a cause for daily family gatherings in many households and has become less structured. Meals are more of a necessity than the social events they used to be, and many people don't even know how to prepare meals at home. This is necessary information for all the major food companies to have, and Campbell's, likewise, is watching. They look at trends in lifestyles to determine what kinds of soups to offer and how to advertise those soups.

One factor in our changing lifestyle is that there are a lot more working moms today than there were several years ago. Women are becoming an increasingly larger part of the work force. In 1970, 43 percent of American women were part of the work force. By 1990, that percentage had increased to over 57 percent and continued to rise to over 59 percent by 1996. In addition, almost 80 percent of young women are working. As a result of these demographic trends, Americans have less time for food preparation in most households and are seeking convenient solutions to the everyday questions of what they are going to eat.

It turns out that this is good news for Campbell's. As women work more, there is less time to prepare both lunch and dinner. Campbell's believes that soups will become increasingly popular because of their convenience and home-style quality. Because soups are perceived by many people to be part of old-fashioned family meals, Campbell's is marketing them as such. Research shows that working moms want to be able to provide a stable environment for their children, similar to their own childhood experiences, and soup is reminiscent of that time in their lives.

American consumers have, in recent years, also shown increasing demand for foods perceived to be healthy, according to data from the Calorie Control Council. The share of U.S. adults regularly consuming low-fat, sugar-free, and low-calorie foods and beverages reached 92 percent in 1996, significantly up from the 81 percent share recorded in 1993.

Growth in the soup industry has also been partly influenced by a segment from a popular comedy television program, *Seinfeld*, about a "Soup Nazi" in late 1995. The segment was based on the real-life Al Yegeaneh, the owner of Manhattan's Soup Kitchen International. The show gave immediate popularity to his establishment; the restaurant was ranked as one of the distinguished eateries in the *1998 Zagat Restaurant Survey* in New York. The increased attention on soup has led to greater profits for Campbell's and other soup companies.

In late 1997, of the top brands in soup, Campbell's had over 70 percent of the market. This means that out of all the soup sold in the United States, 70 percent was a Campbell's brand.

As you can see from the chart below, Campbell's makes many brands of soup:

BRAND	COMPANY	PARENT COMPANY
Baked Ramen	Campbell's	Campbell Soup Co.
Campbell's	Campbell's	Campbell Soup Co.
Chunky	Campbell's	Campbell Soup Co.
Creative Chef	Campbell's	Campbell Soup Co.
Healthy Request	Campbell's	Campbell Soup Co.
Home Cookin'	Campbell's	Campbell Soup Co.
Low Fat Ramen	Campbell's	Campbell Soup Co.
98% Fat Free	Campbell's	Campbell Soup Co.
Premium in a Jar	Campbell's	Campbell Soup Co.
Swanson Broth	Campbell's	Campbell Soup Co.
Swanson 99% Fat Free	Campbell's	Campbell Soup Co.
Swanson Natural Goodness	Campbell's	Campbell Soup Co.
Healthy Choice	ConAgra	ConAgra *(continued)*

BRAND	COMPANY	PARENT COMPANY
Knorr	Best Foods	CPC International
Progresso	Pet, Inc.	Grand Metropolitan
Mrs. Grass Noodle Soup	Borden	Kohlberg, Kravis & Roberts
Wyler's Soup Starter	Borden	Kohlberg, Kravis & Roberts
Ramen	Maruchen	
Cup-O-Noodles	Nissin Foods	Nissin Foods
Oodles O'Noodles	Nissin Foods	Nissin Foods
Top Ramen	Nissin Foods	Nissin Foods
Kettle Creations	Lipton	Unilever
Lipton Cup-A-Soup	Lipton	Unilever
Lipton Soup Secrets	Lipton	Unilever

Source: Supermarket Business.

Campbell's is the recognized leader in the soup industry. It has strong customer loyalty and is seen as a promoter of family values. However, in recent years, it has had difficulty with employee satisfaction, which could affect its image. Because Campbell's dominates the soup market so thoroughly, and because soup is a mature product in the United States, most companies are seeking to expand their lines internationally. One of Campbell's strategies in the United States is to focus on product development, especially of low-fat, home-style products.

1. What could be an advantage of having so many brands of soup?

2. Get a can of soup and analyze the label for its readablity—what is in large type? What pictures are used? Symbols? Is it easy to read the information?

3. How would you market soup if you were Campbell's? Would you target a specific group of people?

4. What other companies might be affected by the changing lifestyles of Americans?

5. Look in the soup aisle at your local grocery store and determine what soups take up most of the aisle. What does this tell you about popular brands?

6. How can a television show or movie affect sales of a food product? Can you think of other examples of television shows or movies that have affected product sales?

Internet Exercise

If you do not have an email account, set one up now. There are several free services that you can use if your school does not offer free email. The free email services are supported by advertising money in lieu of membership receipts. Access the following site, or any other preferred service, and set up an email account:

www.hotmail.com

1. Exchange email messages with another person in your class, and print out your messages. The subject of your message should be a topic you plan to write about (either as a course requirement or as a personal project).
2. Before you write your email, brainstorm a list of ideas or an outline of your topic.
3. Enter your topic as the subject line of the email.
4. Use the freewriting technique to compose the message you are sending.
5. Remember to print out a copy of your freewriting.

Journal

Name _____ Date _____

7

Listening, Memory, and Test Taking

Taking In, Retaining, and Demonstrating Knowledge

C ollege exposes you daily to facts, opinions, and ideas. It is up to you to take in, retain, and demonstrate knowledge of what you learn, for use in or out of school. You can accomplish these goals through active listening, focused use of your memory skills, and thorough preparation for taking tests.

Listening is one of the primary ways of taking in information. Memory skills can help you retain what you've listened to so that you can recall it for a paper, a discussion, or a test. After you've listened and remembered, test taking is your key to demonstrating what you have learned to your instructor or others. In this chapter, you will learn strategies to improve your ability to take in, remember, and show knowledge of what you have learned.

In this chapter, you will explore answers to the following questions:

◆ How can you become a better listener?

◆ How does memory work?

◆ How can you improve your memory?

◆ How can tape recorders help you listen, remember, and study?

◆ How can preparation help improve your test scores?

◆ What strategies can help you succeed on tests?

◆ How can you learn from test mistakes?

HOW CAN YOU BECOME A BETTER LISTENER?

The act of hearing isn't quite the same as the act of listening. While *hearing* refers to sensing spoken messages from their source, *listening* involves a complex process of communication. Successful listening results in the speaker's intended message reaching the listener. In school and at home, poor listening results in communication breakdowns and mistakes, and skilled listening promotes progress and success.

Ralph G. Nichols, a pioneer in listening research, studied 200 students at the University of Minnesota over a nine-month period. His findings, summarized in Table 7-1, demonstrate that effective listening depends as much on a positive attitude as on specific skills.[1]

Listening is a teachable—and learnable—skill. Improving your learning skills involves managing listening challenges and becoming an active listener. Although becoming a better listener will help in every class, it is especially important in subject areas that are difficult for you.

Manage Listening Challenges

Classic studies have shown that immediately after listening, students are likely to recall only half of what was said. This is partly due to particular listening challenges, including divided attention and distractions, the tendency to shut out the message, the inclination to rush to judgment, and partial hearing loss or learning disabilities.[2] To help create a positive listening environment, in both your mind and your surroundings, explore how to manage these challenges.

Divided Attention and Distractions

Internal and external distractions often divide your attention. *Internal distractions* include anything from hunger to headache to personal worries. Something the speaker says may also trigger a recollection that may cause

LISTENING IS HELPED BY . . .	LISTENING IS HINDERED BY . . .	Table 7-1
making a conscious decision to work at listening; viewing difficult material as a listening challenge.	caring little about the listening process; tuning out difficult material.	What helps and hinders listening.
fighting distractions through intense concentration.	refusing to listen at the first distraction.	
continuing to listen when a subject is difficult or dry, in the hope that one might learn something interesting.	giving up as soon as one loses interest.	
withholding judgment until hearing everything.	becoming preoccupied with a response as soon as a speaker makes a controversial statement.	
focusing on the speaker's theme by recognizing organizational patterns transitional language, and summary statements.	getting sidetracked by unimportant details.	
adapting note-taking style to the unique style and organization of the speaker.	always taking notes in outline form, even when a speaker is poorly organized, leading to frustration.	
pushing past negative emotional responses and forcing oneself to continue to listen.	letting an initial emotional response shut off continued listening.	
using excess thinking time to evaluate, summarize, and question what one just heard and anticipating what will come next.	thinking about other things and, as a result, missing much of the message.	

your mind to drift. In contrast, *external distractions* include noises (whispering, honking horns, screaming sirens) and even excessive heat or cold. It can be hard to listen in an overheated room that is putting you to sleep.

Your goal is to reduce distractions and focus on what you're hearing. Sitting where you can see and hear clearly will help you listen well. Dress comfortably and try not to go to class hungry or thirsty.

Shutting Out the Message

Instead of paying attention to everything the speaker says, many students fall into the trap of focusing on specific points and shutting out the rest of the message. Creating a positive listening environment includes accepting responsibility for listening. While the instructor communicates information to you, he or she cannot force you to listen. You are responsible for taking in that information. Instructors often cover material from outside the textbook during class and then test on that material. If you work to take in the whole message in class, you will be able to read over your notes later and think critically about what is most important.

The Rush to Judgment

People tend to stop listening when they hear something they don't like. If you rush to judge what you've heard, your focus turns to your personal reaction rather than the content of the speaker's message. Judgments also involve reactions to the speakers themselves. If you do not like your instructors or if you have preconceived notions about their ideas or cultural background, you may decide that their words have little value.

Work to recognize and control your judgments. Being aware of what you tend to judge will help you avoid putting up a barrier against incoming messages that clash with your opinions or feelings. Try to see education as a continuing search for evidence, regardless of whether it supports or negates your point of view.

Partial Hearing Loss and Learning Disabilities

"No one cares to speak to an unwilling listener. An arrow never lodges in a stone; often it recoils upon the sender of it."
ST. JEROME

Good listening techniques don't solve every listening problem. Students who have a partial hearing loss have a physical explanation for why listening is difficult. If you have some level of hearing loss, seek out special services that can help you listen in class. You may require special equipment or might benefit from tutoring. You may be able to arrange to meet with your instructor outside of class to clarify your notes.

Other disabilities, such as attention deficit disorder (ADD) or a problem with processing heard language, can cause difficulties with both focusing on and understanding that which is heard. People with such disabilities have varied abilities to compensate for and overcome them. If you have a disability, don't blame yourself for having trouble listening. Your counseling center, student health center, advisor, and instructors should be able to give you particular assistance in working through your challenges.

How DOES MEMORY WORK?

You need an effective memory in order to use the knowledge you take in throughout your life. Human memory works like a computer. Both have essentially the same purpose: to encode, store, and retrieve information.

During the *encoding stage*, information is changed into usable form. On a computer, this occurs when keyboard entries are transformed into electronic symbols and stored on a disk. In the brain, sensory information becomes impulses that the central nervous system reads and codes. You are encoding, for example, when you study a list of chemistry formulas.

During the *storage stage*, information is held in memory (the mind's version of a computer hard drive) for later use. In this example, after you complete your studying of the formulas, your mind stores them until you need to use them.

During the *retrieval stage*, memories are recovered from storage by recall, just as a saved computer program is called up by name and used again. In this example, your mind would retrieve the chemistry formulas when you had to take a test or solve a problem.

Memories are stored in three different storage banks. The first, called *sensory memory*, is an exact copy of what you see and hear and lasts for a second or less. Certain information is then selected from sensory memory and moves into *short-term memory*, a temporary information storehouse that lasts no more than ten to twenty seconds. You are consciously aware of material in your short-term memory. While unimportant information is quickly dumped, important information is transferred to *long-term memory*—the mind's more permanent storehouse.

Having information in long-term memory does not mean that you will be able to recall it when needed. Particular techniques can help you improve your recall.

How can you improve your memory?

Your accounting instructor is giving a test tomorrow on the use of bookkeeping programs. You feel confident, since you spent hours last week memorizing the material. Unfortunately, by the time you take the test, you may remember very little. That's because most forgetting occurs within minutes after memorization.

In a classic study conducted in 1885, researcher Hermann Ebbinghaus memorized a list of meaningless three-letter words such as CEF and LAZ. Within one short hour, he measured that he had forgotten more than 50 percent of what he learned. After two days, he knew fewer than 30 percent. Although his recall of the syllables remained fairly stable after that, the experiment shows how fragile memory can be, even when you take the time and energy to memorize information.[3]

People who have superior memories may have an inborn talent for remembering. More often, though, they have mastered techniques for improving recall. Remember that techniques aren't a cure-all for memory difficulties, especially for those who may have disabilities such as ADD. If you have a disability, the following memory techniques may help you but may not be enough. Seek specific assistance if you consistently have trouble remembering.

Memory Improvement Strategies

As a student, your job is to understand, learn, and remember information, from general concepts to specific details. The following suggestions will help improve your recall.

Develop a Will to Remember

Why can you remember the lyrics to dozens of popular songs but not the functions of the pancreas? Perhaps this is because you want to remember the lyrics, you connect them with a visual image, or you have an emotional tie to them. To achieve the same results at school or on the job, tell yourself that what you are learning is important and that you need to remember it. Saying these words out loud can help you begin the active, positive process of memory improvement.

Understand What You Memorize

Make sure that everything you want to remember makes sense. Something that has meaning is easier to recall than something that is gibberish. This basic principle applies to everything you study—from biology and astronomy to history and English literature.

Recite, Rehearse, and Write

When you *recite* material, you repeat it aloud in order to remember it. Reciting helps you retrieve and retain information as you learn it and is a crucial step in studying (see Chapter 5). *Rehearsing* is similar to reciting but is done in silence, in your mind. It involves the process of repeating, summarizing, and associating information with other information. *Writing* is rehearsing on paper. The act of writing solidifies the information in your memory.

Separate Main Points From Unimportant Details

If you use critical-thinking skills to select and focus on the most important information, you can avoid overloading your mind with extra clutter. To focus on key points, highlight only the most important information in your texts, and write notes in the margins about central ideas. When you review your lecture notes, highlight or rewrite the most important information to remember.

Study During Short but Frequent Sessions

Research shows that you can improve your chances of remembering material if you learn it more than once. To get the most out of your study sessions, spread them over time. A pattern of short sessions followed by brief periods of rest is more effective than continual studying with little or no rest. Even though you may feel as if you accomplish a lot by studying for an hour without a break, you'll probably remember more from three 20-minute sessions. Try sandwiching study time into breaks in your schedule, such as when you have time between classes.

Separate Material Into Manageable Sections

When material is short and easy to understand, studying it start to finish may work. For longer material, you may benefit from dividing it into logical sections, mastering each section, putting all the sections together, and then testing your memory of all the material. Actors take this approach when learning the lines of a play, and it can work just as well for students.

Use Visual Aids

Any kind of visual representation of study material can help you remember. You may want to convert material into a think link or outline. Write material in any visual shape that helps you recall it, and link it to other information.

Flash cards are a great visual memory tool. They give you short, repeated review sessions that provide immediate feedback. Make them from 3-by-5-inch index cards. Use the front of the card to write a word, idea, or phrase you want to remember. Use the back side for a definition, explanation, and other key facts. Figure 7-1 shows two flash cards for studying psychology.

Here are some additional suggestions for making the most of your flash cards:

◆ *Use the cards as a self-test.* Divide the cards into two piles: the material you know and the material you are learning. You may want to use rubber bands to separate the piles.

◆ *Carry the cards with you and review them frequently.* You'll learn the most if you start using cards early in the course, well ahead of exam time.

◆ *Shuffle the cards and learn information in various orders.* This will help avoid putting too much focus on some information and not enough on others.

◆ *Test yourself in both directions.* First, look at the terms or ideas and provide definitions or explanations. Then turn the cards over and reverse the process.

Mnemonic Devices

Certain show business performers entertain their audiences by remembering the names of 100 strangers or flawlessly repeating thirty 10-digit phone numbers. These performers probably have superior memories, but genetics alone can't produce these results. They also rely on memory techniques, known as mnemonic (pronounced neh MAHN ick) devices to help them.

TERMS

Mnemonic devices
Memory techniques that involve associating new information with information you already know.

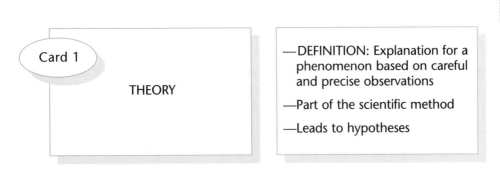

Figure 7-2

Flash cards help you memorize important facts.

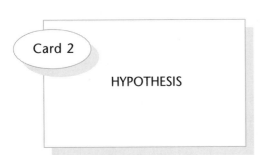

Card 1

THEORY

—DEFINITION: Explanation for a phenomenon based on careful and precise observations

—Part of the scientific method

—Leads to hypotheses

Card 2

HYPOTHESIS

—Prediction about future behavior that is derived from observations and theories

—Methods for testing hypotheses: case studies, naturalistic observations, and experiments

Mnemonic devices work by connecting information you are trying to learn with simpler information or information that is familiar. Instead of learning new facts by rote (repetitive practice), associations give you a hook on which to hang these facts and retrieve them. Mnemonic devices make information familiar and meaningful through unusual, unforgettable mental associations and visual pictures.

"The true art of memory is the art of attention."

SAMUEL JOHNSON

Here's an example to prove the power of mnemonics. Suppose you want to remember the names of the first six presidents of the United States. The first letters of their last names—Washington, Adams, Jefferson, Madison, Monroe, and Adams—together read W A J M M A. To remember them, you might add an "e" after the "J" and create a short nonsense word, "wajemma." To remember their first names—George, John, Thomas, James, James, and John—you might set the names to the tune of "Happy Birthday" or any musical tune that you know.

Visual images and acronyms are a few of the more widely used kinds of mnemonic devices. Apply them to your own memory challenges.

Create Visual Images and Associations

Visual images are easier to remember than images that rely on words alone. In fact, communication through visual images goes back to the prehistoric era, when people made drawings that still exist on cave walls. It's no accident that the phrase "a picture is worth a thousand words" is so familiar. The best mental pictures often involve colors, three-dimensional images, action scenes, and disproportionate, funny, or ridiculous images.

Especially for visual learners, turning information into mental pictures helps improve memory. To remember that the Spanish artist Picasso painted "The Three Women," you might imagine the women in a circle dancing to a Spanish song with a pig and a donkey (pig-asso). Don't reject outlandish images—as long as they help you.

Create Acronyms

TERMS

Acronym
A word formed from the first letters of a series of words, created in order to help you remember the series.

Another helpful association method involves the use of the acronym. The acronym "Roy G. Biv" often helps students remember the colors of the spectrum. Roy G. Biv stands for Red, Orange, Yellow, Green, Blue, Indigo, Violet. In history, you can remember the big three Allies during World War II—Britain, America, and Russia—with the acronym BAR.

When you can't create a name like Roy G. Biv, create an acronym from an entire sentence in which the first letter of each word in the sentence stands for the first letter of each memorized term. When science students want to remember the list of planets in order of their distance from the Sun, they learn the sentence: My Very Elegant Mother Just Served Us Nine Pickles (Mercury, Venus, Earth, Mars, Jupiter, Saturn, Uranus, Neptune, and Pluto).

Improving your memory requires energy, time, and work. In school, it also helps to master PQ3R, the textbook study technique that was introduced in Chapter 5. By going through the steps in PQ3R and using the specific memory techniques described in this chapter, you will be able to learn more in less time—and remember what you learn long after exams are over.

HOW CAN TAPE RECORDERS HELP YOU LISTEN, REMEMBER, AND STUDY?

The selective use of a tape recorder can provide helpful backup to your listening and memory skills and to your study materials. It's important, though, not to let tape-recording substitute for active participation. Not all students like to use tape recorders, but if you choose to do so, here are some guidelines and a discussion of potential effects.

Guidelines for Using Tape Recorders

Ask the instructor whether he or she permits tape recorders in class. Some instructors don't mind, while others don't allow students to use them.

Use a small, portable tape recorder. Sit near the front for the best possible recording.

Participate actively in class. Take notes just as you would if the tape recorder were not there.

Use tape recorders to make study tapes. Questions on tape can be like audio flash cards. One way to do it is to record study questions, leaving ten to fifteen seconds between questions for you to answer out loud. Recording the correct answer after the pause will give you immediate feedback. For example, part of a recording for a writing class might say, "The three elements of effective writing are . . . (10–15 seconds) . . . topic, audience, and purpose."

Potential Positive Effects of Using Tape Recorders

- You can listen to an important portion of the lecture over and over again.
- You can supplement or clarify sections of the lecture that confused you or that you missed.
- Tape recordings can provide additional study materials to listen to when you exercise or drive in your car.
- Tape recordings can help study groups reconcile conflicting notes.
- If you miss class, you might be able to have a friend record the lecture for you.

Potential Negative Effects of Using Tape Recorders

- You may tend to listen less in class.
- You may take fewer notes, figuring that you will rely on your tape.
- It may be time-consuming. When you attend a lecture in order to record it and then listen to the entire recording, you have taken twice as much time out of your schedule.
- If your tape recorder malfunctions or the recording is hard to hear, you may end up with very little study material, especially if your notes are sparse.

Think critically about whether using a tape recorder is a good idea for you. If you choose to try it, let the tape recorder be an additional resource for you instead of a replacement for your active participation and skills. Tape-recorded lectures and study tapes are just one study resource you can use in preparation for the tests that will often come your way.

HOW CAN PREPARATION HELP IMPROVE YOUR TEST SCORES?

Many people don't look forward to taking tests. If you are one of those people, try thinking of exams as preparation for life. When you volunteer, get a job, or work on your family budget, you'll have to apply what you know. This is exactly what you do when you take a test.

Like a runner who prepares for a marathon by exercising, eating right, taking practice runs, and getting enough sleep, you can take steps to master your exams. Your first step is to study until you know the material that will be on the test. Your next step is to use the following strategies to become a successful test taker: Identify test type, use specific study skills, prepare physically, and conquer test anxiety.

Identify Test Type and Material Covered

Before you begin studying, try to determine the type of test and what it will cover:

- ◆ Will it be a short-answer test with true/false and multiple-choice questions, an essay test, or a combination?
- ◆ Will the test cover everything you studied since the semester began, or will it be limited to a narrow topic?
- ◆ Will the test be limited to what you learned in class and in the text, or will it also cover outside readings?

Your instructors may answer these questions for you. Even though they may not tell you the specific questions that will be on the test, they might let you know what blocks of information will be covered and the question format. Some instructors may even drop hints throughout the semester about possible test questions. While some comments are direct ("I might ask a question on the subject of ___ on your next exam"), other clues are subtle. For example, when instructors repeat an idea or when they express personal interest in a topic ("One of my favorite theories is . . . "), they are letting you know that the material may be on the test.

Here are a few other strategies for predicting what may be on a test:

Use PQ3R to identify important ideas and facts. Often, the questions you write and ask yourself when you read assigned materials may be part of the test. In addition, any textbook study questions are good candidates for test material.

If you know people who took the instructor's course before, ask them about class tests. Try to find out how difficult the tests are and whether the test focuses more on assigned readings or class notes. Ask about instructor preferences. If you learn that the instructor pays close attention to details, such as facts or grammar, plan your work accordingly.

Examine old tests if instructors make them available in class or on reserve in the library. If you can't get copies of old tests, use clues from the class to predict test questions. After taking the first exam in the course, you will have a lot more information about what to expect in the future.

Use Specific Study Skills

Certain study skills are especially useful for test taking. They include choosing study materials, setting a study schedule, using critical thinking, and taking a pretest.

Choose Study Materials

Once you have identified as much as you can about the subject matter of the test, choose the materials that contain the information you need to study. You can save yourself time by making sure that you aren't studying anything you don't need to. Go through your notes, your texts, any primary source materials that were assigned, and any handouts from your instructor. Set aside any materials you don't need so they don't take up your valuable time.

Set a Study Schedule

Use your time-management skills to set a schedule that will help you feel as prepared as you can be. Consider all the relevant factors—the materials you need to study, how many days or weeks until the test date, and how much time you can study each day. If you establish your schedule ahead of time and write it in your date book, you will be much more likely to follow it.

Schedules will vary widely according to situation. For example, if you have only three days before the test and no other obligations during that time, you might set two 2-hour study sessions for yourself during each day. On the other hand, if you have two weeks before a test date, classes during the day, and work three nights a week, you might spread out your study sessions over the nights you have off work during those two weeks.

Use Critical Thinking

Using the techniques from Chapter 4, approach your test preparation critically, working to understand rather than to just pass the test by repeating facts. As you study, try to connect ideas to examples, analyze causes and effects, establish truth, and look at issues from different perspectives. Although it takes work, critical thinking will promote a greater understanding of the subject and probably a higher grade on the exam. Using critical thinking is especially important for essay tests. Prepare by identifying potential essay questions and writing your responses.

Take a Pretest

Use questions from the ends of textbook chapters to create your own pretest. Choose questions that are likely to be covered on the test; then answer them under testlike conditions—in a quiet place, with no books or notes to help you, and with a clock to tell you when to quit. Try to duplicate the conditions of the actual test. If your course doesn't have an assigned text, develop questions from your notes and from assigned outside readings.

Prepare Physically

When taking a test, you often need to work efficiently under time pressure. If your body is tired or under stress, you will probably not think as clearly or perform as well. If you can, avoid pulling an all-nighter. Get some sleep so that you can wake up rested and alert. If you are one of the many who press the snooze button in their sleep, try setting two alarm clocks and placing them across the room from your bed. That way you'll be more likely to get to your test on time.

Eating right is also important. Sugar-laden snacks will bring your energy up only to send it crashing back down much too soon. Similarly, too much caffeine can add to your tension and make it difficult to focus. Eating nothing will leave you drained, but too much food can make you want to take a nap. The best advice is to eat a light, well-balanced meal before a test. When time is short, grab a quick-energy snack such as a banana, some orange juice, or a granola bar.

Conquer Test Anxiety

A certain amount of stress can be a good thing. Your body is on alert, and your energy motivates you to do your best. For many students, however, the time before and during an exam brings a feeling of near-panic known as *test anxiety*. Described as a bad case of nerves that makes it hard to think or remember, test anxiety can make your life miserable and affect how you do on tests. When anxiety blocks performance, here are some suggestions:

Prepare so you'll feel in control. The more you know about what to expect on the exam, the better you'll feel. Find out what material will be covered, the format of the questions, the length of the exam, and the percentage of points assigned to each question.

Put the test in perspective. No matter how important it may seem, a test is only a small part of your educational experience and an even smaller part of your life. Your test grade does not reflect the kind of person you are or your ability to succeed in life.

Make a study plan. Divide the plan into a series of small tasks. As you finish each one, you'll feel a sense of accomplishment and control.

Practice relaxation. When you feel test anxiety coming on, take some deep breaths, close your eyes, and visualize positive mental images related to the test, like getting a good grade and finishing confidently with time to spare.

Test Anxiety and the Returning Adult Student

If you're returning to school after a layoff of five, ten, or even twenty years, you may wonder if you can compete with younger students or if your mind is still able to learn new material. To counteract these feelings of inadequacy, focus on how your life experiences have given you skills you can use. For example, managing work and a family requires strong time management,

REAL WORLD PERSPECTIVE

How can I prepare for exams?

Jeff Felardeau, Selkirk College, Nelson, British Columbia

I've been out of school for quite a long time, so when I returned and had to memorize material for exams, I just wasn't prepared. The labor work I was doing didn't require me to use my memorization skills. I had the most difficulty memorizing for classes like biology and any of the sciences where you have to memorize a lot of facts. I'd work hard by repeating the information over and over in my mind, but I'd only be able to recall it for a short time afterwards—long-term learning wasn't there. Whenever I'd prepare for an exam, I'd find myself in a "cram" mode because I didn't remember any of the material from class. It was like learning the material all over again.

I took a class called College Success, which gave me some good study tips. They taught me things like mind mapping, listening skills, and note-taking styles. They also taught me to use word associations and visualization to help remember the material. It's helped me improve a lot, but I still get stuck in old habits and patterns and forget to apply the methods that will really help me improve. I know that if I don't change these old study patterns and habits, I'll hit the wall sooner or later. I can't keep using methods that served me in the past but are no longer effective for where I am today. What do you suggest?

Miriam Kapner, New England Conservatory, Boston

Even though you have a good understanding of what it takes to prepare for an exam, the key is to remain disciplined. If your mind is wandering in class and you find you're staring out the window looking at those clouds, remember that you have control of your mind. By staying focused in class, you will not have to study so much when exam time rolls around. Although we all fall victim to daydreaming, try and gain control of your mind by thinking of your goals or by using simple mind tricks. Even if the class has a very dry teacher, there are ways to keep focused. One day a friend and I sat down and figured out exactly how much each class was costing us. When we realized the amount of money we were spending for that hour, it was a real eye-opener. If I'm really having a hard time, then I make sure I ask at least two questions per class. This forces me to pay attention.

In order to memorize, you need to be able to find some order. It helps if you have a reference point to begin with and then look for certain patterns or categories. I also use mnemonic devices to help me remember. In fact, I can still remember one I learned in elementary school: Every Good Boy Does Fine for the lines in the treble clef. But mainly, whatever steps you take to improve your preparation for exams, remember that you are in control of your mind—not the other way around.

planning, and communication skills that can help you plan your study time, juggle school responsibilities, and interact with students and instructors.

In addition, your life experiences give you examples with which you can understand ideas in your courses. For example, your relationship experiences may help you understand concepts in a psychology course; managing your finances may help you understand economics or accounting practices; and work experience may give you a context for what you learn in a business management course. If you let yourself feel positive about your knowledge and skills, you may improve your ability to achieve your goals.

WHAT STRATEGIES CAN HELP YOU SUCCEED ON TESTS?

Even though every test is different, there are general strategies that will help you handle almost all tests, including short-answer and essay exams.

Write Down Key Facts

Before you even look at the test, write down any key information—including formulas, rules, and definitions—that you studied recently or even right before you entered the test room. Use the back of the question sheet or a piece of scrap paper for your notes. (Make sure it is clear to your instructor that this scrap paper didn't come into the test room already filled in!) Recording this information right at the start will make forgetting less likely.

Begin With an Overview of the Exam

Even though exam time is precious, spend a few minutes at the start of the test to get a sense of the kinds of questions you'll be answering, what kind of thinking they require, the number of questions in each section, and the point value of each section. Use this information to schedule the time you spend on each section. For example, if a two-hour test is divided into two sections of equal point value—an essay section with four questions and a short-answer section with sixty questions—you can spend an hour on the essays (fifteen minutes per question) and an hour on the short-answer section (one minute per question).

As you make your calculations, think about the level of difficulty of each section. If you think you can handle the short-answer questions in less than an hour and that you'll need more time with the essays, rebudget your time in a way that works for you.

Know the Ground Rules

A few basic rules apply to any test. Following them will give you the advantage.

Read test directions. While a test made up of 100 true/false questions and one essay may look straightforward, the directions may tell you to answer 80, or that the essay is an optional bonus. Some questions or sections may be weighted more heavily than others. Try circling or underlining key words and numbers that remind you of the directions.

Begin with the parts or questions that seem easiest to you. Starting with what you know best can boost your confidence and help you save time to spend on the harder parts.

Watch the clock. Keep track of how much time is left and how you are progressing. You may want to plan your time on a scrap piece of paper, especially if you have one or more essays to write. Wear a watch or bring a small clock with you to the test room. A wall clock may be broken, or there may be no clock at all! Also, take your time. Rushing is almost always a mistake, even if you feel you've done well. Stay till the end so you can refine and check your work.

Master the art of intelligent guessing. When you are unsure of an answer, you can leave it blank, or you can guess. In most cases, guessing will benefit you. First, eliminate all the answers you know—or believe—are wrong. Try to narrow your choices to two possible answers; then, choose the one that makes more sense to you. When you recheck your work, decide if you would make the same guesses again, making sure there isn't a qualifier or fact that you hadn't noticed before.

Follow directions on machine-scored tests. Machine-scored tests require that you use a special pencil to fill in a small box on a computerized answer sheet. Use the right pencil (usually a number 2) and mark your answer in the correct space. Neatness counts on these tests because the computer can misread stray pencil marks or partially erased answers. Periodically check the answer number against the question number to make sure they match. One question skipped can cause every answer following it to be marked incorrect.

Use Critical Thinking to Avoid Errors

When the pressure of a test makes you nervous, critical thinking can help you work through each question thoroughly and avoid errors. Following are some critical-thinking strategies to use during a test.

Recall facts, procedures, rules, and formulas. You base your answers on the information you recall. Think carefully to make sure you recall it accurately.

Think about similarities. If you don't know how to attack a question or problem, consider any similar questions or problems that you have worked on in class or while studying.

Notice differences. Especially with objective questions, items that seem different from what you have studied may indicate answers you can eliminate.

Think through causes and effects. For a numerical problem, think through how you plan to solve it and see if the answer—the effect of your plan—makes sense. For an essay question that asks you to analyze a condition or situation, consider both what caused it and what effects it has.

> **TERMS**
>
> **Qualifier**
> A word, such as *always*, *never*, or *often*, that changes the meaning of another word or word group.

Find the best idea to match the example or examples given. For a numerical problem, decide what formula (idea) best applies to the example or examples (the data of the problem). For an essay question, decide what idea applies to or links the examples given.

Support ideas with examples. When you put forth an idea in an answer to an essay question, be sure to back up your idea with an adequate number of examples that fit.

Evaluate each test question. In your initial approach to any question, evaluate what kinds of thinking will best help you solve it. For example, essay questions often require cause-and-effect and idea-to-example thinking, while objective questions often benefit from thinking through similarities and differences.

The general strategies you have just explored can also help you address specific types of test questions.

Master Different Types of Test Questions

Although the goal of all test questions is to discover how much you know about a subject, every question type has its own way of asking what you know. Objective questions, such as multiple-choice or true/false, test your ability to recall, compare, and contrast information and to choose the right answer from among several choices. Subjective questions, usually essay questions, demand the same information recall but ask that you analyze the mind actions and thinking processes required, then organize, draft, and refine a written response. The following guidelines will help you choose the best answers to different types of questions.

TERMS

Objective questions
Short-answer questions that test your ability to recall, compare, and contrast information and to choose the right answer from a limited number of choices.

Subjective questions
Essay questions that require you to express your answer in terms of your own personal knowledge and perspective.

Multiple-Choice Questions

Multiple-choice questions are the most popular type on standardized tests. The following strategies can help you answer these questions:

Read the directions carefully. While most test items ask for a single correct answer, some give you the option of marking several choices that are correct.

First read each question thoroughly. Then look at the choices and try to answer the question.

Underline key words and phrases in the question. If the question is complicated, try to break it down into small sections that are easy to understand.

Pay special attention to qualifiers such as *only* **and** *except.* For example, negative words in a question can confuse your understanding of what the question asks ("Which of the following is *not* . . .").

If you don't know the answer, eliminate those answers that you know or suspect are wrong. Your goal is to narrow down your choices. Here are some questions to ask:

- ◆ Is the choice accurate in its own terms? If there's an error in the choice— for example, a term that is incorrectly defined—the answer is wrong.

◆ Is the choice relevant? An answer may be accurate, but it may not relate to the essence of the question.

◆ Are there any qualifiers, such as *always, never, all, none,* or *every?* Qualifiers make it easy to find an exception that makes a choice incorrect. For example, the statement that "children *always* begin talking before the age of 2" can be eliminated as an answer to the question, "When do children generally start to talk?"

◆ Do the choices give you any clues? Does a puzzling word remind you of a word you know? If you don't know a word, does any part of the word (prefix, suffix, or root) seem familiar to you?

> "A little knowledge that acts is worth infinitely more than much knowledge that is idle."
>
> KAHLIL GIBRAN

Look for patterns that may lead to the right answer; then use intelligent guessing. Test-taking experts have found patterns in multiple-choice questions that may help you get a better grade. Here is their advice:

◆ Consider the possibility that a choice that is more *general* than the others is the right answer.

◆ Look for a choice that has a middle value in a range (the range can be from small to large, from old to recent). This choice may be the right answer.

◆ Look for two choices with similar meanings. One of these answers is probably correct.

Make sure you read every word of every answer. Instructors have been known to include answers that are right except for a single word.

When questions are keyed to a long reading passage, read the questions first. This will help you focus on the information you need to answer the questions.

In the box below are some examples of the kinds of multiple-choice questions you might encounter in an Introduction to Psychology course[4] (the correct answer follows each question).

---

1. Arnold is at the company party and has had too much to drink. He releases all of his pent-up aggression by yelling at his boss, who promptly fires him. Arnold normally would not have yelled at his boss, but after drinking heavily he yelled because ___.
   a. parties are places where employees are supposed to be able to "loosen up"
   b. alcohol is a stimulant
   c. alcohol makes people less concerned with the negative consequences of their behavior
   d. alcohol inhibits brain centers that control the perception of loudness

(The correct answer is c)

2. Which of the following has not been shown to be a probable cause of or influence in the development of alcoholism in our society?
   a. intelligence
   b. culture
   c. personality
   d. genetic vulnerability

(The correct answer is a)

True/False Questions

True/false questions test your knowledge of facts and concepts. Read them carefully to evaluate what they truly say. Try to take these questions at face value without searching for hidden meaning. If you're truly stumped, guess (unless you're penalized for wrong answers).

In true/false questions, look for qualifiers—such as *all, only, always, because, generally, usually,* and *sometimes*—that can turn a statement that would otherwise be true into one that is false, or vice versa. For example, "The grammar rule, 'I before E except after C,' is *always* true" is *false*, whereas "The grammar rule, 'I before E except after C,' is *usually* true" is *true*. The qualifier makes the difference. Here are some examples of the kinds of true/false questions you might encounter in an Introduction to Psychology course.

Are the following questions true or false?

1. Alcohol use is always related to increases in hostility, aggression, violence, and abusive behavior. (False)
2. Marijuana is harmless. (False)
3. Simply expecting a drug to produce an effect is often enough to produce the effect. (True)

Essay Questions

An essay question allows you to use writing to demonstrate your knowledge and express your views on a topic. Start by reading the questions and deciding which to tackle (sometimes there's a choice). Then focus on what each question is asking, the mind actions you will have to use, and the writing directions. Read the question carefully, and do everything you are asked to do. Some essay questions may contain more than one part.

Watch for certain action verbs that can help you figure out what to do. Figure 7-2 explains some words commonly used in essay questions. Underline these words as you read any essay question, and use them as a guide.

Next, budget your time and begin to plan. Create an informal outline or think link to map your ideas, and indicate examples you plan to cite to support those ideas. Avoid spending too much time on introductions or flowery prose. Start with a thesis idea or statement that states in a broad way what your essay will say (see Chapter 6 for a discussion of thesis statements). As you continue to write your first paragraph, introduce the essay's points, which may be sub-ideas, causes and effects, or examples. Wrap it up with a concise conclusion.

Use clear, simple language in your essay. Support your ideas with examples, and look back at your outline to make sure you are covering everything. Try to write legibly. If your instructor can't read your ideas, it doesn't matter how good they are. If your handwriting is messy, try printing, skipping every other line, or writing on only one side of the paper.

Do your best to save time to reread and revise your essay after you finish getting your ideas down on paper. Look for ideas you left out and sentences that

Analyze Break into parts and discuss each part separately.

Compare Explain similarities and differences.

Contrast Distinguish between itms being compared by focusing on differences.

Criticize Evaluate the positive and negative effects of what is being discussed.

Define State the essential quality or meaning. Give the common idea.

Describe Visualize and give information that paints a complete picture.

Discuss Examine in a complete and detailed way, usually by connecting ideas to examples.

Enumerate/List/Identify Recall and specify items in the form of a list.

Explain Make the meaning of something clear, often by making analogies or giving examples.

Evaluate Give your opinion about the value or worth of something, usually by weighing positive and negative effects, and justify your conclusion.

Illustrate Supply examples.

Interpret Explain your personal view of facts and ideas and how they relate to one another.

Outline Organize and present the sub-ideas or main examples of an idea.

Prove Use evidence and argument to show that something is true, usually by showing cause and effect or giving examples that fit the idea to be proven.

Review Provide an overview of ideas, and establish their merits and features.

State Explain clearly, simply, and concisely, being sure that each word gives the image you want.

Summarize Give the important ideas in brief.

Trace Present a history of the way something developed, often by showing cause and effect.

Figure 7-2

Common action verbs on essay tests.

might confuse the reader. Check for mistakes in grammar, spelling, punctuation, and usage. No matter what subject you are writing about, having a command of these factors will make your work all the more complete and impressive.

Here are some examples of essay questions you might encounter in your Introduction to Psychology course. In each case, notice the action verbs from Figure 7-2.

1. Summarize the theories and research on the causes and effects of daydreaming. Discuss the possible uses for daydreaming in a healthy individual.
2. Describe the physical and psychological effects of alcohol and the problems associated with its use.

HOW CAN YOU LEARN FROM TEST MISTAKES?

The purpose of a test is to see how much you know, not merely to achieve a grade. The knowledge that comes from attending class and studying should allow you to correctly answer test questions. Knowledge also comes when you learn from your mistakes. If you don't learn from what you get wrong on a test, you are likely to repeat the same mistake again on another test and in life. Learn from test mistakes just as you learn from mistakes in your personal and business life.

Try to identify patterns in your mistakes by looking for:

◆ *Careless errors*—In your rush to complete the exam, did you misread the question or directions, blacken the wrong box, skip a question, or use illegible handwriting?

◆ *Conceptual or factual errors*—Did you misunderstand a concept or never learn it in the first place? Did you fail to master certain facts? Did you skip part of the assigned text or miss important classes in which ideas were covered?

You may want to rework the questions you got wrong. Based on the feedback from your instructor, try rewriting an essay, recalculating a math problem, or redoing the questions that follow a reading selection. As frustrating as they are, remember that mistakes show that you are human, and they can help you learn. If you see patterns of careless errors, promise yourself that next time you'll try to budget enough time to double-check your work. If you pick up conceptual and factual errors, rededicate yourself to better preparation.

When you fail a test, don't throw it away. First, take comfort in the fact that a lot of students have been in your shoes and that you are likely to improve your performance. Then recommit to the process by reviewing and analyzing your errors. Be sure you understand why you failed. You may want to ask for an explanation from your instructor. Finally, develop a plan to really learn the material if you didn't understand it in the first place.

ཤེས་ས་ཡེང་ཞིག

In Sanskrit, the written language of India and other Hindu countries, the characters above read *sem ma yeng chik*, meaning, "do not be distracted." This advice can refer to the focus on a task or job at hand, the concentration required to critically think and talk through a problem, or the mental discipline of meditation.

Think of this concept as you strive to improve your listening and memory techniques. Focus on the task, the person, or the idea at hand. Try not to be distracted by other thoughts, other people's notions of what you should be doing, or any negative messages. Be present in the moment to truly hear and remember what is happening around you. Do not be distracted.

Success in the Real World

Elizabeth Del Ferro

Elizabeth "Liz" Del Ferro, Director of Latin American Operations for Storage Tek, came to the United States to live when she was twelve years old, having spent her childhood in Italy. In the United States, she found a rich blending of cultures and languages and knew that she wanted to be involved in some type of international commerce.

Before she went to college, she looked around at many universities to determine  which ones were offering both an international program and a solid foundation of business courses. Liz knew that, even at that time, she would need to have a good understanding of all aspects of business, no matter what type of position she eventually landed. Throughout her education, she was conscious of her ultimate goal; she joined international groups and arranged to spend a semester in Mexico. She chose to go to the international graduate school Thunderbird to receive an MBA and enhance her understanding of business issues.

When Elizabeth hires new employees, she looks for a broad base of courses. A finance major should have had some marketing courses, for example. She believes that it is really important for people to have exposure to a variety of classes and experiences.

Liz has also learned other skills, which she finds crucial for her success, including flexibility. In her position, she needs to know how to really understand other people and their cultures. She does not want to impose her way on others but wants to understand their ways. As we do in our personal lives with our friends, Liz believes, we can open ourselves up to understanding others in

business. Liz also finds that patience has helped her succeed. Especially when dealing with other cultures, she finds that sometimes things take a little longer than she wants, or telephones may be out in the country where she is doing business. However, even in her home office, she finds that patience with others helps.

We, as a society, determine success, Liz believes, by income and job title just because these are concrete and easy to measure. For Liz, her success comes by simply being able, at the end of the day, to feel good about the job she has done. If she can either learn something new that day or teach someone else something new, she feels she has been successful. In the same way, she reviews each year, judging her success by the knowledge she has gained and shared.

Critics of her policies and managerial decisions certainly exist, and Liz sees that disagreements and criticism ease when she takes the time to thoroughly explain her position. A lot of criticism comes, she thinks, because people form an opinon based on what they think they know. She tries to do a lot to communicate with others about her reasons for a decision.

She suggests that students get as much general business into their curriculum as possible. Even if people believe they definitely know what they want to do, they should still get as much experience in other areas as possible. The world we live in now is changing so rapidly that a broad understanding of business is becoming much more important. Liz also thinks initiative is very important. Students should be responsible for their own learning and pose a lot of questions—to their teachers, interviewers, employers—because a lot of curiosity paves the road to success.

Chapter 7 Applications

Name _____ Date _____

KEY INTO YOUR LIFE
Opportunities to Apply What You Learn

 7.1 Optimum Listening Conditions

Describe a recent classroom situation in which you had an easy time listening to the instructor:

Where are you? _____

What is the instructor discussing? _____

Is it a straight lecture, or is there give-and-take between instructor and students? _____
_____

What is your state of mind? (List factors that might affect your ability to listen.) _____
_____
_____
_____

Are there any external barriers to communication? If yes, what are they, and how do they affect your concentration? _____
_____
_____
_____

Now describe a situation where you have found it more difficult to listen.

Where are you? _____

What is the instructor discussing? _____

Is it a straight lecture, or is there give-and-take between instructor and students? _____
_____

What is your state of mind? (List factors that might affect your ability to listen.) _____

_____

_____

_____

Are there any external barriers to communication? If yes, what are they, and how do they affect your concentration? _____

_____

_____

_____

Examine the two situations. Based on your descriptions, name three conditions that are crucial for you to listen effectively.

1. _____

2. _____

3. _____

What steps can you take to re-create these conditions in more difficult situations like the second one you described? _____

_____

_____

_____

7.2 *Create a Mnemonic Device*

Look back at all the memory principles examined in this chapter. Using what you learned about mnemonic devices, create a mnemonic that allows you to remember these memory principles quickly. You can create a mental picture or an acronym. If you are using a mental picture, describe it here; if you are using an acronym, write it and then indicate what each letter stands for.

_____

_____

_____

_____

_____

_____

_____

_____

Think of other situations in which you used a mnemonic device to remember something. What was the device? How effective was it in helping you remember the information?

_____

_____

_____

_____

7.3 *Learning From Your Mistakes*

For this exercise, use an exam on which you made one or more mistakes.

Why do you think you answered the question(s) incorrectly?

_____

_____

Did any qualifying terms, such as *always, sometimes, never, often, occasionally, only, no,* and *not*, make the question(s) more difficult or confusing? What steps could you have taken to clarify the meaning?

_____

_____

_____

Did you try to guess the correct answer? If so, why do you think you made the wrong choice?

_____

_____

Did you feel rushed? If you had had more time, do you think you would have gotten the right answer(s)? What could you have done to budget your time more effectively?

_____

_____

_____

If an essay question was a problem, what do you think went wrong? What will you do differently the next time you face an essay question on a test?

_____

_____

_____

7.4 Team-Building Exercise: Hone Your Listening Skills

Improve listening through teamwork. Divide into groups of five to nine to play a game called *Celebrity*. Each group will have two or three teams, each with two or three people (for example, a group of seven will have two teams of two and one of three). Using small slips of paper, each person must write down the names of five well-known people, one on each slip. The people may be living or dead and can have achieved celebrity status in any field—sports, entertainment, politics, arts and literature, science and medicine, and so on. Each scrap of paper should be folded to conceal the name written on it. Put all of the scraps together in one container. The only other equipment you need is a watch with a second hand.

Within each team of two, there is a giver and a receiver (team members switch roles every time they have a new turn). Teams take turns guessing. While a member of a nonguessing team times the pair for one minute, the giver of the guessing team picks a piece of paper and describes the named celebrity to the receiver without saying any part of the person's name. The giver can use words, sounds, motion, singing, anything that will help the receiver. (For Jackie Robinson: "Famous baseball player, first black man on a pro team, first name is the same as President Kennedy's wife," etc.) If and when the receiver guesses correctly, the giver keeps that scrap and chooses another, continuing to go through as many names as possible before the minute is up. When time is called, the container of names (minus the names guessed) moves to the next team. (If a name remains unguessed when time is called, that paper has to go back into the container without the giver revealing the name.)

When all the names have been guessed, teams count their papers to learn their scores. Then come together as a class and take some time to exchange views about your experience. How did the time limit, teamwork atmosphere, or noise affect your ability to listen? Which names were you more able to guess? Which gave you trouble, and why? Evaluate your skills.

Does Women's Communication Style Hinder Them in Business?*

Case Studies

Deborah Tannen says there's a distinct difference between the genders in the way they communicate. She calls them male and female rituals and she says they can get in the way of achieving work-related goals.

One of Tannen's findings relates to directness. Tannen says women often tend to avoid directness and cast themselves in an inferior light. This is seen in this conversation between two *Money Magazine* writers—Lesley Alderman and Gary Belsky:

---

*Case Study from *Managing Today* by Stephen P. Robbins. Copyright © 1997 by Prentice-Hall, Inc., Upper Saddle River, NJ. Used by permission. Case study based on "He Says She Says," *20/20;* ABC News; aired on October 21, 1994.

Gary: Well, do you have anything that you're considering?

Lesley: Here are things we . . . we were . . . that we've been thinking about. I'm just throwing things up.

Gary: Go on.

Lesley: So that's good. Then this one's really out, but . . . you're going to think I'm completely insane . . . but you know, there's like this whole like spiritual kind of drive thing. I can see you . . . like you're saying, 'Oh, no.'

I don't even know if that's the angle, exactly. I'm not sure if that's the angle. All I'm saying is . . . I'm sort of throwing that out as something . . .

Gary: OK.

Lesley: Maybe there's something in that. It's a little way out, perhaps.

Another gender-related ritual is apologizing. Women tend to apologize when they haven't done anything wrong. Why? They use it as a ritual way to get into the interaction. Men, on the other hand, seem to apologize only when they absolutely need to.

Tannen says women use a communication style that allows others to save face. They avoid directness and prefer subtlety. But this can create real problems in organizations. Female managers may appear to be lacking in confidence. They may also appear to be tentative when giving orders. According to Tannen, these conversational rituals can be the basis for underestimating a woman's capbilities. She can be seen as incompetent, whereas she thinks she's being considerate. She can be seen as lacking in confidence, whereas she feels she's simply being a good person by not flaunting her authority.

Women may be in a "can't win" situation. If they try to be considerate through indirctness, they may receive lower performance evaluations. Their bosses may assume they are not aggressive or confident enough to handle their jobs. But if they talk too much like men, they suffer because their bosses and subordinates may see them as too aggressive.

QUESTIONS

1. Do you think gender stereotypes of communication styles can be generalized to the entire workforce?

2. Do you think these gender styles are influenced by national culture? Explain.

3. Do you think adults can unlearn specific gender-related communication styles? Defend your position.

4. What suggestions would you make so women can communicate more effectively at work?

5. What suggestions would you make for men?

Internet Exercise

There are many sites on the Internet devoted to shopping. You can purchase products over the Internet using a credit card, but beware. Make sure that the site is secured before you do this. One shopping site that has some useful information is the popular online bookstore:

www.amazon.com

This site is set up for selling books and music but also has reviews and descriptions of many books. Several of the books also have excerpts that are included on the site.

1. Access the site, find a description of one of the available books, and print it out.

2. Analyze and list what Amazon.com has to offer that you couldn't get at a major bookstore chain.

   a. _____

   _____

   b. _____

   _____

   c. _____

   _____

3. Analyze and list what a bookstore has to offer that you couldn't get at Amazon.com.

   a. _____

   _____

   b. _____

   _____

   c. _____

   _____

4. Which one is doing a better job of listening to its customers? Why?

   _____

   _____

   _____

Journal

Name _____   Date _____

Business Communication

Reporting Results

C ommunicating should come naturally; after all, we've been communicating since childhood. We made it through elementary and
secondary school where they taught us even more, especially about
how to read and write, and maybe even about giving a presentation. Still,
the process seems overwhelming and scary. But it doesn't have to be. It
may never be totally easy because it is complex, but it certainly can
become less intimidating. And you can gain skills that become your tools
to success.

In this chapter, you will start with self-awareness to help you learn how
to share results. The way we share results is part of the communication
process. This chapter gives you guidelines for effective oral presentations
(public speaking), since so much of the time we share results by talking
about them. Keys to effective business-writing techniques are also presented in this chapter because written reports are often used in business
and generally accompany any oral presentation.

In this chapter, you will explore answers to the following questions:

◆ How does self-awareness affect communication?

◆ What is the communication process?

◆ What makes communication difficult?

◆ What are the keys to effective public speaking?

◆ How do nonverbal clues give meaning in communication?

◆ What are the keys to effective business writing?

HOW DOES SELF-AWARENESS AFFECT COMMUNICATION?

The Four Selves in Communication

The Johari Window is a simple model that can give you insight into how communication works. The name of the window comes from the developers, Joe and Harry (Joseph Luft and Harrington Ingham). In the Johari Window, communication involves yourself and others. Some things are known to you, some to others, and some to both. The window thus gives us four selves: the open, the hidden, the blind, and the unknown. Figure 8-1 shows these selves.

The Open Self

The open self means all the information, behaviors, attitudes, feelings, desires, motivations, and ideas that we and others know about us. The type of information may vary from name, color of skin, and sex to age, political affiliations, and the car we drive. According to Joseph Luft, the smaller the first quadrant, the poorer the communication. Communication depends on how much we open ourselves up to others. If we do not allow others to know us, we keep the open self small, making communication between them and us more difficult.

Figure 8-1

The four selves of the Johari Window.

Open Self	Blind Self
Hidden Self	Unknown Self

The Hidden Self

The hidden self consists of all you know of yourself and of others but that you keep to yourself. This area includes all the successfully kept secrets about yourself and others. In relating to others, some people are overdisclosers. They keep nothing hidden about themselves or others. They tell you their family history, marital difficulties, children's problems, financial status, successes, and failures. They do not distinguish to whom such information should or should not be disclosed; nor do they distinguish what types of information should be disclosed. The underdisclosers tell nothing. They talk about you, but not about themselves. We might feel they are afraid to tell anyone anything for fear of being laughed at or rejected, or we may feel rejected for their refusal to trust us. Most people fall in between—they are selective disclosers.

The Blind Self

The blind self represents all the things others know about us, but which we ourselves do not know. Such things may include the rather insignificant habit of saying "you know" or raising your eyebrows when you get angry; or it may include having a body odor or a defense mechanism. Some people have a very large blind self, oblivious to their own faults and even their own virtues. Others have a rather small blind self, being mostly self-aware. The majority of us are in the middle. However, as we open ourselves up to other people and accept their feedback, we move information from our blind selves to our open selves.

The Unknown Self

The unknown self represents truths that exist, but which neither we nor others know. Mostly this unknown is good, for we need to forget much information if we are to survive as humans; otherwise, we would face constant overload. Sometimes the unknown is revealed through temporary changes induced by drugs, hypnosis, dreams, or projective tests. On occasions when we demonstrate some peculiar behavior or are affected in unexplained ways, we may need to seek psychological help to discover more of our unknown self. Needing help at such times is normal; otherwise, we have no way to move information from our unknown self to either the open or hidden self.

WHAT IS THE COMMUNICATION PROCESS?

Communication is best understood as a system. A basic system consists of inputs, some activity, some outputs, and feedback. For example, take the heating system for our house. The inputs are the desired temperature we set and the actual temperature. The integrating process compares the two; then it determines the need to turn on the furnace to increase heat. The output is the heat from the furnace. Feedback will take the new temperature and add that as new input to the system. When we reach the right temperature, the

"The mind celebrates a little triumph every time it formulates a thought."
EMERSON

TERMS

Self-Aware
Conscious of oneself as an individual entity or personality.

TERMS

Communication
The exchange of ideas, messages, or information, by speech, signals, or writing; to express oneself effectively.

integrating process turns off the furnace. Mechanical systems like a furnace are relatively simple compared to human communication.

Input

Communication begins with who we are. Objectively, we have unique physical features, come from a particular background, have completed a specific type of education, and have work experiences and friendships. Subjectively, we bring our own set of expectations and assumptions to any communication. We may only see or hear what we expect rather than what is actually there. We tend to tune out what doesn't fit our preconceptions. Our unspoken assumptions help to create our blind self, since we may not even be aware of our assumptions.

Purpose

Central to any communication is our purpose—what we hope to achieve and the audience we are dealing with. Our purpose can be to gain a willing listener, to be understood, to make a sale, to fulfill legal requirements, or to provide the basis for a long-term relationship. The audience may be someone we know quite well or a stranger, a family member or a clerk behind a desk.

Method

After we are sure of our purpose, we then select the method to use. The form that our communication could take might be a conversation, a telephone call, a meeting, a formal speech, a written letter, a Post-it note, or a videoconference. Regardless of the form we intend to use, we must still create the process. Process concerns the sequence of ideas, word choice, pictures, or drawings to accompany the words, and any drafts of our ideas before we begin to create the communication.

We may not even realize how we create our communication. We don't always follow a straight line from purpose (intentions and audience) to method (form and process). We may start out thinking of a quick note but, after jotting down our ideas, realize that we should send a letter. So we often change our approach as we develop the purpose and method.

Output

After some preparation, we produce something seen or heard. We speak our words, write or type them, or enter them onto a computer screen. Regardless of the method used, we end up with some output message. However, the real communication is not the message we send, but the message that someone else interprets. I may have said, "We mustn't go"; but you heard, "We must go." Perhaps I was too soft in saying the words and you couldn't hear the *n't* ending; or if you were expecting to go, maybe your preconceptions prevented you from hearing the actual words.

Feedback

If we take the system's approach to communication, we don't stop after we present our message. We look for feedback so we can ensure that our intended message matches what the other person interprets. We may ask the other person to repeat what we've said, or we may ask a follow-up question that lets us know that we're both on the same page. Feedback that matches our intentions may indicate successful communication; unexpected feedback means regrouping and continuing the process. Put another way, feedback will let us see our blind self, the message obvious to the listener but one that we were not aware of.

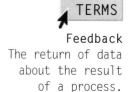

WHAT MAKES COMMUNICATION DIFFICULT?

Communication would be easy if we were machines. When you press the keys *k*, *n*, *o*, and *w* on the computer keyboard, you have the word *know*. As long as you physically hit the correct keys, the computer has the word. If you save your message and then call it back in an hour, the same word will come back to you. The machine program will not arbitrarily change the word the next time you call up your document.

But people are not machines. People may hear one thing and think another; someone may expect to hear *no* or *snow* or *glow*, so the person hears that word when you say *know*. Someone may not understand your words or think that you had a different intention behind saying them (proud to be "in the know"). People may forget after a while or think that they heard something quite different (such as the word *show*). Computers have no such problems. Computers follow machine logic, but as people, we follow our own train of assumptions, prejudices, and impressions, which we believe are real. But now comes the difficult part. Whether or not what we see matches reality, what we interpret is very real for us. Communication tries to ensure that the interpretation is real for others as well.

WHAT ARE THE KEYS TO EFFECTIVE PUBLIC SPEAKING?

Most people fear having to stand up in front of a group to speak, whether the group is a class of fellow students or a meeting of sports fans. We may ask a question from our seat but don't want to walk to the front of the room and address the crowd. Many business courses will require either group or individual presentations during the term, so it is a good idea to know how to do these effectively.

Looked at objectively, the act of speaking remains the same, whether to one person, a small group, or a large audience. But as we've seen, communication is what we perceive. Psychologically, the formality of the setting brings an added level of nervousness called stage fright; thus, many people are reluctant to engage in public speaking.

TERMS

Feedback
The return of data about the result of a process.

The stage fright and anxiety are quite real; but if you learn to live with them, you can gain a skill that will help you succeed both in the classroom and in the workplace. Knowing how the process works and learning how to prepare can reduce the impact of nervousness.

Conversation and Formal Presentations

Since speaking is a normal activity, as we prepare for a formal presentation, we can adapt conversational speech to a new set of circumstances. To maintain the normalcy of the spoken word, the formal speaker usually does not read or memorize the text. Listeners will interpret both the message you are giving and your credibility as a person. If you *talk to* your audience rather than *read at* them, they will more likely respond both to your message and to you as a credible person.

Although formal presentations resemble conversations, you must adapt to the occasion. In particular, you must slow down, speak louder, and enunciate clearly for the audience to hear:

Slow—Loud—Enunciate

These three requirements actually work to your advantage, especially the first one: Speaking slowly gives you more time to think about both the content of your information and the mechanics of your presentation, such as looking at the audience or pointing to visuals.

Another difference between conversation and formal presentation is in the use of visuals. In conversation, you might draw imaginary pictures with your hands or scribble an idea on a scrap of paper. But in formal presentations, you need to prepare more complete visuals to help keep your audience on track throughout your presentation.

The most significant difference between conversation and formal presentation is nervousness. But here you must always remember an important point:

Nervousness is normal.

"Our doubts are traitors and make us lose the good we often might win by fearing to attempt."
SHAKESPEARE

Even Academy Award–winning actors and actresses are nervous. But most of your nervousness will stay in your hidden self, not in the open self. You may feel and hear your heart pounding, but even so, it makes no difference because that feeling is hidden. Your presentation may *look* calm, cool, and professional even if you *feel* absolutely petrified. With some practice, and with feedback that reveals your blind self, you may actually come to *believe* that you can give a speech, despite your nervousness. The following guidelines will help you reach that point.

General Guides for Effective Presentations

PERSPECTIVE

◆ Remember that individuals, not a group, hear your presentation. You are talking to individual people, and you want them to recognize you as another individual, just like them. Don't let the size of the audience get in the way of your talking to other individuals.

◆ Recognize your nervousness and tell yourself, "This is normal and will remain hidden."

◆ Learn to live with nervousness. For some people, practice and experience will reduce the nervousness; others will always be nervous. But in either case, nervousness will probably not affect the audience, since your feelings are in your hidden self. You know your material, you know that you are prepared, and the audience is actually waiting to hear what you have to say. You can't eliminate nervousness; just live with it. You can become an effective speaker, nervous or not.

PURPOSE

◆ As with all communication, you must determine your goals in the speech. And usually, you have many goals.

Class presentation:	Inform my classmates.
	Show that I did my research.
	Impress the instructor and get a good grade.
Community meeting:	Point out an issue that people have forgotten.
	Sound credible so they can actually hear me.
	Get the others to vote with me.

Your goal is not just to make an appearance. You must be aware of and clear about what you hope to accomplish.

◆ Identify your audience. In the classroom, you have two separate audiences—your fellow students and your instructor. Each has different expectations: Students want you to be interesting; the instructor wants you to know the material. When speaking to other groups outside the classroom, you may need to do a little more work to find out about the audience. What is their background? How much do they already know? What have they done before related to this topic? How significant is my topic to them? What do they need to know so they can use my information? How much time will they give me for my presentation?

PREPARATION

◆ Outline your ideas so that your sequence will make sense to your audience. Don't stop with the first sequence that comes to mind—that sequence may be OK for you but not for your audience.

◆ Use details and examples to get your point across. Use different types of examples so more of your audience can relate to your points. For instance, don't talk about a proposal to "improve the environment." Rather, say that this proposal will reduce carbon dioxide by 15 percent, will cut in half the number of "brown cloud" days in the city, or will cost about the same as buying one candy bar a day. Use details and examples that make your idea come alive for your audience.

◆ Prepare notes, but not a full script—don't read to the audience. You know what you want to say and have practiced it ahead of time, so you only need note cards. Don't try to put your entire speech on the cards word for word; rather, use a few key ideas as reminders as you go. Also remember that if you focus on reading notes, you may state all of your words and ideas but not communicate yourself as a person, so your impact will be less.

◆ Practice so you are comfortable with the material. When you speak more slowly and louder than usual, you will sound different to yourself, so you need to hear that difference and get used to it. A speech will also take longer than merely reading or just talking in conversation, so you need to know how long it takes.

◆ Practice the gestures and accept feedback.

◆ Use visuals to reinforce the content: slides, overhead projections, video-tapes, and handouts. We'll talk more about visuals later in this chapter.

◆ Practice with visuals to ensure coordination between speaker, visuals, and audience. Just having the visuals isn't enough; you must practice so you know what they contain and when to display them.

METHOD

◆ Speak slowly and loudly enough to be heard within the given physical layout, platform, and microphones. You probably need to fight the tendency to just rush through it and get it over with. Instead, you need to take a deep breath and remind yourself—*slow and loud.*

◆ Enunciate clearly—otherwise, large audiences can't hear. To enunciate, you need to open your mouth more widely, which forces you to slow down, helps you speak louder, and calms your nervous tendency to speed up.

◆ Slow, loud, and enunciate are a package deal that works together and gives you the advantage. You can stay in control of your thoughts and your presentation.

◆ Keep eye contact with the audience. Since you have prepared, you know the material; now you must convince your audience. Unless you look at them, they will not be convinced. Even if the group is large, remember that each listener is one person (like you), wanting to hear what you have to say. When you look at them, they can relate to you as a person.

◆ Use meaningful gestures. You want to appear natural rather than forced; you want the gestures to emphasize rather than distract. See Figure 8-2.

Use of Visuals

For a formal presentation, you need to use visual aids, or visuals, to help keep the audience on track. People tend to get distracted or have their minds wander. They may even latch on to an idea of yours and start to see how to take and use that idea themselves, which means they are no longer listening to your next points. Visuals help keep the audience on track or help them return to the track after their mental wanderings.

◆ Keep visuals simple. Too much detail confuses and distracts. You want to highlight your key topics, give an example or illustration, or rein-

PREPARE	Sequence for main ideas
	Note cards
	Visuals
	Room setup
DELIVER	Take a deep breath before speaking.
	Speak clearly and distinctly.
	Speak more slowly than in normal conversation: slower speech allows listeners to hear more clearly; slower speech gives the speaker time to organize thoughts.
	Time to think reduces the need for verbal fillers ("ah," "ahm").
	Keep eye contact with the audience.
	Use note cards with key words as reminders.
	Don't read extensively from a full text.
REMEMBER	Nervousness is normal: You feel the nervousness more intensely than the audience perceives it.

Figure 8-2

Tips for public speaking.

force a point you are talking about. If you put too much information on a visual, your audience will spend time reading rather than listening to you.

◆ Adapt visuals from books or magazines. Remove portions not relevant for your audience's needs or change the emphasis for your needs. You don't have to be an artist yourself to make visuals, especially with computer scanners and clip art. But make sure that the visual fits your particular material.

◆ Use sharp colors for contrast. Pastel colors tend to wash out toward gray when projected in a large room. Color printers and slide makers can use all shades of color, but you want clear colors that project into a room. Don't go in for fancy shades just because a color printer can do it—use clear colors for your audience.

◆ Use minimal wording and short labels. Too many words make the visual a liability rather than an asset. Even though you often hear, "A picture is worth a thousand words," those thousand words may be much more than your audience needs. Visuals don't stand alone but should go along with your verbal presentation.

◆ If you must use a complex visual, build up to it by presenting smaller parts, then showing how the parts fit together in the more complex figure. Here you take the "divide and conquer" approach—break a complex topic into small parts, and use visuals of just the small parts. As a final visual, show all of the parts together. If you start with a complex visual, most audiences will tune you out. They see you as too complicated and confusing, so you lose credibility. See Figure 8-3.

Figure 8-3

General
guidelines for
visuals.

◆ Keep visuals simple. Too much detail confuses and distracts.

◆ Adapt visuals from books or magazines. Remove portions not relevant for your audience's needs or change the emphasis for your needs.

◆ Use sharp colors for contrast. Pastel colors tend to wash out toward gray when projected in a large room.

◆ Use minimal wording and short labels. Too many words make the visual a liability rather than an asset.

◆ If you must use a complex visual, build up to it by presenting smaller parts, then showing how the parts fit together in the more complex figure.

Source: Adapted from Charles E. Beck and William J. Wallisch, Jr., "Technical Illustration," in *Courses, Components, and Exercises in Technical Communication,* ed. Dwight W. Stevenson. Urbana, IL: National Council of Teachers of English, 1981, pp. 123-125.

HOW DO NONVERBAL CLUES GIVE MEANING IN COMMUNICATION?

Nonverbals affect all people consciously and unconsciously. People may react to nonverbal stimuli, interpreting a message even if one was not meant to be sent. For our discussion here, we will focus on four significant areas of nonverbal communication: gestures, facial expressions, dress and physical appearance, and context.

Gestures

Gestures serve as an original language through pointing to an object or motioning (come, go). Our demonstrative pronouns (this, that, these, those) are words to accompany the gesture of pointing; without the accompanying gesture, such words are vague or meaningless. When we use a demonstrative adjective with a gesture ("this tool"), the adjective now has a referent; otherwise, a vague "this" lacks a referent or gesture to clarify the meaning.

Gestures may have specific references, as in pointing, or they may be a way to show emphasis. Gesticulating may be a personality or an ethnic trait of an individual speaker ("She's Italian"). But gestures can convey emotional feelings, such as slamming a door in anger or throwing a document on a desk in disgust. Pounding the fist or pointing an index finger at someone may indicate emphasis. Of course, gestures can misrepresent one's intention: Your looking at someone else with intense interest may occur because that person looks familiar or reminds you of something, but the other person thinks you are directly interested in him or her.

We usually consider gestures as obvious, yet they are culturally bound. An American's friendly wave with the left hand to say "hi" may be an insult in some cultures where the left hand is considered unclean (the hygiene or toilet hand). The American "thumbs up" gesture to indicate OK is an obscene gesture in other cultures. While Americans may nod their heads up and down to indicate agreement, people in another culture nod the head to indicate no;

while Americans shake their heads left to right to indicate no, in another culture the head turns to the left to indicate yes. Differing interpretations of gestures lead to the cultural aversion to foreigners who appear insulting and uncouth to the host culture. Since Americans frequently travel abroad, they may unwittingly communicate a poor image of themselves with wrong gestures. Most likely, they will not realize the wrong message, since that message is what the host culture perceives, not the intended message of the gesture.

Gestures may seem normal and natural or may seem contrived. Perceivers may interpret these gestures as inappropriate or emphatic, or they may remain oblivious to them because they seem so appropriate. Gestures depend on context. A "high five" or a "pat on the rear" may be appropriate on the athletic field but not in an office. Gestures may also evoke annoyance: Why doesn't he just get to the point without all the theatrics. Sitcoms on television consistently use interpretations of nonverbal messages and their unintended communication problems as the source of humor.

Facial Expressions

Aside from words, facial expressions contain the greatest amount of communication in interpersonal relationships. Involuntary expressions may include blushing, lowering of eyes, and sometimes smiling. More voluntary expressions include grimaces, wrinkling of eyebrows, smiles, and turning away.

Nonverbals can become the source of misinformation as well. For example, someone with a slight scar that tends to give a wrinkled expression to the eyes may always be interpreted as angry or unhappy, even though an expression may have nothing to do with an actual mood.

To the extent possible, we try to control our expressions so that the nonverbal reflects the verbal. Regardless of the extent of our control, however, others may see and interpret a message that differs from the words conveyed. Or the listener may be unsure how to interpret something when a different message comes through the words than through the expressions. The proverbial "poker face" acknowledges the reality of interpretation of facial expressions. The better poker player can assume a common expression regardless of the type of hand dealt; the novice will give away a good hand by the slight changes of expression conveyed while interpreting the hand dealt. Either way, the communicated message is not the intention but the interpretation by others.

Dress and Physical Appearance

People must dress for all kinds of occasions. We gauge the attire required for a particular encounter, ranging from informal (shorts and T-shirt) to casual (sport shirt and slacks) to semiformal (coat and tie) to formal (tuxedo). Some positions require a specific uniform, which relieves doubt concerning the status and role of the person, reducing uncertainty in the communication. Sports stores target different clothing for different activities: walking, hiking, running, and biking. As this uniform code becomes widely accepted, participants are expected to conform to the rules that apply to a given sports activity.

Although dress and appearance help determine the context for communication, they (like other aspects of the communication process) are subject to misinterpretations. A manager was once called from work because of an injury to his daughter, who was rushed to the hospital and taken for X-rays. While waiting for the results of the X-rays, the manager was looking at some work information on a clipboard. Later the X-ray technician came up to the manager and started to explain the X-rays, believing him to be the attending physician. To the technician, the person holding the clipboard was the doctor.

Dress and appearance may assist a person in interpreting a particular communication event. People use physical dress and appearance as a way to provide the context for interpreting a given communication event.

Context

TERMS

Context
It provides a key
to interpretation.

As with the verbal aspect of communication, context also affects the nonverbal. Perhaps it impacts negatively even more than positively. For example, a person who is not dressed for the occasion seems out of place, which is another phrase for out of context. The person just doesn't fit into the circumstances. The person in casual dress does not command the importance of the sharp dresser. Comedies and fairy tales use this incongruence to heighten the effect—the beggar is actually the executive, or the frog becomes the prince.

The context distorts communication in other ways as well. People tend to interpret the polished presentation as professional, when it may be a scam. On the other hand, people tend to hesitate in supporting an ingenious idea that comes from a basement or a garage, regardless of the importance of the invention or discovery.

When the nonverbal context complements the verbal, it reinforces communication in a way that seems appropriate to the occasion. The nonverbal sets up expectations for the receiver, so it can help you as you communicate.

WHAT ARE THE KEYS TO EFFECTIVE BUSINESS WRITING?

Many of the ideas discussed in verbal communication also apply to business writing. Just as in formal presentations and the writing basics you learned in Chapter 6, business writing also begins with identifying a clear purpose, your goals, and your audience. Letters, memos, email, and formal reports are frequently used as forms of business communication.

Letters And Memos

Both letters and memos serve as short guides to action. The following are general tips to use when writing either a letter or a memo:

- Keep to one page if possible, two pages maximum.
- Use 1-inch top margins, and $3/4$ to 1 inch on the sides and bottom.

◆ Most readers groan if they see a long document—the shorter the better; otherwise, your correspondence may get put aside for later, "when we have time," which often means *never*.

◆ In the first sentence, tell readers what you expect of them in this communication. Readers need to know immediately if you are giving them a task, asking for information, asking for approval, or merely providing supplemental information.

◆ Don't keep readers guessing by giving extensive background first. Unless readers know their role in the communication, they cannot interpret the background information.

◆ Keep the tone *informal*. Use words or phrases such as I, we, you, please regard, and in case you need to know. Avoid bureaucratic talk such as "this office believes" or "pursuant to the aforementioned request." Remember, ALL communication occurs at the level of individuals. You want each individual to respond to you as a person, not as a mechanical cog in a wheel.

◆ Use short paragraphs. Divide or "chunk" information into short paragraphs that aid the reader in rapidly scanning the text. Long paragraphs seem oppressive, making readers want to avoid the document rather than feel invited into the conversation.

◆ If you have extensive information, write a short letter or memo with an attachment. The short letter or memo clarifies the readers' role and summarizes the attached information.

◆ An attachment to a letter or memo can take on a life of its own. The attachment may be a list of instructions, a proposal, a progress report, an outline of pros and cons for an upcoming decision, minutes of a meeting—almost any kind of document. The short letter or memo gains the reader's attention, but the attachment can serve new purposes as the reader sees fit. The reader may use it as a handout at a staff meeting, post it on a bulletin board, or create a new memo and send copies to others in the organization. If the information were embedded in a letter or memo and the reader forwards a copy to someone else, that person may glance at the document and say, "Well, this isn't addressed to me," and pitch it. But a self-contained attachment provides greater flexibility.

Letters

Letters appear on company letterhead, usually on higher-quality stationery. The letterhead contains the company logo (often in color), mailing address, and phone number for ease of reference.Letters contain the date, name and address of the recipient, and salutation. Letters should use short paragraphs and maintain the length limit (one to two pages). Longer information should appear in a self-contained attachment.

The letter ends with a closing, signature element, and job title. The letter is signed rather than initialed. Other information may appear after the signature, such as carbon copy, attachment, and the initials of the typist.

The letter format may be full block, modified block, or semi-block; companies give their own guidance so that the documents appear standardized. See Figure 8-4.

Figure 8-4	Sample letter.

Computer Consultants, Inc.
1235 Macro Trail
Los Angeles, CA 90211
(203) 222-2222

January 22, 1999

Customer Service
Best Buy #298
Los Angeles, CA 92222

RE: Computer Equipment
Acct: 123456789-987654321

Dear Customer Service Manager:

I need to exchange the modem I purchased for a similar item. The one that I bought does not work properly since it has no dial tone.

On December 15, 1998, I purchased a modem upgrade for my computer. I did not immediately install the modem after Christmas since I also needed a memory upgrade to install an HP ScanJet. At that time, you were out of the memory upgrades. After repeated checks, you did have the memory upgrade on January 19, so I bought the memory and installed the memory and modem.

Upon installation, the memory checked out fine. I followed the modem installation instructions for hardware and software:

1. The software acknowledged the modem installation on Comm-port 2.
2. My Windows program acknowledged the proper modem installed on Comm-port 2.
3. The phone connected through this modem worked properly (dial tone, able to call out, rings for in-coming calls).
4. However, attempting any computer connection through this modem resulted in a prompt of "No Dial Tone."

I followed the checks both in the modem instructions and in my Windows manual, and all settings were fine. All tests identified the proper mode configuration— yet no dial tone.

As a result, I want to exchange this defective modem for a new one.

Thank you for your help.

Sincerely,

Karl P. Bach

Memos

Memos are internal, with the assumption that all parties involved have some working relationship with each other. The memo appears on plain paper rather than on letterhead. The memo contains four main categories:

From:

Date:

Subject:

To:

Memos may contain two additional categories for attachments and copies:

atch:

cc:

Authors initial after their name as sender. Memos do not contain additional salutations, addresses, or signature elements. See Figure 8-5.

Email

Electronic mail tends to follow the conventions of the memo, using categories established by the software or the server program. Since most computer screens are smaller than the typical page of text, email tends to be shorter than memos. Readers can respond more quickly to the email if they can see the entire text. If they must scroll down too much, they tend to lose the train of thought.

Be sure to proofread email before sending. Because you can send email immediately, you tend to type quickly and send without proofreading. As a result, you can send errors much more quickly than with a printed document.

Figure 8-5

From: K. P. Bach
Date: 1/22/99
Subject: Modem Not Working
To: Purchasing Department

The modem that we purchased in December doesn't work. I'm attempting to get it exchanged at Best Buy.

We purchased the modem last month to take advantage of the Christmas sale price. However, we didn't install it until we could get the expanded memory. When we added the new upgrade memory this past week, we found out that the modem didn't work.

I've attached a copy of my letter to Best Buy for your records. Hopefully, we'll get a new one quickly. I'll keep you posted.

Sample memo.

Email has many advantages, the biggest of which is the speed at which you can communicate with others. However, this speed can also be dangerous. Once you hit the "send" key, you cannot change your mind. Therefore, it is a good idea not to write an email message when you are angry or emotional; you may regret sending it. Also, beware of your use of humor and sarcasm in email, as these are sometimes difficult for others to interpret in their context.

Formal Reports

A formal report sends information to decision makers or those who need the information. In college courses, the instructor is the decision maker who will use your report to determine how well you know the topic and how well you can present it.

The structure for a major report can be a variation of the following:

A. Memo or letter explaining the type and purpose of report (Discuss anything unusual that came up or that you learned while completing the report. List the report itself as an attachment to the memo.)

B. Title Page:
   - Title of the report
   - Author
   - Submitted to
   - Date

C. Abstract or executive summary (page i) (one-page summary of the report)

D. Table of contents (page ii)

E. List of visuals (figures and tables) (If this is short, place it on the same page as the contents; if it is long, start a new page iii.)

F. The report itself:
   - Place page numbers at bottom, centered.
   - Use plenty of headings and subheadings.
   - Use references: footnotes, author/date, or numbered references.
   - Pay attention to page layout, visual appeal.

G. Bibliography/references (last main heading of the report)

H. Appendix/appendices

Note: For a short (two to ten-page) report, you don't need an abstract or table of contents. Just attach the report to a memo or letter.

Joie de Vivre

The French have a phrase *joie de vivre*, which literally means "joy of living." A person with *joie de vivre* is one who finds joy and optimism in all parts of life, who is able to enjoy life's pleasures and find something positive in its struggles. Without experiencing difficult and sometimes painful challenges, people might have a hard time recognizing and experiencing happiness and satisfaction.

REAL WORLD PERSPECTIVE

How can I adjust to diversity?

Carrie Nelson, University of Guadalajara

Once I made the decision to study Spanish, the idea of studying abroad in a Spanish-speaking country was simultaneous. I have always been fascinated with learning about other cultures and being introduced to new ideas. Once I started filling out forms for the school in Mexico and buying my plane ticket, however, I began to question my decision. I wondered if I could really handle this big of a change in my life. But in my heart I knew that I had made the right decision.

Now that I am actually studying in Guadalajara, Mexico, I cannot imagine how I could have been nervous. This is one of the best decisions I have ever made, although I have had to adjust to living here. In some aspects the Mexican and American cultures are very similar, but in other regards they can be very different. For example, in the U.S. the customer is considered the most important person and expects to be served very quickly. In Mexico the customer is important but the way of life is much more relaxed. Therefore, if a clerk gets a personal phone call, they will most likely talk to that person whether there is a customer waiting or not.

Every day I experience something new or begin to better understand the differences in our cultures. By learning about other people, I am learning more about myself and the beauty and complexity of people. Still, I would like to deepen my relationship with the people of Guadalajara. I realize I am just scratching the surface of this experience. Do you have any suggestions?

Tan Pham, Gonzaga University, Spokane, Washington

In 1981, I escaped from Vietnam after having tried unsuccessfully 13 different times. Like you in Guadalajara, I found being in a new country both wonderfully enriching and overwhelming at the same time.

When I first arrived in the U.S., I was amazed at the way the people value time. In Vietnam, as in Guadalajara, things are much slower. But here, time is seen as money. I learned it was very important to arrive at my appointments at the exact time they were scheduled. I was also amazed at the technology: the computers and the transportation.

When you visit another country there is so much to learn. My recommendation is that you stay open to the experience. Let go of your past and fully embrace the new life you have accepted. Remember not to isolate yourself. Talk to the people. Avoid socializing just with people from your own country. Try to immerse yourself fully in the new culture. Also, ask for help. Most people are very sincere in their desire to help you. Each land has unique opportunities. Take advantage of them as you explore your new world.

Success in the Real World

Monty Roberts

Some might say that Monty Roberts had little chance for success. He grew up with a physically abusive father and endured beatings so severe that, as a child, he ended up in the hospital with broken bones and spinal processes. Yet Monty not only stopped the cycle of abuse in his life, he also significantly improved the way that human beings communicate with horses, other animals, and each other.

For many years, it was thought that cowboys had to "break" their horses—they had to beat them into submission, breaking their will. The "breaking" process took anywhere from four to six weeks. The young Monty identified with the beaten horses and began to watch them closely. By observing a group of wild mustangs for a period of several days, he started to notice additional patterns in the way they communicated with each other. Since that time, he has refined and enhanced his knowledge of their communication system; by using their own "language," he can communicate with them using the position of his body, head, and eyes. He can now take a horse that has never before had a saddle on its back and get the horse to accept a saddle and rider without ever using physical force—in less than half an hour. He trains other people in the horse language he has termed Equus, and he has demonstrated his gentle method of horse training several thousand times. He also continues to train the Queen of England's horses.

Modified versions of this language have been found to work with other animals, including deer; Monty also uses the ideas behind the language to communicate with people. Central to the concept is the idea that humans and some animals, including horses, are social beings. We are group ani-

mals and need to be around others. By reinforcing positive behavior from the horse with positive rewards, and negative behavior with negative consequences, Monty modifies the horse's behavior, much as a parent can modify the behavior of an unruly child. The system of rewards and negative consequences has to be used continually in the training phase. Using this system with people, Monty and his wife, Pat, have also helped almost fifty foster children.

Several years ago, a business institute was founded by Monty and his team because, as Monty sees it, many of the problems with businesses today revolve around the motivation of the employees. IBM and Volkswagen are two of the companies that have benefited from Monty's way of thinking. According to Monty, many companies tend to put a safety net under their employees, trying to prevent any type of failure. However, Monty believes that failure is essential to long-term success because only when people fail do they see the consequences of negative behavior.

Managers can train their employees in the same way Monty trains horses—by "making positive choices great and negative choices awful." Too often employees are rewarded for negative actions—the person promoted may have hurt others to get there, for example. Employees' negative behavior has to always be met with negative consequences, while positive behavior has to always result in rewards.

Monty believes that success is a measure that other people put on you after you've finished what you can do. For himself, his measure is always moving, and he is continually improving upon his latest "success." Monty considers his desire to continually improve the reason he has accomplished what he has; he knows he will continue his

(continued)

Success in the Real World

work as long as his brain is still functioning and there are still people who doubt his methods. His critics hurt him, but they are also what drive him and make him more tenacious—he believes critics and doubters are the reason he exists.

Monty doesn't believe that the future will be much different from the past, apart from the use of technology. He thinks that students need to be more technically skilled than he is because their future

will depend on it. He also says to students and all people looking for success:

When you think that you've put in a hard day's work and done enough for the day, go another hour and do something or learn something you didn't think you would. Try not to seek the pleasant things so much—they will come when you've earned them. The real joys in your life will be in your accomplishments.

Chapter 8   Applications

Name _____   Date _____

KEY INTO YOUR LIFE
Opportunities to Apply What You Learn

8.1   *Analyze Your Audience*

In this exercise your topic is Choosing a College and Major, and the two audiences you need to analyze are: high school juniors and parents of high school juniors.

First, consider your topic. Then, answer the following questions for both of your audiences in terms of the topic:

QUESTIONS:	AUDIENCE 1 HIGH SCHOOL JUNIORS	AUDIENCE 2 PARENTS OF HIGH SCHOOL JUNIORS
1. What are their expectations?		
2. What do they already know about the topic?		

QUESTIONS:	AUDIENCE 1 HIGH SCHOOL JUNIORS	AUDIENCE 2 PARENTS OF HIGH SCHOOL JUNIORS
3. What experience do they have with the topic?	_____	_____
4. Does this topic matter to them? Why?	_____	_____
5. What do they need from me, in order to use or act on the information?	_____	_____

8.2 *Design a Visual*

Pictures can help us communicate, whether we are writing or speaking. This chapter gave a list of ideas or tips on designing good visuals. Use that list and design a set of visuals to go with the topic from Exercise 1 (Choosing a College and Major). For each visual, respond to the following requirements.

For each visual:

Describe what the visual will illustrate or demonstrate to the audience:

_____

_____

_____

Draw a brief sketch of the visual:

Explain when and how you will use the visual in the presentation:

WHEN _____

_____

_____

HOW _____

_____

_____

Effective Business Writing

Business writing needs to be clear and concise. Two standard business formats are letters and memos. Letters are written to people outside the company you work for (clients, future employers), and memos are written to people within your company (your boss, personnel). Use the information from this chapter to write the following:

1. A letter to a prospective employer explaining why you are the best person for the job (you can make up the job and company)
2. A memo to your boss explaining why you are the best person for a new position in your department (you can make up the position and department)

Team-Building Exercise: Communicating Strengths

Your team will act as a panel of prospective employees, interviewing to fill a position on the team. Each person will take turns and describe what would make him or her a valuable team member.

Panel members can ask questions to clarify what is said, as well as ask for examples to help demonstrate or explain.

Appoint one person to keep a record of what each person described as his or her strengths.

Multilingual Work Force

Case Studies

Given the numbers of people in our country who have a language other than English as their mother tongue, it is not surprising to find several different languages being spoken in workplaces around the country. This has created several problems and has resulted in a number of lawsuits. The following example is a hypothetical situation based on a number of real-life situations.

Lidia Gonzales, a Nicaraguan by birth, is a nurse in a private hospital. She had been employed by the hospital for twenty years when a new supervisor was hired. The supervisor, Betty Daniels, noticed several languages being spoken at the hospital, including Spanish, Tagalog (from the Philippines), and Korean. Betty believed that the safety of the patients required one language to be spoken on the hospital premises. If the Philippine nurses were speaking about a patient in the lounge, for example, the Spanish-speaking nurses wouldn't understand what they were saying and therefore couldn't contribute information that they might have. Also, Betty thought that speaking a different language would cause further stress to the patients.

Betty introduced a new rule to the hospital banning all languages, other than English, from being spoken on the hospital grounds. This ban was all-inclusive. English would have to be used in front of patients, in the hallways, in the lounges, at lunch, on breaks, and on the telephone.

The new rule was met by outrage from the nurses and with concern from minority groups. The nurses objected, saying they never spoke their native tongue in front of patients, and no other supervisor had ever voiced concern. Betty told them that since everyone spoke English perfectly, there were over-riding reasons to speak one language. The nurses believed that Betty was paranoid—thinking they were talking about her at lunch—and thought the ban was for her own benefit, since the care of the patients had never been compromised before.

Lidia strongly objected to the rule because she has an elderly mother at home who only speaks Spanish, and it is necessary for her to use Spanish when she spoke with her mother on the telephone. Because of the all-inclusive ban that she implemented, Betty was going to have to use disciplinary measures (warnings, suspension, and even termination) when she heard other languages being spoken in order to enforce the ban. At present, she had not yet heard Lidia on the phone with her mother. Lidia, however, said she felt like a fugitive, sneaking to the phone on her break and having other nurses look for Betty in order to warn her. Even a warning would go into her file and impact her performance evaluation and raise.

Susana Mores, who is Hispanic and head of the nursing staff, did not approve of the ban and thought Lidia, especially, was in a terrible position. "We should be able to speak any language we want. You can't say to someone that they can't speak their native language. Lidia has been a good employee here for twenty years, and now she feels persecuted."

The nurses gathered together to discuss filing a lawsuit. They scheduled an immediate meeting with Betty and the hospital administrators.

1. What were the reasons for the ban that Betty introduced? Are there other reasons for proposing such a ban or situations where a one-language rule might be advocated?

2. What reasons did the nurses give to oppose the ban? Are there other reasons why such a ban should not be implemented?

3. How does this situation affect the working relationship between the nurses and their new supervisor?

4. What should Betty do now?

5. What should Lidia do?

6. Is this a communication problem? What could have been done differently by Betty to avoid this problem? What could have been done differently by Susana? By Lidia?

Internet Exercise

Many companies and individuals have set up Web sites in order to provide information or sell products. Access Monty Robert's site at:

www.MontyRoberts.com

1. What does Monty's site share with you?

   _____

   _____

2. What advantages do you think the site offers Monty?

   _____

   _____

3. What disadvantages does a Web site have?

   _____

   _____

4. Would you do anything differently to make this site better?

   _____

   _____

5. If you were going to design a Web site for yourself, what would it look like?

   _____

   _____

   _____

Journal

Name _____ Date _____

9

Business Math

Finding Strength in Numbers

I f you were a little anxious when you saw the title of this chapter, you are probably not alone. Some people have a tendency to avoid math and question its usefulness in their lives. Business students, however, will come to realize that the skills presented in this chapter are crucial for success, regardless of their chosen field. You may find that you need to do more with math than use it to count all of your money. You'll want to use those math skills to earn even more money and maximize your profits. Improving efficiency and effectiveness is critical to any type of business, and what you will learn and review in this chapter has been invaluable in almost every profession, including artist, engineer, doctor, marketing director, and manager. So, be prepared to learn more of the secrets to success!

In this chapter, you will review the basic math skills and how they relate to business applications, as well as learn how to analyze graphs ("a picture is worth a thousand words"). You will also discover a graph and business relationship called breakeven analysis. Electronic spreadsheets are discussed in the last part of the chapter. You will discover how the computer is able to "do the math" and give you more time to analyze the results.

In this chapter, you will explore answers to the following questions:

- ◆ What math do you need to know?
- ◆ Charting new territory—How do you use graphs?
- ◆ What is breakeven analysis?
- ◆ How can spreadsheets help you to analyze data?

WHAT MATH DO YOU NEED TO KNOW?

Many of your everyday tasks require math. When you want to pay the correct amount on a bill, ensure that you receive the correct amount of change, balance your checkbook, compute your GPA, figure your interest payments, or plan a trip, you will need math skills.

Arithmetic

The basic building blocks of arithmetic include several activities that you have already learned in your elementary and secondary education:

1. Addition $(4 + 4)$
2. Subtraction $(6 - 4)$
3. Multiplication (4×6)
4. Division $(12 \div 4)$
5. Raising to a power (x^2)
6. Finding a square root $(\sqrt{4})$

If you have several of these operations to do to solve a problem, you will want to know which to do first. An easy way to remember is to use an acronym (a technique you learned in Chapter 7):

PLEASE END MY DREADED ARITHMETIC SCARE

> **P** stands for Parentheses. Do anything you see in parentheses first.
>
> **E** stands for Exponents. Do any exponents next.
>
> **M** stands for Multiplication.
>
> **D** stands for Division.
>
> **A** stands for Addition.
>
> **S** stands for Subtraction.

If you solve math problems in this order when you have more than one function, you shouldn't have any problems. For example:

TERMS

Arithmetic
The art of counting; computation or problem solving involving real numbers and arithmetic operations.

$(7 \times 5) + 4 = ?$

First, solve what is in the parentheses: $7 \times 5 = 35$. Next add the 4. The answer is 39.

Try this one:

$2[10 - (8 \div 2)] = ?$

In this problem, you find two sets of parentheses. Solve what is located in the innermost set of parentheses first: $8 \div 2$, which is 4. Next, solve what is in the next set of parentheses: $[10 - (4)]$, which is 6. Finally, you can multiply by 2, and the answer is 12.

Fractions

If you don't know these well already, you will want to understand fractions and how to add, subtract, multiply, and divide them. You can think of a fraction in one of two ways:

1. A fraction is another way to express division. For example, the expression $1/3$ is another way of saying 1 divided by 3.
2. A fraction symbolizes a part of something in relation to the whole: $4/5$ can be thought of as 4 parts out of a total of 5 parts.

Adding and Subtracting Fractions

If you have fractions with the same denominator (bottom half), it is a simple matter of adding the numerators (top halves). For example:

$$\frac{1}{5} + \frac{3}{5} = \frac{4}{5}$$

The denominator stays the same. This is true for subtraction, as well:

$$\frac{6}{7} - \frac{4}{7} = \frac{2}{7}$$

If you don't have the same denominators, you will have to make them the same. In order to do this, you could multiply each fraction by a number that would give it the same denominator as the other. You can't multiply it by any number other than 1 without changing the value of the fraction. But if you multiply the fraction by 1, the value will stay the same. For example, if you wanted to change $1/3$ into sixths, you could multiply this by $2/2$ (which equals 1):

$$\frac{1}{3} \times \frac{2}{2} = \frac{2}{6}$$

If you wanted to add $2/3 + 1/2$, you could change both the denominators into sixths:

$$\frac{2}{3} \times \frac{2}{2} = \frac{4}{6}$$

$$\frac{1}{2} \times \frac{3}{3} = \frac{3}{6}$$

"First convince yourself, then you can convince others."

SOCRATES

Then you could add:

$$\frac{4}{6} + \frac{3}{6} = \frac{7}{6}$$

Multiplying Fractions

As you just saw in the previous example, when you multiply fractions, you multiply the numerators and the denominators. For example:

$$\frac{5}{6} \times \frac{3}{4} = \frac{15}{24}$$

Reducing Fractions

When you add and multiply fractions, the resulting fractions can sometimes be too large to work with. To reduce a fraction, find a factor of the numerator that is also a factor of the denominator: $^{15}/_{24}$ can be reduced by finding the common factor of 15 and 24, which is 3. If we divide each side of the fraction by 3, we are left with $^{5}/_{8}$, which means the same thing as $^{15}/_{24}$ but is easier to work with.

Dividing Fractions

To divide one fraction by another, just turn the second fraction upside down and multiply. For example:

$$\frac{2}{3} \div \frac{4}{5}$$

is the same thing as

$$\frac{2}{3} \times \frac{5}{4} = \frac{10}{12}$$

Proportions

TERMS

Proportion
A part considered
in relation to
the whole.

As we have seen, a fraction means the same thing in a variety of forms: $^{4}/_{6}$, for example, is the same as $^{2}/_{3}$ and, $^{5}/_{8}$ is the same as $^{15}/_{24}$. A proportion can also be expressed as a fraction. For example: If 2 large barges can ship a total of 14 cars, how many cars can be carried on 3 barges? The way to solve this is to put it into fraction form:

$$\frac{2}{14} = \frac{3}{x}$$

To solve the value for x, you can cross-multiply, which means multiplying the numerators of the fractions by the denominators of the corresponding fraction. In this case:

$$\frac{2}{14} = \frac{3}{x}$$
$$2x = (14 \times 3) = 42$$

Divide both sides by 2 and you have $x = 21$. Therefore, 21 cars can fit on 3 barges.

CHALLENGE YOURSELF

The marketing budget you have is composed of three elements: $^1/_3$ of the budget is promotional material, $^3/_5$ is advertising, and the remaining $12,000 is for salaries. What is the total dollar amount of your marketing budget?

What makes this problem challenging is that the elements of the budget are expressed in two different forms. The promotional material and advertising are given as fractions, while the salaries are expressed in dollar value. The first step to solving this problem is to add the fractions that you have:

$$\frac{1}{3} + \frac{3}{5} = \left(\frac{1}{3} \times \frac{5}{5}\right) + \left(\frac{3}{5} \times \frac{3}{3}\right) = \frac{14}{15}$$

Promotional material and advertising, therefore, make up 14 parts out of the whole of 15. What fraction does the salary dollar value make up, then? What is left out of the whole, or 1/15. If you set this up now as a proportion, you can solve the problem:

$$\frac{\text{Part}}{\text{Whole}} \quad \frac{1}{15} = \frac{12,000}{x}$$

Cross-multiply and discover that $x = 180,000$. You now know that the whole budget is $180,000. Can you check this number by determining the dollar value of promotional materials and advertising?

Decimals

Fractions can be expressed as decimals, just as decimals can be expressed as fractions. For example, we know that $^4/_5$ means both 4 parts out of a whole of 5 and 4 divided by 5. If we divide 4 by 5, we get:

$$\frac{4}{5} = .8$$

Adding And Subtracting Decimals

To add or subtract, simply line the decimal points up, and add or subtract as you normally would. If you add 12, 3.4, and .2, you would set it up like this:

```
 12.0
  3.4
   .2
 15.6
```

Multiplying Decimals

To multiply decimals, don't pay any attention to the decimal points until after you've finished multiplying. Afterwards, count all the digits behind (on the right side of) the decimal points in the original numbers you just multiplied,

> "There are no hopeless situations; there are only people who have grown hopeless about them."
>
> CLARE BOOTHE LUCE

and place the decimal point in your answer so that there is the same number of digits behind (to the right of) the decimal.

In the problem .4 × .8, you would ignore the decimal points and multiply 4 × 8. You get 32. Then you count all the numbers on the right side of the decimal points in the original numbers, .4 and .8. There are a total of 2 numbers behind the decimal point. Next, you place the decimal point in your answer so there are the same number of digits behind the decimal, in this case 2. The answer is .32.

If you multiply 2.43 × .04, you would ignore the decimal points and multiply 243 × 4. You get 972. Next, you count the digits behind the decimal points in the original numbers. You should count a total of 4 digits. Therefore, your answer will be .0972.

Dividing Decimals

The best way to divide one decimal by another is to convert one into a whole number by moving the decimal point to the right as many places as you must. You then have to move the decimal point of the number into which you are dividing over the same number of places. For example:

$$.6 \sqrt{18.0}$$

To make .6 into a whole number, you have to move the decimal point to the right one place. The number then becomes 6. Then, you must move the decimal point of 18.0 over by one place to get 180. Now divide 180 by 6 to get 30.

Ratios

Ratios look like fractions, and you can do everything to them that you can do to fractions (turn them into decimals, multiply, divide, reduce). There is an important difference, however, between ratios and fractions. Remember that fractions symbolize the relation of a part to a whole. A ratio tells us the relationship between variables, but it doesn't give us a part in relation to a whole. For example, when you hear that 4 out 5 doctors recommend a certain aspirin, you don't have any idea how many doctors recommend this—they could number 5 or 1,000. Or when you hear that the ratio of women to men at a university is 2 to 1, you don't have any idea how many people attend the university based on the ratio alone.

Let's say that the ratio of men to women in an accounting class is 3 to 4. What is the number of men in the room if there are 20 women? All you have to do is set this up in fraction form. The ratio is 3:4, or $^3/_4$. Therefore,

$$\frac{3}{4} = \frac{x}{20}$$

Now you can cross-multiply, to arrive at $4x = 60$, or $x = 15$.

Percentages

A percent is also a fraction, where the denominator of every fraction is 100. For example, 20 percent is simply $^{20}/_{100}$, 50 percent is $^{50}/_{100}$, and so on. Like every other fraction, you can reduce, multiply, divide, and turn these into decimals.

CHALLENGE YOURSELF

The ratio of managers to employees in a company is 1 to 4. If there are a total of 200 people in the company, how many managers are there?

This problem is more difficult because you don't know how many managers or employees there are; if you try to set this up as you did before, you get:

$$\frac{1}{4} = \frac{x}{y}$$

You can't solve the problem this way. This is where the difference between ratios and fractions becomes apparent. If you have a ratio of 1 to 4, this means that there is 1 manager to every 4 employees. Out of every 5 people, 1 is a manager and 4 are employees. How many groups of 5 people are there in the total of 200 people? There are 40 groups of 5 people (40 × 5 = 200). If there are 40 groups of 5, then each one of those groups will be made up of 1 manager and 4 employees. The total number of managers would be 40 (40 groups × 1 manager), and the total number of employees would be 160 (40 groups × 4 employees). These problems require a little more thinking about what the numbers mean, but they are solvable!

$$20\% = \frac{20}{100} = \frac{1}{5} = .2$$

The number 3 is what percent of 60? When you see a percent problem, put it in terms of parts to the whole. Here, the part is 3 and the whole is 60:

$$\frac{3}{60}$$

Now, you have to turn this into a percent, whose denominator is 100:

$$\frac{3}{60} = \frac{x}{100}$$

By cross-multiplying, you get $60x = 300$. Solving this, you can determine that the number 3 is 5 percent of 60.

GOOD PERCENTAGES TO REMEMBER:

$$\frac{1}{4} = .25 = 25\%$$

$$\frac{1}{2} = .50 = 50\%$$

$$\frac{1}{3} = .3333 \text{ etc.} = 33^1/_3\%$$

$$\frac{1}{5} = .20 = 20\%$$

Here are some good tips to remember (the first one is helpful for remembering what to tip). You can get 10 percent of any number by moving the decimal point of that number one place to the left. For example:

10% of 50 = 5.0
10% of 500 = 50.0
10% of 5   = 0.5
10% of 550 = 55.0

You can get 20 percent of any number by doubling the answer for 10 percent. For example, to find 20 percent of 50, you can multiply .20 x 50. You can also take 10 percent of 50, which is easy to determine as 5, and multiply this by 2, for the answer of 10.

CHALLENGE YOURSELF

A business has 500 employees, of which 30% are part-time. Of the employees, 20% are using the educational assistance program. This number includes 10 part-time workers. The company would like more of its full-time employees to benefit from the educational program. Can you tell the company what percent of its employees are full-time and not using the plan?

You can solve this problem one step at a time. The first fact you know is that 30% of the employees are part-time:

.30 × 500 = 150

The company has 150 part-time employees, which means that the rest, 350 (500 - 150), are full-time employees.

The next fact you know is that 20 percent of the employees, including 10 part-time workers, are using the educational plan:

.20 × 500 = 100

So 100 employees are using the educational program; 10 of these people are part-time. Therefore, 90 (100 – 10) full-time employees are using the program.

You can now determine how many full-time employees are not using the plan by taking the total number of full-time employees, 350, and subtracting the number of these full-timers who are using the program, 90:

350 – 90 = 260

The answer: 260 full-time employees are not using the educational program.

Percent Increase

A type of percent problem you will see fairly frequently throughout your educational and career experience has to do with percentage increases or decreases. For instance: The sales department in a major department store has determined that the average sale (how much a customer spent, on average, when he or she purchased something at the store) was $150 in 1990. By 1998, this had increased to $210. What was the percent increase in the average sale?

First, find out what the actual increase is:

$210 – $150 = $60

Then, set the problem up in the following manner:

$$\frac{\text{Amount of increase (or decrease)}}{\text{Original amount}} = \frac{x}{100}$$

In this problem, the set-up looks like:

$$\frac{\$\,60}{\$150} = \frac{x}{100}$$

Cross-multiply, and you determine that $150x = 6,000$ and $x = 40$. The percent increase in the average sale between 1990 and 1998 was 40 percent.

Interest And Compound Interest

Computing simple interest is another type of percentage problem. If you had $1,000 in the bank for 1 year at 12 percent interest, you can determine how much you would get at the end of the year:

12% = .12
.12 × $1,000 = $120

At the end of 1 year, you would have $120.

However, if the interest was compounded, you would get slightly more at the end of the year. Let's look at two situations. What would happen if you invested $1,000 in an account that is compounded semiannually (twice a year) and gave you 12 percent interest? And, what would happen if you invested the same amount in an account that is compounded quarterly (four times a year), with the same interest rate?

When you determine compound interest, you first divide the interest into as many parts as are being compounded. For example, if you're compounding interest semiannually, divide the interest into 2 parts; if you are compounding quarterly, divide the interest into 4 equal parts.

In the first case, compounding semiannually, the bank will put the first of the interest into your account halfway through the year. Since $1/2$ of the 12 percent interest rate is 6 percent, in the first 6 months, you will earn:

.06 × $1,000 = $60

The bank will deposit $60 into your account after 6 months. Then, you will have a total of $1,060 in the bank. In the second half of the year, the bank will pay you 6 percent on the new amount in your account:

.06 × $1,060 = $63.60

At the end of 1 year, you would have a total of $1,123.60. You earned $123.60, as compared to the $120 you earned with simple interest.

Now try compounding quarterly. Divide the 12 percent interest rate into 4 equal parts of 3 percent:

1st quarter:	.03 x $1,000 = $30.	Total in bank = $1,030.
2nd quarter:	.03 x $1,030 = $30.90.	Total in bank = $1,060.90.
3rd quarter:	.03 x $1,060.90 = $31.83.	Total in bank = $1,092.73.
4th quarter	.03 x $1,092.727 = $32.78.	Total in bank = $1,125.51.

> "Worry gives a small thing a big shadow."
> SWEDISH PROVERB

Note: When you compute interest, don't round your numbers until the very end.

By compounding quarterly, you will get more interest than with simple interest or semiannually compounded interest. While a few dollars here and there may not seem like very much, try computing this over a period of several years, while also increasing the amount you deposit into your account, and see what happens!

Word Problems

In math, the single largest stumbling block is word problems. There is a famous *Far Side* cartoon titled "Hell's Library," which shows a shelf filled with books entitled *Story Problems*, *More Story Problems*, and so on. Word problems represent the number one fear of students of math. The bottom line is that word problems will be the most common way you will encounter mathematics throughout your life. Therefore, the ability to solve word problems is a necessary skill.

Why do people have so many difficulties with word problems? The reason lies with the fact that word problems force you to translate between two languages, English and mathematics. Math is a language in and of itself, and an extremely precise one. English and other living languages, however, are not precise. Although this lack of precision helps such languages achieve their richness in poetry and literature, it makes the process of translating more difficult.

Steps to Solving Word Problems

Translating from English or any other language to math takes a lot of practice. George Polya, in his 1945 classic, *How to Solve It*, devised a four-step method for attacking word problems. This procedure has been adopted in one form or another in nearly every math textbook.[1] The basic steps are as follows:

1. Understand the problem. This means reading the problem carefully. Understand what it is asking. Know what information you have. Know what information is missing. Draw a picture, if possible.

2. Devise a plan. Try to decide how you want to solve the problem. Think about similar problems. Try to relate the given information. This is the translation step, where you need to develop and use your problem-solving strategies.

3. Carry out your plan. Solve the problem. Check each of your steps.

4. Review your result. Check your answer, if possible. Make sure you've answered the question the problem is asking. Does your result make sense in the context of the problem? Are there other ways to do the problem?

The best way to develop your skills in solving word problems is by doing a lot of them. Do extra problems. Practice a lot. The following section lays out several problem-solving strategies by working through different types of word problem examples.[2]

Problem-Solving Strategies

Strategy 1. Look for a pattern. G. H. Hardy (1877–1947), an eminent British mathematician, described mathematicians as makers of patterns and ideas. The search for patterns is one of the best strategies in problem solving. This process is used in police work as well as in mathematics.

Example 1: Find the next three entries in the following sequences:

a. 1, 2, 4, ____ , ____ , ____
b. O, T, T, F, F, S, S, ____ , ____ , ____
c. 1, 1, 2, 3, 5, 8, 13, ____ , ____ , ____

Solutions to Example 1:

a. One important thing to remember about trying to identify patterns is that you may very well make connections and find a different pattern than someone else. This doesn't mean yours is wrong. In example 1a, there are actually several possible answers. Here are two:

   1. First, you might recognize that each succeeding term of the sequence is twice the previous term. In that case, the next three values would be 8, 16, 32.
   2. Another possibility is that you might notice the second term is 1 more than the first term and the third term is 2 more than the second. This might lead you to guess the fourth term is 3 more than the third term, the fifth term is 4 more than the fourth term, and so on. In that case, the next three terms are 7, 11, 16.

b. Example 1b is a famous pattern that often appears in puzzle magazines. The key to it is that O is the first letter of one, T is the first letter of two, and so on. Therefore, the next three terms would be E, N, and T for eight, nine, and ten.

c. Example 1c is another famous sequence called the Fibonacci sequence. It's named after Leonardo of Pisa (c.1170–1250), an Italian mathematician who was also called Fibonacci. In 1202, he wrote a book about algebra called *Liber Abaci* in which he introduced this sequence. You determine each succeeding term by adding the two immediately preceding terms together, so term three is 1 + 1 = 2, term four is 1 + 2 = 3, and so on. This means the next three terms are 21 = 8 + 13, 34 = 13 + 21, and 55 = 21 + 34. The Fibonacci sequence occurs frequently in nature. The seeds of a sunflower spiral out from the center in a Fibonacci number of rows, for example, and the scales of a pineapple spiral in a Fibonacci number of rows as well.

Strategy 2. Make a table. A table can be used to help organize and summarize information. This then may enable you to see a pattern that lets you solve a problem.

TABLE A.

Quarters	0	0	0	0	0	0	0	0	0	0	0	0	0	0	0	0	0	0
Dimes	0	0	0	0	0	0	0	0	0	0	0	1	1	1	1	1	1	1
Nickels	0	1	2	3	4	5	6	7	8	9	10	0	1	2	3	4	5	6
Pennies	50	45	40	35	30	25	20	15	10	5	0	40	35	30	25	20	15	10

TABLE B.

Quarters	0	0	0	0	0	0	0	0	0	0	0	0	0	0	0	0	0	0
Dimes	1	1	2	2	2	2	2	2	2	3	3	3	3	3	4	4	4	5
Nickels	7	8	0	1	2	3	4	5	6	0	1	2	3	4	0	1	2	0
Pennies	5	0	30	25	20	15	10	5	0	20	15	10	5	0	10	5	0	0

TABLE C.

Quarters	1	1	1	1	1	1	1	1	1	1	1	1
Dimes	0	0	0	0	0	0	1	1	1	1	2	2
Nickels	0	1	2	3	4	5	0	1	2	3	0	1
Pennies	25	20	15	10	5	0	15	10	5	0	5	0

Example 2: How many ways can you make change for a half dollar using only quarters, dimes, nickels, and pennies?

Solution to Example 2: To attack the half-dollar problem, you might construct several tables and go through every possible case. You could start by seeing how many ways you can make change for a half dollar without using a quarter, which would produce the results shown in Tables A and B above. There are 36 ways to make change for a half dollar without using a quarter.

Using one quarter results in the options shown in Table C above. Using one quarter, you get twelve different ways to make change for a half dollar.

Lastly, using two quarters, there's only one way to make change for a half dollar. Therefore, the solution to the problem is that there are 36 + 12 + 1 = 49 ways to make change for a half dollar using only quarters, dimes, nickels, and pennies.

Strategy 3. Identify a sub-goal. Breaking the original problem into smaller and easier problems may lead to a solution of the original problem. This is often the case in writing a computer program.

Example 3: Arrange the nine numbers 1, 2, 3, . . . , 9 into a square subdivided into nine sections in such a way that the sum of every row, column, and main diagonal is the same. This is what is called a *magic square*.

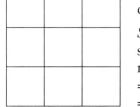

Solution to Example 3: Since each number will go into one of the squares, the sum of all the numbers will end up being three times the sum of any given row, column, or main diagonal. The sum of 1 + 2 + 3 + 4 + 5 + 6 + 7 + 8 + 9 = 45. Therefore, each row, column, and main diagonal needs to sum to 45/3 = 15. Now you need to see how many ways you can add three of the numbers from 1 to 9 and get 15. In doing this, you should get:

$$9 + 1 + 5 = 15 \qquad 8 + 2 + 5 = 15 \qquad 7 + 3 + 5 = 15$$
$$9 + 2 + 4 = 15 \qquad 8 + 3 + 4 = 15 \qquad 6 + 4 + 5 = 15$$
$$8 + 1 + 6 = 15 \qquad 7 + 2 + 6 = 15$$

Now, looking at your magic square, notice that the center position will be part of four sums (a row, a column, and the two main diagonals). Looking back at your sums, you see that 5 appears in four different sums; therefore 5 is in the center square. The number in each corner appears in 3 sums (row, column, and a diagonal). Looking through your sums, you find that 2, 4, 6, and 8 each appear in three sums. Now you need to place them in the corners in such a way that your diagonals add up to 15.

2		6
	5	
4		8

To finish, all you need to do is fill in the remaining squares to get the needed sum of 15 for each row, column, and main diagonal. The completed square is as follows:

2	7	6
9	5	1
4	3	8

Strategy 4: Work backwards. With some problems, you may find it easier to start with the perceived final result and work backwards.

Example 4: In the game of "Life," Carol had to pay $1500 when she was married. Then she lost half the money she had left. Next she paid half the money she had for a house. Then the game ended and she had $3000 left. With how much money did she start?

Solution to Example 4: Carol ended up with $3000. Right before that she paid half her money to buy a house. Since her $3000 was half of what she had before her purchase, she had 2($3000) = $6000 before buying the house. Prior to buying the house, Carol lost half her money. This means that the $6000 is the half she didn't lose. So, before losing half her money, Carol had 2($6000) = $12,000. Prior to losing half her money, Carol had to pay $1500 to get married. This means she had $12,000 + $1500 = $13,500 before getting married. Since this was the start of the game, Carol began with $13,500.

Strategy 5: Draw a diagram. Drawing a picture is often an aid to solving problems. Pictures are especially useful in gaining insight into geometrical problems. However, the use of pictures and drawings can be helpful in many other types of problems.

Example 5: There were twenty people at a round table for dinner. Each person shook hands with the person to his or her immediate right and left. At the end of the dinner, each person got up and shook hands with everybody except the people who sat on his or her immediate right and left. How many handshakes took place after dinner?

Solution to Example 5: To solve this with a diagram, it might be a good idea to examine several simpler cases to see if you can determine a pattern of any kind that might help. Starting with two or three people, you can see there are no handshakes after dinner, since everyone is adjacent to everyone else.

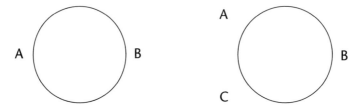

In the case of four people, we get the following diagram, connecting those people who shake hands after dinner:

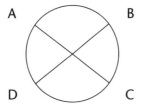

In this situation, you see there are two handshakes after dinner, AC and BD. In the case of five people, you get this picture:

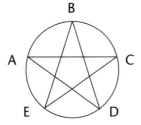

In this case, you have five after-dinner handshakes: AC, AD, BD, BE, and CE. Looking at one further case of six people seated around a circle gives the following diagram:

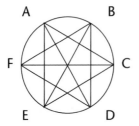

In this diagram, there are now a total of nine after-dinner handshakes: AC, AD, AE, BD, BE, BF, CE, CF, and DF. In noticing from the diagrams what is happening, you realize that if there are N people, each person would shake N − 3 people's hands after dinner (they don't shake their own hands or the hands of the two people adjacent to them). Since there are N people, that would lead to N(N − 3) after-dinner handshakes. However, this would double-count every handshake, since AD would also be counted as DA. Therefore, this is twice as many handshakes as actually took place. So, the correct number of handshakes is [N(N − 3)]/2. So finally, if there are twenty people, there would be 20(17)/2 = 170 after-dinner handshakes.

CHARTING NEW TERRITORY: HOW DO YOU USE GRAPHS?

A graph or chart is a picture of information. Some charts can give several pieces of information, while others convey only one point. In business, you will need to understand several types of charts. In this section, we will look at two types: the pie chart and the line graph.

The Pie Chart

You saw the pie chart in Figure 9-1 in Chapter 1.

Why was this chart used? It makes it easy to see that, compared to other fields, there are a lot of jobs in business. Almost half of the jobs, in fact, that were offered were in the business field. What other information does it tell you?

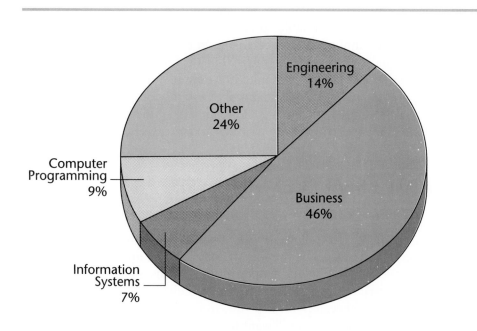

Figure 9-1

Jobs offered— 1998.

Source: Salary Survey, April 1998 (figures from September 1997–March 1998).

Figure 9-2

Job offers.

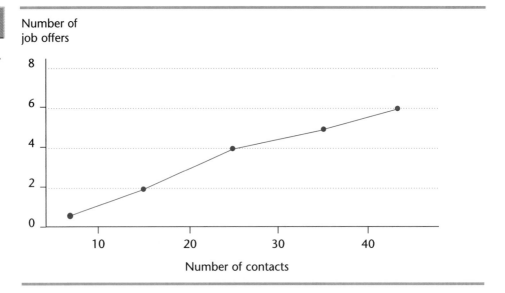

Number of job offers

The Line Graph

A line graph will generally have two axis—the x axis and the y axis. It is used to show the relationship between two things, or variables. For instance, you can see from the graph in Figure 9-2 that the more contacts students make with potential employers, the more job offers they get.

In a line graph, there is an x axis and a y axis. The x axis, in this case, tells how many contacts were made. On the y axis, we see how many job offers were given. We can see from this graph that after 10 contacts with potential employers, 1 job offer was made; 20 contacts led to 2 job offers.

The two variables we plot (in this case, the number of contacts and the number of job offers) are called the independent and dependent variables. Independent variables are variables that we have control over. For example, we can control the number of contacts made, so that is the independent variable, which is usually plotted on the x axis. The dependent variable *depends* on what we do to the independent variable. For example, if we make more contacts with potential employers, the number of job offers will likely rise because job offers depend on contacts. The number of job offers, then, is the dependent variable, which is usually plotted on the y axis.

WHAT IS BREAKEVEN ANALYSIS?

The artist, Mary Hey, wants to know how many paintings she must sell in order to cover all her costs, including her paint, her canvas materials, her easels, and her studio lease. The number of paintings she must sell in order to cover all of her costs is her breakeven point (BEP). This is a very useful number to know in every business because if you are below this number, you lose money; above the breakeven point is profit. In order to determine this point, there are a couple of concepts you'll want to understand. The first is fixed cost.

Fixed cost is what you will have to pay if you stopped working today and didn't produce anything else. If Mary stopped painting, she would still have

TERMS

Fixed costs
Costs that are
not affected in
the short term by
production level.

to pay her studio lease. She may also have insurance, phone service, or any other long-term obligations that wouldn't go away just because she stopped producing. This is the same for any business. Harry's Wonder Widgets, for instance, could stop making widgets but still owe money for equipment, leases, and possibly salaries. Of course, in the longer term, all of these costs can be eliminated, so we are looking at the shorter term when we analyze breakeven point. Fixed costs, therefore, are costs you can't easily eliminate if you stopped production. If Harry's fixed cost, for instance, totaled $100,000 a month, he would have to pay that money whether he produced 1 widget or 500,000 widgets in the month.

Variable costs are the costs that change with how many units you produce. For instance, if Mary paints one picture a month, she will buy a certain amount of paint and canvas material. If she paints ten paintings, she will have to spend more money on paint and canvas. This is the variable cost associated with any type of business. The more business you do, the more money you will spend. Of course, you'd like to sell enough to more than cover all of these costs. In order to do that, you have to know what they are. Variable costs are costs that increase depending on the number of products you produce. Harry's Wonder Widgets has determined that its variable costs include electricity to run the machines, oil for the machines, hourly wages to pay the machine operators, and the cost of the raw materials. They have computed this cost to be $2 per widget. For every widget they make, it costs them $2 in addition to their $100,000 per month of fixed cost.

Total costs are the variable costs added to the fixed costs. If they made 10,000 widgets this month, it would cost them ($2 × 10,000) + $100,000 = $120,000. How many wonder widgets will they have to sell in order to cover this cost? It depends on their price, of course. If Harry has determined that the market will pay $6 per widget, we can then determine the breakeven point for the month. The formula for this is fairly straightforward:

> **TERMS**
>
> Variable costs
> Costs that change
> depending on pro-
> duction level.

$$\text{Quantity (BEP)} = \frac{\text{Total Fixed Cost}}{(\text{Price per Unit - Variable Cost per Unit})}$$

If we plug in the numbers for Harry, we get:

$$\text{Quantity (BEP)} = \frac{\$100,000}{(\$6 - \$2)}$$

$$= \frac{\$100,000}{\$4}$$

$$= 25,000 \text{ widgets}$$

Harry has to sell 25,000 widgets in order to break even or just cover his costs. Using this formula, we can also determine how many widgets he will need to sell in order to make a certain amount of money. If Harry wanted to make $10,000 profit, for example, how many widgets would he have to sell?

$$\text{Quantity (\$10,000)} = \frac{\text{Total Fixed Cost} + \$10,000}{(\text{Price per Unit - Variable Cost per Unit})}$$

$$\text{Quantity} = \frac{\$100,000 + \$10,000}{(\$6 - \$2)}$$

$$= 27,500$$

We can see this relationship on a line graph in Figure 9-3.

Figure 9-3

Breakeven line graph.

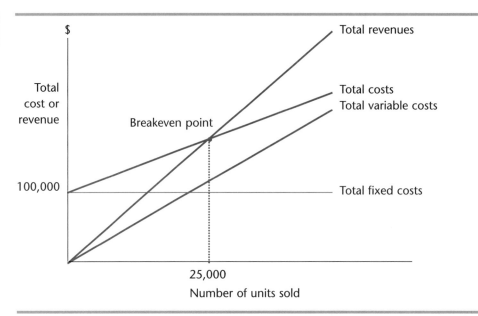

How CAN YOU USE SPREADSHEETS?

Spreadsheets are software programs where you can keep data that you may want to use to compute other information. You can collect, interact with, and display the data in rows and columns in a spreadsheet. You can build in formulas that will compute mathematical problems easily. There are several spreadsheet applications, including Microsoft Excel and Lotus 1-2-3. Spreadsheets are essential, powerful business tools. By completing the case study at the end of the chapter, you will have a better idea of how to use spreadsheets.

Electronic spreadsheets can look like spreadsheets prepared by hand when they are printed, but don't be fooled. They are much more powerful because of format designs and imbedded commands (formulas and functions).

Format designs allow you to add columns and rows, change titles, and add dollar signs, all without having to erase and redo the whole spreadsheet. You can make a column as wide or narrow as you want, rather than having to use a "one size fits all" approach.

Imbedded commands often take the form of what we know as math shorthand, or formulas and functions. If you were going to add three numbers, you could write a formula $(x + y + z = a)$ and then define what each term stood for. The computer software in a spreadsheet program allows you to enter a formula or perform a function (for example, SUM, IF) and then have the software calculate or perform the imbedded commands for you. The power in the electronic spreadsheet is the speed with which it can "crunch" the numbers, as well as make changes and quickly recalculate the results. Spreadsheets also allow us to analyze the data with graphs and pie charts, which are prepared by the computer, based on your directions (commands).

When you combine the power of format and imbedded commands, and extra features such as graphic capabilities, you see that spreadsheets are the way to go for calculations. You may have to spend a little more time setting up the spreadsheet on the computer, but it is worth the time investment, especially if you will reuse the same data.

PUTTING MATH TO WORK: HOW CAN YOU CREATE A BUDGET THAT WORKS?

Every time you have some money in your pocket and have to figure out whether it will pay for what you want at that moment, you are budgeting your money. It takes some thought and energy to budget efficiently. The more money you can save each month, the more you will thank yourself later when you need it. Consider your resources (money coming in) and expenditures (money flowing out). A smart budget adjusts the money flow for the best pos-

---

REAL WORLD PERSPECTIVE

What should I do about all these credit-card offers?

Brett Cross, University of Washington

Recently, I have been receiving a number of credit-card applications offering a low interest rate. In fact, I get at least one offer a week. I've been thinking it would be nice to establish credit, but I'm not sure if getting a credit card right now is a good idea. Even though I have a part-time job hauling and have financial aid, it seems like there's never enough to make it to the end of the semester. Should I apply for one of these credit cards? It would be really great to have some extra cash every now and then.

Tim Short, Washington State University

Dealing with financial hardships while in college is a part of life for many people these days. Credit-card offers are in abundance for college students, and for good reason. Credit companies know that most college students won't be able to pay off their cards until after they graduate, and that they tend to carry balances and pay interest and hefty fees until they are solvent. Believe me, I know. Throughout my past four years at college, I have acquired several credit cards. On them I have charged things such as books, car repairs, auto insurance, and other personal items. I am still paying interest on these cards monthly and will not be able to pay them off until after I graduate.

My suggestion to you is this: Don't take out a credit card unless you absolutely have to. If you can take out student loans or borrow from your parents, do that instead. Most academic loans hold a 6 to 8 percent interest rate which is much lower than the 18 to 21 percent that most credit card companies charge. Don't be fooled by offers for a card with a low rate. These invariably expire after one year and then the rate jumps up. If you miss a payment during that year, some companies will raise your rates immediately. Rationalizing that you will pay the card off before that time frame is up is also not a good idea. Unless you are on the verge of graduation, you will probably not have any more cash in a year than you do now. Overall, my advice is this: If you can avoid borrowing from credit-card companies, do so! You will be a lot happier in the long run.

sible chance that what comes in will be more than what goes out. Smart budgeting is a worthwhile investment in your future.

The Art of Budgeting

Budgeting involves following a few basic steps in order. These steps are: determining how much money you make, determining how much money you spend, subtracting the second number (what you spend) from the first number (what you make), evaluating the result, and making decisions about how to adjust your spending or earning based on that result. Budgeting regularly is easiest. Use a specified time frame, such as a week or month. Most people budget on a month-by-month basis.

Determine How Much You Will Make

Do this by adding up all your money receipts from the month. If you currently have a regular full-time or part-time job, add your pay stubs. If you have received any financial aid, loan funding, or scholarship money, determine how much of that you can allow for each month's income and add it to your total. For example, if you received a $1,200 grant for the year, each month would have an income of $100. Be sure, when you are figuring your income, to use the amounts that remain *after* taxes have been taken out.

Figure Out How Much You Spend

You may or may not have a handle on your spending. Many people don't take the time to keep track. If you have never before paid much attention to how you spend money, examine your spending patterns. Over a month's time, record expenditures in a small notebook or on a piece of paper on a home bulletin board. You don't have to list everything down to the penny. Just indicate expenditures over $5, making sure to count smaller expenditures if they are frequent (a bus pass for a month, soda or newspaper purchases per week). In your list, include an estimate of the following:

- ◆ Rent/mortgage/school room fees
- ◆ Tuition or educational loan payments (divide your annual total by 12 to arrive at a monthly figure)
- ◆ Books, lab fees, and other educational expenses
- ◆ Regular bills (heat, gas, electric, phone, car payment, water)
- ◆ Credit card or other payments on credit
- ◆ Food, clothing, toiletries, and household supplies
- ◆ Child care
- ◆ Entertainment and related items (eating out, books and publications, movies)
- ◆ Health, auto, and home/renters' insurance
- ◆ Transportation and auto expenses

Subtract what you spend from what you make. Ideally, you will have a positive number. You may end up with a negative number, however, especially if you haven't made a habit of keeping track of your spending. This indicates that you are spending more than you make, which over a long period of time can create a nasty debt.

Evaluate the Result

After you arrive at your number, determine what it tells you. If you have a positive number, decide how to save it if you can. If you end up with a negative number, ask yourself questions about what is causing the deficit—where you are spending too much or earning too little. Of course, surprise expenses during some months may cause you to spend more than usual, such as if you have to replace your refrigerator, pay equipment fees for a particular course, or have an emergency medical procedure. However, when a negative number comes up for what seems to be a typical month, you may need to adjust your budget over the long term.

Make Decisions About How to Adjust Spending or Earning

Looking at what may cause you to overspend, brainstorm possible solutions that address those causes. Solutions can involve either increasing resources or decreasing spending. To deal with spending, prioritize your expenditures and trim the ones you really don't need to make. Do you eat out too much? Can you live without cable, a beeper, a cellular phone? Be smart. Cut out unaffordable extras. As for resources, investigate ways to take in more money. Taking a part-time job, hunting down scholarships or grants, or increasing hours at a current job may help.

A Sample Budget

Table 9-1 shows a sample budget of an unmarried student living with two other students. It will give you an idea of how to budget (all expenditures are general estimates, based on averages).

To make up the $190 that this student went over budget, he can adjust his spending. He could rent movies or check them out of the library instead of going to the theater. He could socialize with friends at someone's apartment instead of paying high prices and tips at a bar or restaurant. Instead of buying CDs and tapes, he could borrow them. He could also shop for specials and bargains in the grocery store or go to a warehouse supermarket to stock up on staples at discount prices. He could make his lunch instead of buying it and walk instead of taking public transportation.

Not everyone likes the work involved in keeping a budget. While linear, factual, reflective, and verbal learners may take to it more easily, active, holistic, theoretical, and visual learners may resist the structure and detail (see Chapter 2). Visual learners may want to create a budget chart like the one shown in the example or construct a think link that shows the connections between all the month's expenditures. Use images to clarify ideas, such as picturing a bathtub you are filling that is draining at the same time. Use strategies that make budgeting more tangible, such as dumping all of your receipts into a big jar and tallying them at the end of the month. Even if you have to force yourself to do it, you will discover that budgeting can reduce stress and help you take control of your finances and your life.

Table 9-1

A student's sample budget.

Part-time salary: $10 an hour, 20 hours a week. 10 × 20 = $200 a week, × 4 ¹/₃ weeks (one month) = $866. Student loan from school's financial aid office: $2,000 divided by 12 months = $166. Total income per month: $1,032.

MONTHLY EXPENDITURES	AMOUNT
Tuition ($6,500 per year)	$ 542
Public transportation	$ 90
Phone	$ 40
Food	$ 130
Medical insurance	$ 120
Rent (including utilities)	$ 200
Entertainment/miscellaneous	$ 100
TOTAL SPENDING	$1,222

$1,032 (income) − $1,222 (spending) = −$190 ($190 over budget).

Savings Strategies

You can save money and still enjoy life. Make your fun less expensive fun—or save up for a while to splurge on a really special occasion. Small amounts can add up to big savings after a while. Here are some suggestions for saving a little bit of money here and there:

- Rent movies or attend bargain matinees.
- When safe for the fabric, hand-wash items you ordinarily dry-clean.
- Check movies, CDs, tapes, and books out of your library.
- Make popcorn instead of buying bags of chips.
- Walk instead of paying for public transportation.
- If you have storage space, buy detergent, paper products, toiletries, and other staples in bulk.
- Shop in secondhand stores.
- Keep your possessions neat, clean, and properly maintained—they will last longer.
- Take advantage of weekly supermarket specials, and bring coupons when you shop.
- Reuse grocery bags for food storage and garbage instead of buying bags.
- Return bottles and cans for deposits if you live in a state that accepts them.
- Trade clothing with friends and barter services (plumbing for baby-sitting, for example).
- Buy display models of appliances or electronics (stereo equipment, TVs, VCRs).
- Take your lunch instead of buying it.
- Find a low-rate long-distance calling plan, use email, or write letters.

◆ Save on heat by dressing warmly and using blankets; save on air conditioning by using fans.

◆ Have potluck parties; ask people to bring dinner foods or munchies.

◆ Add your own suggestions here!

_____

_____

_____

You can also maximize savings and minimize spending by using credit cards wisely.

Managing Credit Cards

Most credit comes in the form of a powerful little plastic card. Credit-card companies often solicit students on campus or through the mail. When choosing a card, pay attention to the *annual fee* and *interest rates*, the two ways in which a credit card company makes money from you. Some cards have no annual fee; others may charge a flat rate of $10 to $70 per year. Interest rates can be fixed or variable. A variable rate of 12 percent may shoot up to 18 percent when the economy slows down. You might be better off with a mid-range fixed rate that will always stay the same.

Following are some potential effects of using credit.

Positive Effects

A good credit history. If you use your credit card moderately and pay your bills on time, you will make a positive impression on your creditors. Your *credit history* (the record of your credit use, including positive actions, such as paying on time, and negative actions, such as going over your credit limit) and *credit rating* (the score you are given based on your history) can make or break your ability to take out a loan or mortgage. How promptly you make loan payments and pay mortgage and utility bills affects your credit rating as well. Certain companies track your credit history and give you a credit rating. Banks or potential employers will contact these companies to see if you are a good credit risk.

Emergencies. Few people carry enough cash to handle unexpected expenses. Your credit card can help you in emergency situations, such as when you need towing.

Record of purchases. Credit-card statements give you a monthly record of purchases made, where they were made, and exactly how much was paid. Using your credit card for purchases that you want to track, such as work expenses, can help you keep records for tax purposes.

Negative Effects

Credit can be addictive. Credit can be like a drug, seeming like fun because the pain of paying is put off until later. If you get hooked, though, you can wind up thousands of dollars in debt to creditors. The high interest will

> TERMS
>
> **Creditors**
> People to whom debts, usually money, are owed.

> "Put not your trust in money, but put your money in trust."
> OLIVER WENDELL HOLMES

enlarge your debt, your credit rating may fall (potentially hurting your eligibility for loans and mortgages), and you may lose your credit cards altogether.

Credit spending can be hard to monitor. Paying by credit can seem so easy that you don't realize how much you are spending. When the bill comes at the end of the month, the total can hit you hard.

You are taking out a high-interest loan. Buying on credit is similar to taking out a loan—you are using money with the promise to pay it back. Loan rates, however, especially on fixed-interest loans, are often much lower than the 11 to 23 percent on credit card debt: 15 percent interest per year on a credit card debt averaging $2000 is approximately $300; 5 percent interest per year on a loan in the same amount is $100.

Bad credit ratings can haunt you. Any time you are late with a payment, default on a payment, or in any way misuse your card, a record of that occurrence will be entered on your credit history, lowering your credit rating. If a prospective employer or loan officer discovers a low rating, you will seem less trustworthy and may lose the chance at a job or a loan.

Managing Credit Card Debt

There are ways to manage credit card debt so that it doesn't get worse. Stay in control by having only one or two cards and paying bills regularly and on time. Try to pay in full each month. If you can't, at least pay the minimum. Make as much of a dent in the bill as you can.

If you get into trouble, three steps will help you deal with the situation. First, *admit* that you made a mistake, even though you may be embarrassed. Then, *address* the problem immediately and honestly in order to minimize the damages. Call the bank or credit card company to talk to someone about the problem. They may draw up a payment plan that allows you to pay your debt gradually, in amounts that your budget can manage. Creditors would rather accept small payments than nothing at all.

Finally, *prevent* this problem from happening again. Figure out what got you into trouble and take steps to avoid it in the future if you can. Some financial disasters, such as medical emergencies, may be beyond your control. Overspending on luxuries, however, is something you have the power to avoid. Make a habit of balancing your checkbook. Cut up a credit card or two if you have too many. Don't let a high credit limit tempt you to spend. Pay every month, even if you pay only the minimum. If you work to clean up your act, your credit history will gradually clean up as well.

Sacrifici

In Italy, parents often use the term *sacrifici*, meaning "sacrifices," to refer to tough choices that they make in order to improve the lives of their children and family members. They may sacrifice a larger home so that they can afford to pay for their children's sports and after-school activities. They may sacrifice a higher-paying job so that they can live close to where they work. They give up something in exchange for something else that they have decided is more important to them.

Success in the Real World

Scott Lehman

Scott "Opie" Lehman founded Software Configuration Management Labs eight years ago to provide software services and products to large corporate clients. Scott's love

for computer programming began when he worked his way through school in the computer lab. IBM showed up one day and asked Scott to write a program to coordinate all the radio carbon labs in the world. After

that, he knew he didn't want to do anything else—he had found his passion. Scott believes that if people do what they love, and if they try to be the best at it, they will stick with it through the tough times and eventually find great success.

Scott began his consulting company and saw his company grow at an explosive rate. He had to hire many more people, and he used his steadfast rule when hiring: surround yourself with people of high integrity who are committed to excellence. Scott tries to do this, not only when hiring people for his company but in all aspects of his life. He looks for people who are smarter than he is because he thinks that it is beneficial for him to put his ego aside and learn from others. In fact, continual learning is extremely important to Scott—his survival and that of his company depend on it. Scott believes that school teaches you how to learn. In the technical field, the knowledge Scott acquired in school was not enough. New information continues to be published, and you have to be on top of it. School is not so much about learning specific applications or skills like Windows 98. "You have to know that it runs on top of instructions that run in a chip, and you have to understand how the chip works." School helps give you a history and understanding of how things came to be, so that they are not a mystery anymore.

Even in his technical field, Scott has found communication and relationship building two of the most important pieces of success. He became very knowledgeable technically but did not put much energy into building business relationships, at first. Now he believes that relationships are at least half, though probably more, of the factors contributing to success. He reads the book *How to Win Friends and Influence People* every year just to remind himself of the basic points: Don't criticize or complain, but say only good things and be positive. All things tend to decay if you don't put time and energy into them. Even businesspeople want to be loved, so focus on relationships and success will just start happening. Scott now tries to be what he terms a "karma broker," accepting help from others and also giving it away.

Scott has three basic rules for his life:

1. Remember that life is a verb and not a noun—it is a process, not something to achieve, which requires action.

2. It is better to be a stream than a pond—when a stream hits a rock, it goes around it. Find the path of least resistance and continue along. Ponds are stagnant.

3. Gravity and light explain everything. There are thousands of laws, but you can boil them down to common denominators. Silicon chips start with sand. If you can see things in different ways, you can notice similarities, and skills become interchangeable. Debugging a memory leak, for example, requires going all the way to the lowest core.

Scott prepared himself to take advantage of opportunities. He saw the need for his consulting service and learned the necessary skills to make it happen. He attributes

(continued)

Success in the Real World

his success to several factors: 30% is due to luck, he says—being in the right place at the right time; 30% is because others helped him; and 40% because he was smart, worked hard, and knew how to do what was neces-

sary. Great things have happened to him because, he believes, he is eternally optimistic, builds relationships, and knows how important it is to give back to the world.

Chapter 9   Applications

Name _____   Date _____

KEY INTO YOUR LIFE
Opportunities to Apply What You Learn

 Where Are You When It Comes to Math?

Math anxiety seems to afflict many people in today's world. As everyday life, society, and business become more technological, anxiety can become a serious problem. The severity of math anxiety is causing critical shortages of people who are qualified to handle this emerging technology. How do you deal with the challenges of mathematics? Respond to the following statements as accurately as possible in light of your own experiences and the information provided in the chapter.

1. When I make an error on a math problem, I _____
   _____
   _____

2. When I get embarrassed about doing math, I _____
   _____
   _____

3. When I'm unable to solve a particular problem, I _____
   _____
   _____

4. If I were able to do mathematics, I would _____

_____

_____

5. When I'm able to solve a problem that was difficult, I feel _____

_____

_____

6. One thing I enjoy about doing math is _____

_____

_____

7. Working on mathematics makes me feel _____

_____

_____

9.2 *Which Strategies Did You Use?*

Using a math or science book, copy down three questions from the text. For each question, name a problem-solving strategy or strategies from this chapter that will help you solve the problem. Solve the problem on a separate piece of paper. Afterwards, state here why you chose the strategies you did. Are there other ways to solve the same problem?

Problem 1: _____

_____

_____

Strategies: _____

_____

_____

_____

_____

_____

_____

Problem 2: _____

_____

_____

Strategies: _____

_____

_____

_____

_____

_____

_____

Problem 3: _____

_____

_____

Strategies: _____

_____

_____

_____

_____

_____

_____

_____

9.3 *Team-Building Exercise*

Choose one or two people from your class—fellow students with whom you feel comfortable working. Use problems from any math text.

Choose one problem. Each of you work on the same problem separately. After finishing the problem, come together to share your methods of solution. Discuss how each of you approached the problem and eventually solved it.

Case Studies

Spreadsheet Practice

In this exercise, you will use a spreadsheet (Microsoft Excel or other application) to analyze the breakeven point for a manufacturing company. You will become familiar with how to enter data and formulas in cells of a spreadsheet, format the information, and use different imbedded formulas.

HERE WE GO!

1. Open the application (i.e., Microsoft Excel) and open a new spreadsheet.

2. Type the title and subtitle of the spreadsheet in cell A1 and A2 (see the sample spreadsheet at the end of this exercise):

CDs R US
Breakeven Analysis

Note what happens when the length of the words in the cell exceeds the width of the cell. You can center text within a cell by using the center command on the toolbar. Next to the center command is the right alignment command. Next to this is the "Merge and Center" command.

Use the Merge and Center command to center the text across columns A through G as it appears on the sample spreadsheet at the end of this exercise.

3. Type in the titles of the rows as you see them on the sample spreadsheet (Units, Revenue, etc.) in column A, starting in row 4.

4. Next, make column A 25 characters wide. There are at least two ways to adjust column width. One way is to use the Format command on the main menu; choose Column and Width and set to 25. Can you discover the other way? (Hint: Click on the column line and drag.)

5. Make columns B through G 8 characters wide. Which of the ways noted above did you use?

6. We will be looking at the effect of selling several quantities. Enter 25 in cell B4, 50 in cell C4, 75 in cell D4, 100 in cell E4, 125 in cell F4, 150 in cell G4.

7. Now enter $200 for Rent in column B, row 16, and fill in columns C through G with the same amount. You can highlight columns C through G and use Edit-Fill-Right or copy and paste from column B by highlighting the cell and using Edit-Copy and Edit-Paste to fill in the same number of units in columns C through G.

USING FORMULAS AND RELATIVE ADDRESSING

8. Next, you will enter formulas in column B that match the definitions below. Note the difference between entering data (as in the number of units, which you entered above) text, functions, and formulas.

- TOTAL VARIABLE COSTS are the sum of the four individual variable costs. There are at least two ways to sum, or add, figures. One way to do this is to highlight cell B11. Then click on the SUM character on the toolbar, Σ. Then highlight cells B7 through B10 and click Enter. Another way is to highlight cell B11 and type =SUM(B7:B10). Copy and paste this formula in the rest of the columns. (After you copy the formula, highlight cell C11 and note that the program has automatically copied the formula using the values in column C—this is what is known as RELATIVE ADDRESSING.)

♦ CONTRIBUTION MARGIN is REVENUE minus TOTAL VARI-ABLE COSTS. You can enter this formula by highlighting cell B13 and typing =B5-B11. Copy and paste the formula to the rest of the columns.

♦ TOTAL FIXED COSTS are the sum of the two fixed costs (Rent and Depreciation). Enter this formula for all columns.

♦ TOTAL COST is the sum of the TOTAL VARIABLE COSTS and TOTAL FIXED COSTS.

♦ NET INCOME is REVENUE minus TOTAL COST (we are ignoring income taxes for this example).

USING ABSOLUTE ADDRESSING AND A DATA INPUT AREA

9. Now you will start a new data entry area on your spreadsheet. This will allow you to see the effect of different selling prices and costs. Scroll or Tab to column I through K, row 1, and enter the following in two columns:

BREAKEVEN DATA INPUT AREA

Per-Unit Costs

Selling Price	$ 12
Direct Material	$ 5
Direct Labor	$ 2

Other Costs

Variable Overhead	50%
(per labor dollar)	
Depreciation	$400

10. Enter the following formulas using "absolute addressing." Absolute addressing is used so that when you copy the formulas from column B to columns C through G, the correct values are generated.

♦ REVENUE is equal to UNITS times the selling price per unit. To enter this formula, highlight cell B5 and type =B4*K4, if cell K4 is where you have the selling price. Copy and paste this formula to the remaining columns.

♦ DIRECT MATERIALS is equal to UNITS times DIRECT MATER-IAL COST. Can you determine what formula to input?

♦ DIRECT LABOR is equal to UNITS times DIRECT LABOR COST.

♦ VARIABLE OVERHEAD is equal to a percentage of DIRECT LABOR. The percentage in this first case is 50%. To input this formula, entered in cell B9, highlight the cell and type =B8*K9, if K9 is where you entered the VARIABLE OVERHEAD figure of 50%.

♦ DEPRECIATION is equal to the figure in the data input area; in this initial case, it is $400.

11. After you enter in the numbers, can you tell how many units you need to sell in order to break even (the number that must be sold so that revenue equals costs)?

12. What would happen if the price of CDs came down to $11? What if Direct Labor costs also increased to $3? Change the data in your data input area to determine the effects of these changes on the net income. How does the breakeven point change?

	A	B	C	D	E	F	G	
1	CDs R US							
2	Breakeven Analysis							
3								
4	UNITS	25	50	75	100	125	150	
5	REVENUE							
6	VARIABLE COSTS							
7	Direct Materials							
8	Direct Labor							
9	Variable Overhead							
10	Advertising							
11	TOTAL VARIABLE COSTS							
12								
13	CONTRIBUTION MARGIN							
14	FIXED OVERHEAD							
15	Depreciation							
16	Rent	$200	$200	$200	$200	$200	$200	
17	TOTAL FIXED COSTS							
18								
19	TOTAL COST							
20	NET INCOME BEFORE TAXES							
21	INCOME TAX							
22								
23	NET INCOME							

Internet Exercise

The Securities and Exchange Commission has a lot of information for investors. Access the site at:

www.sec.gov

On the left-hand side of the site, you will see several choices. Double-click on the **Edgar** database. Next, click on **"Search the Edgar Database."** Double-click on **"Quick Forms Lookup."**

The 10K form is the annual report form that all publicly traded companies must file with the government. It will tell you the revenues and expenses these companies incurred during the year. First select the form, 10K, in the appropriate box. Then go to the Company name box and enter exactly as it appears here:

Campbell Soup Co

You should see a 10K report. Click on this. You will have to scroll down past a lot of writing to almost the end of the report to arrive at the financial figures. Use the report to answer the following questions:

1. What are Campbell's net sales for the first quarter of this year?

   _____

2. What was its net income:

   a. In dollars? _____

   b. As a percent of sales? _____

3. Was this an increase or decrease over *the same quarter* last year?

   _____

   a. What percentage increase/decrease? _____

4. Can you find the name of the company's president and chief executive officer?

   _____

5. Print out a copy of the financial figures and attach to this exercise.

Journal

Name _____   Date _____

Journal

Name _____ Date _____

10

Moving Ahead

Building a Flexible Future

The end of one path can be the beginning of another. For example, graduation is often referred to as commencement because the end of your student career is the beginning or renewal of your life as a working citizen. As you come to the end of your work in this course, you have built up a wealth of knowledge. Now you have more power to make decisions about what directions you want your studies, your career, and your personal growth to take.

This chapter will explore how to manage the constant change you will encounter. Developing your flexibility will enable you to adjust goals, make the most of successes, and work through failures. You will consider what is important about giving back to your community and continuing to learn throughout your life. Finally, you will revisit your personal mission, exploring how to revise it as you encounter changes in the future.

In this chapter, you will explore answers to the following questions:

◆ How can you live with change?

◆ What will help you handle failure and success?

◆ Why give back to the community and the world?

◆ Why is college just the beginning of lifelong learning?

◆ How can you live your mission?

How CAN YOU LIVE WITH CHANGE?

Even the most carefully constructed plans can be turned upside down by change. In this section, you will explore some ways to make change a manageable part of your life by accepting the reality of change, maintaining flexibility, and adjusting your goals.

Accept the Reality of Change

As Russian-born author Isaac Asimov once said, "It is change, continuing change, inevitable change, that is the dominant factor in society today. No sensible decision can be made any longer without taking into account not only the world as it is, but the world as it will be."[1] Change is a sure thing. Two significant causes of change on a global level are technology and the economy.

Technological Growth

Today's technology has spurred change. Tasks that people have performed for years are now taken care of by computer in a fraction of the time and for a fraction of the price. Advances in technology come into being daily: Computer companies update programs, new models of cars and machines appear, and scientists discover new possibilities in medicine and other areas. People make changes in the workplace, school, and home to keep up with the new systems and products that technology constantly offers. People and cultures are linked around the world through the Internet and World Wide Web.

The dominance of the media, brought on by technological growth, has increased the likelihood of change. A few hundred years ago, no television or magazines or Internet existed to show people what was happening elsewhere in the world. A village could operate in the same way for years with very little change because there would be little to no contact with anyone from the outside who could introduce new ideas, methods, or plans. Now, the media constantly presents people with new ways of doing things. When people can see the possibilities around them, they are more likely to want to find out whether the grass is truly greener on the other side of the fence.

Economic Instability

The unpredictable economy is the second factor in this age of constant change. Businesses have had to cut costs in order to survive, which has affected many people's jobs and careers. Some businesses discovered the speed and cost-effectiveness of computers and used them to replace workers. Some businesses have had to downsize and have laid off people to save money. Some businesses have merged with others, and people in duplicate jobs were let go. The difficult economy has also had an effect on personal finances. Many people face money problems at home that force them to make changes in how much they work, how they pursue an education, and how they live.

TERMS

Downsize
To reduce in size; streamline.

Maintain Flexibility

The fear of change is as inevitable as change itself. When you become comfortable with something, you tend to want it to stay the way it is, whether it is a relationship, a place you live, a job, a schedule, or the racial/cultural mix of people with whom you interact. Change may seem to have only negative effects, and consistency only positive effects. Think about your life right now. What do you wish would always stay the same? What changes have upset you and thrown you off balance?

You may have encountered any number of changes in your life to date, many of them unexpected. You may have experienced ups and downs in relationships, perhaps marriage or divorce. You may have changed schools, changed jobs, or moved to a new home. You may have shifted your course of study. You may have added to your family or lost family members. Financial shifts may have caused you to change the way you live. All of these changes, whether you perceive them as good or bad, cause a certain level of stress. They also cause a shift in your personal needs, which may lead to changing priorities.

Change Brings Different Needs

Your needs can change from day to day, year to year, and situation to situation. Although you may know about some changes ahead of time, such as when you plan to attend school or move in together with a partner, others may take you completely by surprise, such as unemployment, illness, or an unexpected pregnancy. Even the different times of year bring different needs, such as a need for extra cash around the holidays or a need for additional child care when your children are home for the summer.

Some changes that shift your needs will occur within a week or even a day. For example, an instructor may inform you that you have a quiz or extra assignment at the end of the week, or your supervisor at work may give you an additional goal for the week. During the course of a day, your daughter might tell you that she needs you to drive her somewhere that evening, or a friend may call and need your help with something that has come up suddenly. Table 10-1, on page 260, shows how the effects of certain changes can lead to new priorities.

Inflexibility vs. Flexibility

When change affects your needs, *flexibility* will help you shift your priorities so that you address those needs. You can react to change with either inflexibility or flexibility, each with its resulting effects.

Inflexibility. Not acknowledging a shift in needs can cause trouble. For example, if you lose your job and continue to spend as much money as you

Table 10-1	Change produces new priorities.	
CHANGE	**EFFECTS AND CHANGED NEEDS**	**NEW PRIORITIES**
Lost job	Loss of income; need for others in your household to contribute more income	Job hunting; reduction in your spending; additional training or education in order to qualify for a different job
New job	Change in daily/weekly schedule; need for increased contribution of household help from others	Time and energy commitment to new job; maintaining confidence; learning new skills
Started school	Fewer hours for work, family, and personal time; responsibility for class work; need to plan semesters ahead of time	Careful scheduling; making sure you have time to attend class and study adequately; strategic planning of classes and of career goals
Relationship/marriage	Responsibility toward your partner; merging of your schedules and perhaps your finances and belongings	Time and energy commitment to relationship
Breakup/divorce	Change in responsibility for any children; increased responsibility for your own finances; possibly a need to relocate; increased independence	Making time for yourself; gathering support from friends and family; securing your finances; making sure you have your own income
Bought car	Responsibility for monthly payment; responsibility for upkeep	Regular income so that you can make payments on time; time and money for upkeep
New baby	Increased parenting responsibility; need money to pay for baby's needs or if you had to stop working; need help with other children	Child care; flexible employment; increased commitment from a partner or other supporter
New cultural environment (from new home, job, or school)	Exposure to unfamiliar people and traditions; tendency to keep to yourself	Learning about the culture with which you are now interacting; openness to new relationships

did before, ignoring your need to live more modestly, you can drive yourself into debt and make the situation worse. Or if you continue to spend little time with a partner who has expressed a need for more contact, you may lose your relationship.

Flexibility. Being flexible means acknowledging the change, examining your different needs, and addressing them in any way you can. As frightening as it can be, being flexible can help you move ahead. Discovering what change brings may help you uncover positive effects that you had no idea were there. For example, a painful breakup or divorce can lead you to discover greater capability and independence. A loss of a job can give you a chance to reevaluate your abilities and look for another job in an area that suits you better. An illness can give you perspective on what you truly value in life. In other words, a crisis can spur opportunity; you may learn that you want to adjust your goals in order to pursue that opportunity.

Sometimes you may need to resist for a while, until you are ready to face an important change. When you do decide you are ready, being flexible will help you cope with the negative effects and benefit from the positive effects.

Adjust Your Goals

Your changing life will often result in the need to adjust goals accordingly: Sometimes goals must change because they weren't appropriate in the first place; some turn out to be unreachable; some may not pose enough of a challenge; others may be unhealthy for the goal setter or harmful to others.

Step One: Reevaluate

Before making adjustments in response to change, take time to *reevaluate* both the goals themselves and your progress toward them.

The goals.   First, determine whether your goals still fit the person you have become in the past week or month or year. Circumstances can change quickly. For example, an unexpected pregnancy might cause a female student to rethink her educational goals.

Your progress.   If you feel you haven't gotten far, determine whether the goal is out of your range or simply requires more stamina than you had anticipated. As you work toward any goal, you will experience alternating periods of progress and stagnation. Sticking with a tough goal may be the hardest thing you'll ever do, but the payoff may be worth it. You may want to seek the support and perspective of a friend or counselor as you evaluate your progress.

Step Two: Modify

If, after your best efforts, it becomes clear that a goal is out of reach, *modifying* your goal may bring success. Perhaps the goal doesn't suit you. For example, an active, interpersonal learner might become frustrated while pursuing a detail-oriented, sedentary career such as computer programming.

Based on your reevaluation, you can modify a goal in two ways:

1. Adjust the existing goal. To adjust a goal, change one or more aspects that define that goal—for example, the time frame, the due dates, or the specifics of the expectations. For example, a woman with an unexpected pregnancy could adjust her educational due date, taking an extra year or two to complete her course work. She could also adjust the time frame, taking classes at night if she had to care for her child during the day.

2. Replace it with a different, more compatible goal. If you find that you just can't handle a particular goal, try to find another that makes more sense for you at this time. For example, a couple who wants to buy a home but just can't afford it can choose to work toward the goal of making improvements to their current living space. Because you and your circumstances never stop changing, your goals should keep up with those changes.

> "Risk! Risk anything! Care no more for the opinion of others, for those voices. Do the hardest thing on earth for you. Act for yourself. Face the truth."
>
> KATHERINE MANSFIELD

Being open to adjusting your goals will help you manage both failure and success along the way.

WHAT WILL HELP YOU HANDLE FAILURE AND SUCCESS?

The perfect, trouble-free life is only a myth. The most wonderful, challenging, fulfilling life is full of problems to be solved and difficult decisions to be made. If you want to handle the bumps and bruises without losing your self-esteem, you should prepare to encounter setbacks along with your successes.

Dealing With Failure

Things don't always go the way you want them to go. Sometimes you may come up against obstacles that are difficult to overcome. Sometimes you will let yourself down or disappoint others. You may make mistakes or lose your motivation. All people do, no matter who they are or how smart or accomplished they may be. What is important is how you choose to deal with what goes wrong. If you can arrive at reasonable definitions of failure and success, accept failure as part of being human, and examine failure so that you can learn from it, you will have the confidence to pick yourself up and keep improving.

Measuring Failure and Success

Most people measure failure by comparing where they are to where they believe they should be. Since individual circumstances vary widely, so do definitions of failure. What you consider a failure may seem like a positive step for someone else. Here are some examples:

◆ Imagine that your native language is Spanish. You have learned to speak English well, but you still have trouble writing it. Making writing mistakes may seem like failure to you, but to a recent immigrant from the Dominican Republic who knows limited English, your command of the language will seem like a success story.

◆ If two people apply for internships, one may see failure as receiving some offers but not the favorite one, while someone who was turned down may see any offer as a success.

◆ Having a job that doesn't pay you as much as you want may seem like a failure, but to someone who is having trouble finding any job, your job is a definite success.

"The word impossible is not in my dictionary."
NAPOLEON I

Accepting Failure

No one escapes failure, no matter how hard he or she may try (or how successful he or she may be at hiding mistakes). The most successful people and organizations have experienced failures and mistakes. For example, the producers of the film *Waterworld* spent over $140 million on a film that made only a fraction of that cost at the box office. America Online miscalculated customer use and offered a flat rate per month, resulting in thousands of customers having trouble logging on to the service. Many an otherwise successful individual has had a problematic relationship, a substance-abuse problem, or a failing grade in a course.

You have choices when deciding how to view a failure or mistake. You can pretend it never happened, blame it on someone or something else, blame yourself, or forgive yourself.

Pretending it didn't happen. Avoiding the pain of dealing with a failure can deny you valuable lessons and could even create more serious problems. HIV is one example of this idea. Imagine that a person has unprotected sex with a potentially HIV-infected partner and then denies it ever happened. If that person later discovers that he or she has contracted HIV from the first partner, the deadly virus may have been passed on to any subsequent partners.

Blaming others. Putting the responsibility on someone else stifles opportunities to learn and grow. For example, imagine that an unprepared and inappropriately dressed person interviews for a job and is not hired. If he or she decides that the interviewer is biased, the interviewee won't learn to improve preparation or interview strategies. Evaluate causes carefully and try not to assign blame.

Blaming yourself. Getting angry at yourself for failing, or believing that you should be perfect, can only result in your feeling incapable of success and perhaps becoming afraid to try. Negative self-talk can become self-fulfilling.

Forgiving yourself. This is by far the best way to cope. First, although you should always strive for your best, don't expect perfection of yourself or anyone else. Expect that you will do the best that you can within the circumstances of your life. Just getting through another day as a student, employee, and/or parent is an important success. Second, forgive yourself when you fail. Your value as a human being does not diminish when you make a mistake. Forgiving yourself will give you more strength to learn from the experience, move on, and try again.

Once you are able to approach failure and mistakes in a productive way, you can explore what you can learn from them.

Learning From Failure

Learning from your failures and mistakes involves thinking critically through what happened. The first step is to evaluate what happened and decide if it was within your control. It could have had nothing to do with you at all. You could have failed to win a job because someone else with equal qualifications was in line for it ahead of you. A family crisis that disrupted your sleep could have affected your studying, resulting in a failing grade on a test. These are unfortunate circumstances, but they are not failures. On the other hand, something you did or didn't do may have contributed to the failure.

REAL WORLD PERSPECTIVE

How can I prepare to make a difference in the world when I finish college?

Norma Espina, University of Texas—El Paso

Right after high school, I tried college and was very unsuccessful at it. I didn't realize what I was getting into. When I was in high school, I was surrounded by my friends. If someone didn't know me personally, they at least knew who I was. College was so different; no one knew me. I wanted to appear grown up so I didn't risk very much. This was one of my downfalls. I was afraid to ask for help or get involved because I wanted to be mature, and I was too afraid to make a mistake. This backfired on me because I started to fall behind in classes. When I didn't understand something, I just let it slide by. Before long, I was avoiding classes. I had excuse after excuse after excuse until finally I didn't want to go to college anymore. That's when I gave up.

Seven years later, after a divorce and two children, I decided to return and finish my education. I was very motivated to succeed. I believe the reason I am successful this time is because I am willing to get involved. I ask questions in class or talk to the professor right after. Through speaking up, I began making friends and forming study groups.

My dream is to finish college so I can begin making a difference in the world. I believe I'm on the right track and have a positive attitude about the direction I'm headed. What specific steps do you recommend I take as I prepare for my future outside of college?

Mike Jackson, Baltimore City Community College

Whether you are in school or beginning your career, one of the things that will contribute to your success is to feel positive about who you are and the dreams you have. Sometimes people who enter the work force allow the job or the group they're in to define them. I personally feel it's better to let the group or the job *enhance* who you are, but not control your life. That's why it's also important to have balance between your work and your personal life. The more balanced you are, the greater the chance you'll have a healthier perspective on your job and on people in general.

I also believe that life is a series of opportunities, so when one comes along, you've got to grab it. It's important to not let life just happen to you. Otherwise you could find yourself in circumstances that are very unpleasant, to say the least. Growing up in an inner-city environment, as I did, opens your eyes to what can occur when you let life happen to you. Fortunately for me, I had parents with very strong values to help point me in the right direction. But even without supportive parents like mine, if you believe that your goals are worth having, you can make it out of the worst of circumstances.

Finally, have a plan. Decide what you want to do with your life, and then formulate steps to achieve that goal. Have some alternatives, too, in case your original ideas don't pan out. But don't worry if you stray from your original plan. Some detours can actually be better than the goal you had in the first place.

If you decide that you have made a mistake, your next steps are to analyze the causes and effects of what happened, make any improvements that you can, and decide how to change your action or approach in the future.

For example, imagine that after a long night of studying you forgot your part-time work-study commitment the next day.

Analyze causes and effects. *Causes:* Your exhaustion and your concern about your test caused you to forget to check your work schedule. *Effects:* Because you weren't there, a crucial curriculum project wasn't completed. An entire class and instructor who needed the project have been affected by your mistake.

Make any possible improvements on the situation. You could apologize to the instructor and see if there were still a chance to finish up part of the work that day.

Make changes for the future. You could set a goal to note your work schedule regularly in your date book—maybe in a bright color—and to check it more often. You could also arrange your future study schedule so that you will be less exhausted.

Think about the people you consider exceptionally successful. They didn't rise to the top without taking risks and making their share of mistakes. They have built much of their success upon their willingness to recognize and learn from their shortfalls. You too can benefit from staying open to this kind of active, demanding, hard-won education. Learning involves change and growth. Let what you learn from falling short of your goals inspire new and better ideas.

Think Positively About Failure

When you feel you have failed, how can you boost your outlook?

Stay aware of the fact that you are a capable, valuable person. People often react to failure by becoming convinced that they are incapable and incompetent. Fight that tendency by reminding yourself of your successes, focusing your energy on your best abilities, and knowing that you have the strength to try again. Realize that your failure isn't a setback as long as you learn from it and rededicate yourself to excellence. Remember that the energy you might expend on talking down to yourself would be better spent on trying again and moving ahead.

Share your thoughts and disappointment with others. Everybody fails. Trading stories will help you realize you're not alone. People refrain from talking about failures out of embarrassment, often feeling as though no one else could have made as big a mistake as they did. When you open up, you may be surprised to hear others exchange stories that rival your own. Be careful not to get caught in a destructive cycle of complaining. Instead, focus on the kind of creative energy that can help you find ways to learn from your failures.

Look on the bright side. At worst, you have at least learned a lesson that will help you avoid similar situations in the future. At best, there may be some positive results of what happened. If your romance flounders, the extra study time you suddenly have may help you boost your grades. If you fail a class, you may discover that you need to focus on a different subject that suits you better. What you learn from a failure may, in an unexpected way, bring you around to where you want to be.

Dealing With Success

Success isn't reserved for the wealthy, famous people you see glamorized in magazines and newspapers. Success isn't money or fame, although it can bring such things. Success is being who you want to be and doing what you want to do. Success is within your reach.

Pay attention to the small things when measuring success. You may not feel successful until you reach an important goal you have set for yourself. However, along the way each step is a success. When you are trying to drop a harmful habit, each time you stay on course is a success. When you are juggling work, school, and personal life, just coping with what every new day brings equals success. If you received a C on a paper and then earned a B on the next one, your advancement is successful.

Remember that success is a process. If you deny yourself the label of "success" until you reach the top of where you want to be, you will have a much harder time getting there. Just moving ahead toward improvement and growth, however fast or slow the movement, equals success.

Here are some techniques to handle your successes.

First, appreciate yourself. You deserve it. Take time to congratulate yourself for a job well done—whether it be a good grade, an important step in learning a new language, a job offer, a promotion or graduation, or a personal victory over substance abuse. Bask in the glow a bit. Everybody hears about his or her mistakes, but people don't praise themselves (or each other) enough when success happens. Praise can give you a terrific vote of confidence.

Take that confidence on the road. This victory can lead to others. Based on this success, you may be expected to prove to yourself and others that you are capable of growth, of continuing your successes and building upon them. Show yourself and others that the confidence is well founded.

Stay sensitive to others. There could be people around you who may not have been so successful. Remember that you have been in their place, and they in yours, and the positions may change many times over in the future. Enjoy what you have, work to build on it and not to take it for granted, and support others as they need it.

Staying sensitive to others is always an important goal, whether you are feeling successful or less than successful. Giving what you can of your time, energy, and resources to the community and the world is part of being aware of what others need. Your contributions can help to bring success to others.

WHY GIVE BACK TO THE COMMUNITY AND THE WORLD?

Everyday life is demanding. You can become so caught up in the issues of your own life that you neglect to look outside your immediate needs. However, from time to time you may feel that your mission extends beyond your personal life. You have spent time in this course working to improve yourself. Now that you've come so far, why not extend some of that energy and effort to the world outside? With all that you have to offer, you have the power to make positive differences in the lives of others. Every effort you make, no matter how small, improves the world.

Your Imprint on the World

As difficult as your life can sometimes seem, looking outside yourself and into the lives of others can help put everything in perspective. Sometimes you can evaluate your own hardships more reasonably when you look at them in light of what is happening elsewhere in the world. There are always many people in the world in great need. You have something to give to others. Making a lasting difference in the lives of others is something to be proud of.

Your perspective may change after volunteering at a soup kitchen. Your appreciation of those close to you may increase after you spend time with cancer patients at the local hospice. Your perspective on your living situation may change after you help people improve their housing conditions.

If you could eavesdrop on someone *talking about you to another person*, what do you think you would hear? How would you like to hear yourself described? What you do for others makes an imprint that can have far more impact than you may imagine. Giving one person hope, comfort, or help can improve his or her ability to cope with life's changes. That person in turn may be able to offer help to someone else. As each person makes a contribution, a cycle of positive effects is generated. For example, Helen Keller, blind and deaf from the age of two, was educated through the help of her teacher Annie Sullivan; then Keller spent much of her life lecturing to raise money for the teaching of the blind and deaf. Another example is Betty Ford, who was helped in her struggle with alcoholism and founded the Betty Ford Center to help others with addiction problems.

How can you make a difference? Many schools and companies are realizing the importance of community involvement and have appointed committees to find and organize volunteering opportunities. Make some kind of volunteering activity a priority on your schedule. Join a group from your company that tutors at a school. Organize a group of students to clean, repair, or entertain at a nursing home or shelter. Look for what's available to you or create opportunities on your own. Table 10-2 lists organizations that provide volunteer opportunities; you might also look into more local efforts or private clearinghouses that set up a number of different smaller projects.

Volunteerism is also getting a great deal of attention on the national level. The government has made an effort to stress the importance of community service as part of what it means to be a good citizen, and it provides support for that effort through AmeriCorps. AmeriCorps provides financial awards for education in return for community service work. If you work for AmeriCorps, you can use the funds you receive to pay current tuition expenses or repay student loans. You may work either before, during, or after your college education. You can find more information on AmeriCorps by contacting this organization:

> The Corporation for National and Community Service
> 1201 New York Avenue, NW
> Washington, DC 20525
> 1-800-942-2677

Sometimes it's hard to find time to volunteer when so many responsibilities compete for your attention. One solution is to combine other activities with volunteer work. Get exercise while cleaning a park or your yard or bring the whole family to sing at a nursing home on a weekend afternoon. Whatever you do, your actions will have a ripple effect, creating a positive impact on those you help and those they encounter in turn. The strength often found in people surviving difficult circumstances can strengthen you as well.

Valuing Your Environment

Your environment is your home. When you value it, you help to maintain a clean, safe, and healthy place to live. What you do every day has an impact on others around you and on the future. One famous slogan says that if you are not part of the solution, you are part of the problem. Every saved bottle, environmentally aware child, or reused bag is part of the solution. Take responsibility for what you can control—your own habits—and develop sound practices that contribute to the health of the environment.

Table 10-2		
Organizations that can use your help.	AIDS-related organizations	Kiwanis/Knights of Columbus/Lions Club/Rotary
	American Red Cross	Libraries
	Amnesty International	Meals on Wheels
	Audubon Society	Nursing homes
	Battered women shelters	Planned Parenthood
	Big Brothers and Big Sisters	School districts
	Churches, synagogues, temples, and affiliated organizations such as the YMCA/YWCA or YMHA/YWHA	Scouting organizations
	Educational support organizations	Share Our Strength/other food donation organizations
	Environmental awareness/support organizations such as Greenpeace	Shelters and organizations supporting the homeless
	Hospitals	Sierra Club/World Wildlife Fund
	Hot lines	

Recycle anything that you can. What can be recycled varies with the system set up in your area. You may be able to recycle any combination of plastics, aluminum, glass, newspapers, and magazines. Products that make use of recycled materials are often more expensive, but if they are within your price range, try to reward the company's dedication by purchasing the products.

Trade and reuse items. When your children have grown too old for the crib, baby clothes, and toys, give away whatever is still usable. Give clothing you don't wear to others who can use it. Organizations, like the Salvation Army, may pick up used items in your neighborhood on certain days or if you make arrangements with them. Wrap presents in plain newspaper and decorate with markers. Use your imagination—there are many, many items all around you that you can reuse.

Respect the outdoors. Participate in maintaining a healthy environment. Use products that reduce chemical waste. Pick up after yourself. Through volunteering, voicing your opinion, or making monetary donations, support the maintenance of parks and the preservation of unspoiled, undeveloped land. Be creative. One young woman planned a cleanup of a local lakeside area as the main group activity for the guests at her birthday party (she joined them, of course). Everyone benefits when each person takes responsibility for maintaining the fragile earth.

Remember that valuing yourself is the base for valuing all other things. Improving the earth is difficult unless you value yourself and think you deserve the best living environment possible. Valuing yourself will also help you understand why you deserve to enjoy the benefits of learning throughout your life.

WHY IS COLLEGE JUST THE BEGINNING OF LIFELONG LEARNING?

Although it may sometimes feel more like a burden, being a student is a golden opportunity. As a student, you are able to focus on learning for a period of time, and your school focuses on you in return, helping you gain access to knowledge, resources, and experiences. Take advantage of the academic atmosphere by developing a habit of seeking out new learning opportunities. That habit will encourage you to continue your learning long after you have graduated, even in the face of the pressures of everyday life.

Learning brings change, and change causes growth. As you change and the world changes, new knowledge and ideas continually emerge. Absorb them so that you can propel yourself into the future. Visualize yourself as a student of life who learns something new every single day.

Here are some lifelong learning strategies that can encourage you to continually ask questions and explore new ideas.

Investigate new interests. When information and events catch your attention, take your interest one step further and find out more. If you are fascinated by politics on television, find out if your school has political clubs that you can explore. If a friend of yours starts to take yoga, try out a class with him. If you really like one portion of a particular class, see if there are other classes that focus on that specific topic. Turn the regretful, "I wish I had tried that," into the purposeful, "I'm going to do it."

Read books, newspapers, magazines, and other writings. Reading opens a world of new perspectives. Check out what's on the best-seller list at your bookstore. Ask your friends about books that have changed their lives. Stay on top of current change in your community, your state, your country, and the world by reading newspapers and magazines. A newspaper that has a broad scope, such as *The New York Times* or *Washington Post*, can be an education in itself. Explore religious literature, family letters, and Internet news groups and Web pages. Keep something with you to read for those moments when you have nothing to do.

Spend time with interesting people. When you meet someone new who inspires you and makes you think, keep in touch. Have a potluck dinner party and invite one person or couple from each corner of your life—your family, your work, your school, a club to which you belong, your neighborhood. Sometimes, meet for reasons beyond just being social. Start a book club, a home-repair group, a play-reading club, a hiking group, or an investing group. Get to know people of different cultures and perspectives. Learn something new from each other.

Pursue improvement in your studies and in your career. When at school, take classes outside of your major if you have time. After graduation, continue your education both in your field and in the realm of general knowledge. Stay on top of ideas, developments, structural changes, and new technology in your field by seeking out continuing education courses. Sign up for career-related seminars. Take single courses at a local college or community learning center. Some companies offer additional on-the-job training or will pay for their employees to take courses that will improve their knowledge and skills. If your company doesn't, you may want to set a small part of your income aside as a "learning budget." When you apply for jobs, you may want to ask about what kind of training or education the company offers or supports.

Nurture a spiritual life. You can find spirituality in many places. You don't have to regularly attend a house of worship to be spiritual, although that may be an important part of your spiritual life. "A spiritual life of some kind is absolutely necessary for psychological 'health,'" says psychologist and author Thomas Moore in his book *The Care of the Soul.* "We live in a time of deep division, in which mind is separated from body and spirituality is at odds with materialism."[2] The words *soul* and *spirituality* hold different meanings for each individual. Decide what they mean to you. Whether you discover them in music, organized religion, friendship, nature, cooking, sports, or anything else, making them a priority in your life will help you find a greater sense of balance and meaning.

TERMS

Continuing education
Courses that students can take without having to be part of a degree program.

Experience what others create. Art is "an adventure of the mind" (Eugene Ionesco, playwright); "a means of knowing the world" (Angela Carter, author); something that "does not reproduce the visible; rather, it makes visible" (Paul Klee, painter); "a lie that makes us realize truth" (Pablo Picasso, painter); a revealer of "our most secret self" (Jean-Luc Godard, filmmaker). Through art you can discover new ideas and shed new light on old ones. Explore all kinds of art and focus on any forms that hold your interest. Seek out whatever moves you—music, visual arts, theater, photography, dance, domestic arts, performance art, film and television, poetry, prose, and more.

Make your own creations. Bring out the creative artist in you. Take a class in drawing, in pottery, or in quilting. Learn to play an instrument that you have always wanted to master. Write poems for your favorite people or stories to read to your kids. Invent a recipe. Design and build a set of shelves for your home. Create a memoir of your life. You are a creative being. Express yourself, and learn more about yourself, through art.

Lifelong learning is the master key that unlocks every door you will encounter on your journey. If you keep it firmly in your hand, you will discover worlds of knowledge—and a place for yourself within them.

How can you live your mission?

As you learn and change, so may your life's mission. Whatever changes occur, your continued learning will give you a greater sense of security in your choices. Recall your mission statement from Chapter 3. Think about how it is changing as you learn and develop. It will continue to reflect your goals, values, and strength if you live with integrity, roll with the changes that come your way, continue to observe the role models in your life, and work to achieve your personal best in all that you do.

Live With Integrity

You've spent a lot of time exploring who you are, how you learn, and what you value. Integrity is about being true to that picture you have drawn of yourself while also considering the needs of others. Living with integrity will bring you great personal and professional rewards.

Honesty and sincerity are at the heart of integrity. Many of the decisions you make and act upon in your life are based on your underlying sense of what is "the right thing to do." Having integrity puts that sense into day-to-day action.

The Marks of Integrity

A person of integrity lives by the following principles:

1. *Honest representation of himself or herself, and his or her thoughts.* For example, you tell your partner when you are hurt over something that he or she did or didn't do.

2. *Sincerity in word and action.* You do what you say you will do. For example, you tell a co-worker that you will finish a project when she has to leave early, and you follow through by completing the work.

3. *Consideration of the needs of others.* When making decisions, you take both your needs and the needs of others into account. You also avoid hurting others for the sake of your personal goals. For example, your sister cares for your elderly father in her home where he lives with her. You spend three nights a week with him so that she can take a course toward her degree.

The Benefits of Integrity

When you act with integrity, you earn trust and respect from yourself and from others. If people can trust you to be honest, to be sincere in what you say and do, and to consider the needs of others, they will be more likely to encourage you, support your goals, and reward your hard work. Integrity is a must for workplace success. To earn promotions, it helps to show that you have integrity in a variety of situations.

Think of situations in which a decision made with integrity has had a positive effect. Have you ever confessed to an instructor that your paper is late without a good excuse, only to find that despite your mistake you have earned the instructor's respect? Have extra efforts in the workplace ever helped you gain a promotion or a raise? Have your kindnesses toward a friend or spouse moved the relationship to a deeper level? When you decide to act with integrity, you can improve your life and the lives of others.

Most importantly, living with integrity helps you believe in yourself and in your ability to make good choices. A person of integrity isn't a perfect person, but one who makes the effort to live according to values and principles, continually striving to learn from mistakes and to improve. Take responsibility for making the right moves, and you will follow your mission with strength and conviction.

Roll With the Changes

Think again about yourself. How has your idea of where you want to be changed since you first opened this book? How has your self-image changed? What have you learned about your values, your goals, and your styles of communication and learning? Consider how your educational, professional, and personal goals have changed. As you continue to grow and develop, keep adjusting your goals to your changes and discoveries.

Stephen Covey says in *The Seven Habits of Highly Effective People,* "Change—real change—comes from the inside out. It doesn't come from hacking at the leaves of attitude and behavior with quick fix personality ethic techniques. It comes from striking at the root—the fabric of our thought, the fundamental essential paradigms which give definition to our character and create the lens through which we see the world."[3]

Examining yourself deeply in that way is a real risk. Most of all, it demands courage and strength of will. Questioning your established beliefs and facing the unknown are much more difficult than staying with how things are. When you have the courage to face the consequences of trying something

> "And life is what we make it, always has been, always will be."
> GRANDMA MOSES

TERMS

Paradigm
An especially clear pattern or typical example.

unfamiliar, admitting failure, or challenging what you thought you knew, you open yourself to growth and learning opportunities. You can make your way through changes you never anticipated if you make the effort to live your mission—in whatever forms it takes as it changes—each day, each week, each month, and for years to come.

Learn From Role Models

People often derive the highest level of motivation and inspiration from learning how others have struggled through the ups and downs of life and achieved their goals. Somehow, seeing how someone else went through difficult situations can give you hope for your own struggles. The positive effects of being true to one's self become more real when an actual person has earned them.

Learning about the lives of people who have achieved their own version of success can teach you what you can do in your own life. Bessie and Sadie Delany, sisters and accomplished African American women born in the late 1800s, are two valuable role models. They took risks, becoming professionals in dentistry and teaching at a time when women and minorities were often denied both respect and opportunity. They worked hard to fight racial division and prejudice and taught others what they learned. They believed in their intelligence, beauty, and ability to give and lived without regrets. Says Sadie in their *Book of Everyday Wisdom*, "If there's anything I've learned in all these years, it's that life is too good to waste a day. It's up to you to make it sweet."[4]

> **TERMS**
> Role model
> A person whose behavior in a particular role is imitated by others

Aim for Your Personal Best

Your personal best is simply the best that you can do, in any situation. It may not be the best you have ever done. It may include mistakes, for nothing significant is ever accomplished without making mistakes and taking risks. It may shift from situation to situation. As long as you aim to do your best, though, you are inviting growth and success.

Aim for your personal best in everything you do. As a lifelong learner, you will always have a new direction in which to grow and a new challenge to face. Seek constant improvement in your personal, educational, and professional life, knowing that you are capable of that improvement. Enjoy the richness of life by living each day to the fullest, developing your talents and potential into the achievement of your most valued goals.

Kaizen is the Japanese word for "continual improvement." Striving for excellence, always finding ways to improve on what already exists, and believing that you can impact change are at the heart of the industrious Japanese spirit. The drive to improve who you are and what you do will help to provide the foundation of a successful future.

Think of this concept as you reflect on yourself, your goals, your lifelong education, your career, and your personal pursuits. Create excellence and quality by continually asking yourself, "How can I improve?" Living by *kaizen* will help you to be a respected friend and family member, a productive and valued employee, and a truly contributing member of society. You can change the world.

Success in the Real World

Dick Rutan

Dick Rutan, adventurer, pilot, and international lecturer, has achieved success more than just a few times in his life. His most notable success was when he piloted the *Voyager*—the first airplane to circumnavigate the globe without refueling. The successful completion of this trip earned him and his crew world records, international fame, financial gain, and a place in the Smithsonian Institute:

"Success for me is when I can stand underneath the airplane at the National Air and Space Museum and say "I built this and flew it around the world." *That,* to me, is my real success."

Dick's philosophy, "If you can dream it, you can do it," has led to his remarkable accomplishments. Dick remembers when he was a boy and the speed of sound was an impossible barrier to break. "Before Chuck Yeager broke the sound barrier, half of the scientists predicted he would die the day that he did it. But he had the courage and did what he said he could do." Dick now dreams of breaking the speed of light barrier— thought by many to be the ultimate barrier. He encourages people to explore and be more adventurous in their lives in order to find their own success.

Detractors and critics aren't a problem, according to Dick. Rather, he sees them as a motivational tool. Not only do they add to the challenge, but they enhance the reward of achieving the goal. "Once you enhance the right and eliminate the wrong, you have to launch your next effort."

Dick finds that accepting the responsibility for your own growth is critical for success. He thinks that we all should be honest about our limitations but make the most of our opportunities. He says we need to find courage when we need it and enjoy the moments in our lives for what they are.

Dick's ten keys for success are:

1. **Be adventurous and willing to take risks.** You have to lead an exciting life in order to have a reason to get out of bed. If you play it safe and follow the blazed path, you probably won't get lost or hurt. But what you'll be totally denied is adventure and exploration.

2. **Decide on a talent or skill you use well.** Everybody has certain aptitudes or capabilities, whether mechanical, artistic, or mathematical, etc. You have to discover these qualities and do something within that discipline.

3. **Have interest and excitement.** Choose a path that elicits your fascination. You have to be interested in it and believe in it.

4. **Select a goal.** Decide what you want to accomplish. Make your goal clear and always concentrate on that. Be very careful about setting a goal too low. Remember, if you can dream it, you can do it.

5. **Look at the long-term outcome.** Don't look at what it's going to take to acheive your goal, you might talk yourself out of it. Imagine sitting in a parking lot and seeing all the street signals down the street. If you wait for all of the signals to turn green, you'll never get out of the parking lot. Don't worry about roadblocks or red lights; deal with them as they come.

6. **Manage your motivation.** Have confidence to keep the motivation alive each day.

7. **Don't ever give up.** Do whatever it takes to accomplish your goal—even if it takes an inordinant amount of effort. One way to surely fail is to quit. The tougher the climb is, the better the view.

(continued)

Success in the Real World

8. **Be competitive.** It's a challenge that keeps your motivation alive. Competition is the catalyst that spurs mankind to greater things.

9. **Don't accept limitations.** Always question limitations. Have the courage to do what some people say can't be done.

10. **See failure as an opportunity.** You can learn a lot from failures, so expect to learn. See it as the first day of your next effort. Enhance what you do right and eliminate the wrong. Then, rebuild, re-evaluate, and learn the lessons.

Chapter 10 Applications

Name _____   Date _____

KEY INTO YOUR LIFE
Opportunities to Apply What You Learn

10.1   *Changes in Goals*

Have you experienced any shifts in your goals? Think about what may have changed since you began this course. List three major goals for each of the five goal areas. In each area, highlight or circle the goal that has changed the most and discuss why the change occurred.

PERSONAL

1. _____

2. _____

3. _____

Discuss changes:

_____

_____

_____

FAMILY

1. _____
2. _____
3. _____

Discuss changes:

_____
_____
_____

LIFESTYLE

1. _____
2. _____
3. _____

Discuss changes:

_____
_____
_____

CAREER

1. _____
2. _____
3. _____

Discuss changes:

_____
_____
_____

FINANCIAL

1. _____
2. _____
3. _____

Discuss changes:

_____
_____
_____

Looking at Change, Failure, and Success

Life can go by so fast that you don't take time to evaluate what changes have taken place, what failures you could learn from, and what successes you have experienced. Take a moment now and answer the following questions for yourself.

What are the three biggest changes that have occurred in your life this year?

1. _____
2. _____
3. _____

Choose one that you feel you handled well. What shifts in priorities or goals did you make?

_____

_____

_____

Choose one that you could have handled better. What happened? What do you think you should have done?

_____

_____

_____

Now name a personal experience, occurring this year, that you would consider a failure. What happened?

_____

_____

_____

How did you handle it—did you ignore it, blame it on someone else, or admit and explore it?

_____

_____

_____

What did you learn from experiencing this failure?

_____

_____

_____

Finally, describe a recent success of which you are the most proud.

_____

_____

_____

How did this success give you confidence in other areas of your life?

_____

_____

_____

10.3   *Volunteering*

Research volunteering opportunities in your community. What are the organizations? What are their needs? Do any volunteer positions require an application, letters of reference, or background checks? List three possibilities for which you have an interest or a passion.

1. _____

2. _____

3. _____

Of these three, choose one that you feel you will have the time and ability to try next semester. Suggestions that don't take up too much time include spending an evening serving in a soup kitchen or driving for Meals on Wheels during a lunch or dinner shift. Name your choice here and tell why you selected it.

_____

_____

_____

Research the suggestion you have chosen. Describe the activity. What is the time commitment? Is there any special training involved? Are there any problematic or difficult elements to this experience?

_____

_____

_____

_____

_____

Lifelong Learning

Review the strategies for lifelong learning in this chapter. Which ones mean something to you? Which do you think you can do, or plan to do, in your life now and when you are out of school? Name them and briefly discuss the role they play in your life.

_____

_____

_____

_____

_____

Team-Building Exercise

Gather in groups of three to five, and make sure that in each group the students are as familiar as possible with one another. Each member of the group should independently write two things on a piece of paper: one specific goal that he or she has attained, and one specific goal that he or she wants to work harder to achieve. When all are ready, sit in a small circle. First, each member should take turns sharing details and thoughts about the successful goal. Show your support and encouragement. If you know a group member well and have seen the difference hard work has made, say so. Then go around the group again, giving each member a chance to bring up the goal that needs work. Offer suggestions and ideas. Boost each other's motivation by discussing the positive effects that can result from working on the goal.

Understanding the U.S. Business System

Hewlett-Packard

Case
Studies

Once upon a time, in 1938, two electrical engineers from Stanford decided to take a risk and start a company in a garage with $538 in working capital. Their company slowly but surely worked its way to the top of the electronics world. Today, Hewlett-Packard is one of the largest suppliers of personal computers, printers and printing supplies, medical and chemical analysis equipment, and other electronic measuring devices. The reach of Hewlett-Packard is staggering—in 1997, it reached almost $43 billion in revenue. How did they do it?

The name of the game has been perseverance and investment in people—Bill Hewlett and Dave Packard developed products that were in demand. They looked at the big picture and used their skills to develop technology that could be used at the time. The demand for electronics was growing, and Hewlett-Packard was there to supply different types of new, useful electronic equipment.

As soon as the company began to see some success, it was time to decide on a management scheme and a list of objectives. Doing this was an important factor in the company's success. Hewlett-Packard knew that to reach its goals of selling products all over the world and becoming a major contributor to the electronics boom, it needed to establish its own internal structure of management and goals. The core belief of the owners and managers is that people are out to do a good job and will do a good job if they are allowed the opportunity. They also believe that people can make sound decisions about business and product development on their own within the company structure. Therefore, Hewlett-Packard structured its group and individual goals around these beliefs, giving the employees room to grow personally and technically. The company split into several divisions that worked and performed as small companies, such as the medical equipment group, chemical analysis equipment group, computers/printers group, research laboratories, software group, and electrical components group (to name a few).

Hewlett-Packard knows that its people are what makes it successful, and what the company tends to invest largely in is employees, ensuring that its employees benefit from the success of the company. Hewlett-Packard is known for its people-oriented environment. The company organizes different activities or resources for social events—orchestras, weight rooms, picnics, etc. Managers interview candidates carefully and actively help to direct the candidates to the appropriate division where their talents and strengths will be best put to use. There has typically been a lot of room for growth in a career at Hewlett-Packard, partly due to its diverse product lines ranging from computers to medical equipment.

This success did not come quickly. In the 1940s and 1950s, the market for the equipment was largely based on government orders. However, Hewlett-Packard decided that it needed to make a large investment to reach the civilian market as well, since much of the world's business lies with private citizens and large corporations not related to the government. One of their first customers was Walt Disney Studios, which had also been started in a garage not long before.

The company shifted from pure electronic sound-testing equipment to medical-testing equipment They continued to search for different, related applications. The product lines branched out and encompassed such areas as computers and printers, photo scanners, and chemical analysis tools for research. The company has grown at a phenomenal rate and continues to fare very well in the global markets in all of its product lines. Its reach includes plants and operations facilities in Europe, Asia, Latin America, Canada, and the Pacific, with its headquarters and main plants in the United States. It is a far cry from the small garage where it all began.

1. What kind of styles do you think most managers at Hewlett-Packard have?

2. What basic philosophy does the company have about its employees? Would you like to work for a company with this philosophy? Why or why not?

3. What do you think it takes for companies like Hewlett-Packard and Disney, starting with very little, to grow into billion-dollar businesses?

a. Describe Hewlett-Packard's strategy.

b. Do you think Hewlett-Packard rewards creativity? Give examples.

Internet Exercise

The Internet can be a great source of information; however, use it with caution! The material and services that are offered are extensive and come from a wide range of sources. Evaluate the sources. Do they provide accurate information? You may find some sources and service agencies to fit your needs, but don't use them all. You'll want to use your time as effectively as possible.

1. The following sites are a few of the sources on the Internet for finding careers. Choose two careers that seem interesting to you. Use the grid on the following page to help you in your research. Access the following sites and research the careers:

   Job Direct: http://www.jobdirect.com

   JobWeb: http://www.jobweb.org

   JobTrak: http://www.jobtrak.com

   Student Center: http://www.studentcenter.com/

	CAREER 1	CAREER 2
Degree required		
Experience needed		
Starting salary		
Demand in next 5 years		
Other		

2. How were these helpful?

   _____

   _____

   _____

   _____

3. What could you do to increase the effectiveness of searching for a job on the Internet?

   _____

   _____

   _____

   _____

   _____

   _____

Journal

Name _____   Date _____

Endnotes

Chapter 2

[1]Barbara Soloman, North Carolina State University, Raleigh, N.C.

[2]Howard Gardner, *Multiple Intelligences: The Theory in Practice* (New York: HarperCollins, 1993), 5–49.

[3]Joyce Bishop, Ph.D., Psychology faculty, Golden West College, Huntington Beach, CA.

Chapter 3

[1]Paul R. Timm, Ph.D., *Successful Self-Management: A Psychologically Sound Approach to Personal Effectiveness* (Los Altos, CA: Crisp Publications, Inc., 1987), 22–41.

[2]Stephen Covey, *The Seven Habits of Highly Effective People* (New York: Simon & Schuster, 1989), 70–144, 309–318.

Chapter 4

[1]Frank T. Lyman, Jr., Ph.D., "Think-Pair-Share, Thinktrix, Thinklinks, and Weird Facts: An Interactive System for Cooperative Thinking." In *Enhancing Thinking Through Cooperative Learning*, ed. Neil Davidson and Toni Worsham (New York: Teachers College Press, 1992), 169–181.

[2]Roger von Oech, *A Kick in the Seat of the Pants* (New York: Harper & Row Publishers, 1986), 5–21.

[3]Dennis Coon, *Introduction to Psychology: Exploration and Application*, 6th ed. (St. Paul: West Publishing Company, 1992), 295.

Chapter 5

[1]U. S. Department of Education, National Center for Education Statistics, *The Condition of Education 1996*, NCES 96–304, by Thomas M. Smith (Washington, DC: U. S. Government Printing Office, 1996), 84.

[2]Sherwood Harris, *The New York Public Library Book of How and Where to Look It Up* (Englewood Cliffs, NJ: Prentice Hall, 1991), 13.

[3]George M. Usova, *Efficient Study Strategies: Skills for Successful Learning* (Pacific Grove, CA: Brooks/Cole Publishing Company, 1989), 45.

[4]Francis P. Robinson, *Effective Behavior* (New York: Harper & Row, 1941).

[5]Sylvan Barnet and Hugo Bedau, *Critical Thinking, Reading, and Writing: A Brief Guide to Argument*, 2nd ed. (Boston: Bedford Books of St. Martin's Press, 1996), 15–21.

[6]John J. Macionis, *Sociology*, 6th ed. (Upper Saddle River, NJ: Prentice Hall, 1997), 174.

[7]Kogan, Sudit, and Vasarhelyi, *The Internet Guide for Accountants.* (Upper Saddle River, NJ: Prentice-Hall, 1998).

Chapter 6

[1]Walter Pauk, *How to Study in College*, 5th ed. (Boston: Houghton Mifflin Company, 1993), 110–114.

[2]Analysis based on Lynn Quitman Troyka, *Simon & Schuster Handbook for Writers* (Upper Saddle River, NJ: Prentice Hall, 1996), 22–23.

Chapter 7

[1]Ralph G. Nichols, "Do We Know How to Listen? Practical Helps in a Modern Age," *Speech Teacher* (March 1961): 118–124.

[2]Ibid.

[3]Hermann Ebbinghaus, *Memory: A Contribution to Experimental Psychology*, trans. H. A. Ruger and C. E. Bussenius (New York: New York Teacher's College, Columbia University, 1885).

[4]Many of the examples of objective questions used in this chapter are from Gary W. Piggrem, Test Item File for Charles G. Morris, *Understanding Psychology*, 3rd ed. (Upper Saddle River, NJ: Prentice Hall, 1996).

Chapter 9

[1]George Polya, *How to Solve It* (London: Penguin, 1990).

[2]Rick Billstein, Shlomo Libeskind, and Johnny W. Lott, *A Problem-Solving Approach to Mathematics for Elementary School Teachers* (Reading, MA: Addison-Wesley Longman, 1993), pp. 5–36.

Chapter 10

[1]Isaac Asimov, "My Own View," in *The Encyclopedia of Science Fiction*, ed. Robert Holdstock (1978).

[2]Thomas Moore, *The Care of the Soul* (New York: Harper Perennial, 1992), xi–xx.

[3]Stephen Covey, *The Seven Habits of Highly Effective People* (New York: Simon & Schuster, 1989), 70–144, 309–318.

[4]Sarah Delaney and Elizabeth Delaney with Amy Hill Hearth, *Book of Everyday Wisdom* (New York: Kodansha International, 1994), 123.

Index

Property of
DeVry University
630 U.S. Highway One
North Brunswick, NJ 08902

DATE	DUE